THE MARSEILLE CONNECTION

The Major Unsolved Crime of the Twentieth Century – Finally Solved!

Kenneth Foard McCallion

Also by Kenneth Foard McCallion

Saving the World One Case at a Time

Profiles in Courage in the Trump Era

Profiles in Cowardice in the Trump Era

COVID–19: The Virus that Changed America and the World

Treason & Betrayal: The Rise and Fall of Individual–1

The Essential Guide to Donald Trump

Shoreham and the Rise and Fall of the Nuclear Power Industry

For more information on these books and Kenneth, please visit www.KennethMcCallion.com

THE MARSEILLE CONNECTION

The Major Unsolved Crime of the Twentieth Century — Finally Solved!

Kenneth Foard McCallion

Bryant Park Press

Bryant Park Press

Published by Bryant Park Press

An imprint of

Copyright © 2023 by Kenneth Foard McCallion

All rights reserved, including the right to reproduce this book or portions thereof in any form whatsoever. For information about permissions, email permissions@hhimedia.net or submit requests by facsimile to +1(203)724–0820

Jacket and book design by Christopher Klaich

Manufactured in the United States of America

Hardback ISBN: 978–1–7371492–9–3   Paperback ISBN: 978–1–7371492–8–6

ACKNOWLEGEMENTS

My deepest and heartfelt thanks goes to Aaron Jerome, and the other intrepid researchers, who, despite formidable obstacles, succeeded in uncovering the well-buried evidence that made this book possible.

ACKNOWLEDGEMENTS

My deepest and heartfelt thanks goes to Aaron Jerome, and the other intrepid researchers, who, despite formidable obstacles, succeeded in recovering the well-buried evidence that made this book possible.

Table of Contents

Cast of Characters i
Introduction xvii
Chapter 1: The Beginning, 1947 1
Chapter 2: Patricia Richardson – The Early Years 19
Chapter 3: Paul–Louis Weiller 29
Chapter 4: The Ex–Nazi Connection 43
Chapter 5: Nixon, The Nazis, and the French Connection 55
Chapter 6: Bebe "The Fixer" Rebozo and Lunch at La Côte Basque 63
Chapter 7: Nixon's Phony "War on Drugs" 69
Chapter 8: Robert Vesco, Nixon, and The Unione Corse 85
Chapter 9: The Watergate Special Prosecutor, Spector and the Saturday Night Massacre 99
Chapter 10: The Big Evidence Hunt 111
Chapter 11: Jerry Barsha, Robin Moore, and "The Real French Connection" 131
Chapter 12: The 1978 Coast Guard Hearings 143
Conclusion 167
Chronology 169
Appendix 189
Endnotes 197

Table of Contents

List of Characters ....
Introduction ....
Chapter 1: The Beginning, 1972 ....
Chapter 2: Hyman Rubinstein - The Early Years ....
Chapter 3: English-born Willie ....
Chapter 4: The Ivy-Nazi Connection ....
Chapter 5: Nixon Unravels and Ivy finds Causes for ....
Chapter 6: Idi Fib - The "Ash" rebounded and "Cover Begin" ....
Chapter 7: From Prison With ....
Chapter 8: Rubinstein, Developed Mature Concerns ....
Chapter 9: The Watergate Syndrome - The Smear of All the Scandals Nightly Journal ...
Chapter 10: The Big Evidence Hunt ....
Chapter 11: Helping Friends, Robbin' Jones, and "The Wall Fund" ....
Funeral of ....
Chapter 12: The 1976 Court Case, the trial ....
Backbiting ....
Summary ....
Appendix ....
Endnotes ....

Cast of Characters

Angleton, James J. – Widely known for serving as the Chief of Counterintelligence for the CIA from 1954 to 1974. Angleton was one of the OSS and Army intelligence officers, who along with William Spector and E. Howard Hunt, negotiated the "Marseille Accord" with the French intelligence services, the French–Corsican syndicate, and Paul–Louis Weiller in 1947 in Marseille, France.

Barroudi, Eduardo – A close associate of Paul–Louis Weiller and Patricia Richardson, Barroudi rose to become a member of the French–Corsican underworld's highest echelon. He provided much of the "on–the–ground" leadership during the Unione Corse's successful efforts in February 1947 to break the strikes paralyzing the Marseille docks.

Barsha, Jerry – A longtime Syracuse radio and TV journalist who befriended William Spector. He ran Spector's story both before and long after the other local and national media outlets had ignored or abandoned it. He died at the Cleveland Clinic on September 10, 2009.

Bartels, John R., Jr. – The Administrator of the DEA from July 1973 to May 1975. Bartels was dismissed from his position after a Congressional investigation suggested that he had refused to fire a close associate in the DEA who had been seen with known and suspected drug dealers.

Beauharnais, Raymond – A local drug dealer on the Island of St. Martin, he was Patricia Richardson's first mentor and lover.

Beidas, Yousef – a Lebanese financier and founder of Intra Bank, which was used by the Unione Corse for money laundering purposes. Beidas was one of the early and most powerful "patrons" of Patricia Richardson after she arrived in Paris.

Biaggi, Mario – As a Congressman from Bronx, New York, Congressman Biaggi chaired the U.S. House of Representatives Coast Guard hearings in 1977. The hearings re–visited the question of why the DEA and other federal agencies had failed to properly investigate the information provided by William Spector about the French–Corsican syndicate behind the "French Connection" shipments of heroin from Marseille to New York.

Bishop, Robert – Major Robert Bishop was one of the officers in the special OSS unit in Romania during World War II, which included Lt. William Spector.

Boucan, Marcel – A close associate of Patricia Richardson, Boucan was arrested in 1972 on a shrimp boat off the coast of Marseille, France, with 935 pounds of heroin.

Bouchard, Conrad – A Corsican by heritage and one of Montreal's leading organized crime figures, Bouchard was the intermediary between the Unione Corse and Frank Peroff, a DEA informant. Peroff recorded Bouchard as saying that the fugitive financier Robert Vesco was financing a significant heroin transaction.

Bruce, David – The U.S. Ambassador to France immediately following the end of World War II.

Buckley, James – The U.S. Senator from New York from 1971 to 1977 and brother of William F. Buckley, the conservative writer. Buckley spearheaded an investigation and hearings on the mishandling by the DEA and other federal agencies of information provided by William Spector as to illegal cash contributions by the French–Corsican organized crime syndicate to Richard Nixon's 1968 presidential campaign.

Bundesnachrichtendienst (BND) – This was the Intelligence arm of the West German Government, which worked closely with the CIA. It acquired many agents from the Gehlen Organization, a group of ex–Nazi intelligence officers who operated throughout Europe under the auspices of the CIA during the post–World War II period.

Cast of Characters · iii

Bureau of Narcotics and Dangerous Drugs (BNDD) – Founded in 1968 and dissolved in 1973, the BNDD was the predecessor agency of the Drug Enforcement Administration.

Christian, Frederic – A member of SAC and the Unione Corse, Christian became Weiller's and Richardson's primary contact in the Caribbean, with headquarters in St. Martin.

Clore, Charles – A noted English industrialist and business tycoon, Clore was one of the early "sponsors" of the ambitious and gorgeous model Patricia Richardson.

Colby, William E. – Executive Director of the CIA from 1971 to 1973, and Director of the CIA from 1973 to 1976.

Conein, Lucien – Born in France in 1919, but raised in the U.S., Conein returned to France in 1939 to fight Nazi Germany. Following the French surrender, he escaped and joined the OSS, supporting Corsican resistance efforts. Conein and E. Howard Hunt became close friends of Paul–Louis Weiller, Patricia Richardson, and other key players in the Unione Corse.

Cotroni, Giuseppe – Along with Conrad Bouchard, Cotroni was one of Montreal's leading organized crime figures. He and Bouchard coordinated closely with other Unione Corse leaders such as Paul–Louis Weiller and Patricia Richardson.

David, Christian – A French SAC member and Unione Corse associate, David was a crucial figure in the ranks of the Unione Corse's operation in the Americas. He was hired by the CIA to assassinate Congo President Patrice Lumumba and by the French SDECE to assassinate Moroccan politician Ben Barka. After being arrested in Brazil, David was extradited to the U.S., where he claimed that another Unione Corse member, Lucien Sarti, was hired to assassinate JFK.

De Gaulle, Charles – The leader of the Free French Forces during World War II, De Gaulle dominated post–war France and became its longstanding President. De Gaulle authorized Paul–Louis Weiller and other representatives of the French government to enter into the

"Marseille Accord" with the French–Corsican syndicate (a/k/a Unione Corse) in February 1947.

Deplarakou, Alika – This world–famous Greek model was Paul–Louis Weiller's second wife.

Docheff, Ivan – This pro–fascist emigree headed the "Bulgarian National Front" and was chairman of the "American Friends of the Anti–Bolshevik Bloc of Nations" (ABN), an organization dominated by war criminals and fugitive fascists. Richard Nixon extensively relied upon the backing of Docheff and other ex–Nazis and fascists as part of his anti–Communist crusade and election campaigns.

Donovan, William "Wild Bill" – Donovan is best known for serving as the head of the Office of Strategic Services (OSS), the precursor to the CIA, during World War II.

Drug Enforcement Administration (DEA) – Founded on July 1, 1973, as successor to the BNDD, the DEA was tasked with combating drug trafficking and distribution within the U.S.

Dulles, Allen – A senior OSS officer during and immediately after World War II, he became the CIA's first civilian and longest–serving Director. In this role, he oversaw the 1953 Iranian coup, the 1954 Guatemalan coup, the U–2 spy plane program, the project MKUltra mind control program, and the Bay of Pigs invasion.

Dulles, John Foster – Principally known as Secretary of State for President Dwight Eisenhower, Dulles was an aggressive anti–communist and, along with his brother Allen, a major backer of Nixon's political career.

Egan, Eddie – Along with Sonny Grasso, NYPD Detective Eddie Egan was one of the detectives responsible for the 1962 arrest in New York of a group of relatively low–level French narcotics traffickers. Their investigation was closed by "higher ups" before the kingpins of the drug organization were exposed and prosecuted.

Cast of Characters · v

Francisci, Marcel – The so-called "Heroin King" of France, Francisci was a highly-decorated veteran of the French resistance. He took advantage of General de Gaulle's offer of immunity in return for wartime service on behalf of Free French forces. After the war, Francisci took a leadership position–along with Paul-Louis Weiller and a few others–in expanding the morphine-based smuggling operations in Marseille and exporting the refined heroin to the American markets.

Gehlen, Reinhard – Nazi Lieutenant General Reinhard was one of the U.S.'s most prized Nazi intelligence assets at the end of World War II. Gehlen's intelligence organization, mainly composed of ex-Nazis, operated under the loose control of the CIA throughout Europe and helped the Unione Corse break the Communist-dominated union strike on Marseille's docks in 1947.

Ghika, Alexandra – Princess Alexandra Ghika, a member of the Romanian aristocracy, married the French industrialist and war hero Paul-Louis Weiller in 1922.

Giscard D'Estaing, Valery – The Free French Finance Minister during World War II, Giscard D'Estaing rose in the post-war French government ranks to eventually serve as the French President.

Grasso, Sonny – Detective Grasso was one of the New York City Police (NYPD) officers who, along with Detective Eddie Egan, broke "the French Connection" case in 1962.

Harriman, W. Averill – A Democratic politician, businessman, and diplomat, Harriman was the U.S. Ambassador-at-Large to Europe in the immediate post-war period.

Helle, Henri – Helle operated a beach resort hotel in St. Martin as a frontman for Paul-Louis Weiller.

Helms, Richard – After serving as an OSS intelligence officer during World War II, Helms eventually served as Director of Central Intelligence (DCI) from 1966 to 1973. Along with Colby, he authorized a secret-CIA staffed inspection and covert intelligence program within the BNDD.

Hoover, J. Edgar – Hoover became the director of the FBI in 1924, and remained in that position for 37 years until his death in 1972. Hoover famously denied the existence of the Mafia for many years and was extremely reluctant to involve the FBI in narcotics investigations. As a staunch anti–Communist, the "Director" had few concerns about Nixon's close association with the Cuban Mafia and the French–Corsican syndicate that dominated the narcotics trade.

Horthy, Miklos – Admiral Horthy was a Hungarian politician and statesman between the two world wars.

The House Un–American Activities Committee (HUAC)–As a member of HUAC, Congressman Richard Nixon made a name for himself as an anti–Communist crusader by helping break the Alger Hiss spy case.

Hughes, Jr., Howard – An American business magnate, investor, record–setting pilot, Hughes was known as one of the most influential and financially successful figures in the aviation industry. Shortly before the 1960 Presidential election, it was revealed that Richard Nixon's brother, Donald, received a $205,000 loan from Hughes. Richard Nixon also received a cash payment from Hughes through his friend and bagman Bebe Rebozo.

Hunt, Jr., E. Howard – A CIA intelligence officer who worked with the OSS during World War II, Hunt helped the CIA maintain close ties with the Unione Corse, which controlled the heroin trade throughout Europe and the Americas. Hunt spent some time working in the CIA's Mexico City office with William F. Buckley, the conservative writer, and brother of Senator James Buckley of New York. Hunt was one of the Nixon White House's "plumbers." Hunt was convicted of burglary, conspiracy, and wiretapping in the Watergate scandal, eventually serving 33 months in prison.

INTERPOL – The International Criminal Police Organization, commonly known as Interpol, was founded in 1923. After falling under Nazi control in 1938, its headquarters were moved to Berlin. Many of its Nazi–collaborationist agents continued to serve in the organization in the post–war period, when its headquarters were moved to Lyon, France.

Kent, Sherman – A history professor who joined the OSS in 1942, Kent is credited with pioneering the art of modern intelligence analysis.

Knight, Paul E. – A longtime CIA officer, Knight used the DEA as "cover" and served as the DEA Agent in Charge of European Operations from 1972 to 1975.

Krogh, Egil – As Deputy to John Ehrlichman, Nixon's senior White House advisor, Krogh was the Nixon White House's primary liaison to the BNDD.

La Côte Basque – The fashionable French restaurant in Manhattan where Paul–Louis Weiller and Patricia Richardson met Richard Nixon and Bebe Rebozo in July 1968. A deal was sealed at this meeting which led to the payment of $2 million in cash to Rebozo for Nixon's 1968 presidential campaign.

Langsford III, John Maynard – At the New York State Select Committee on Crime hearings in 1975, Langsford testified that Patricia Richardson asked him to kill her then–husband, William Spector.

Lansdale, Edward G. – During the French Indochina war, Colonel Edward G. Lansdale made a six–week tour of Indochina for the CIA. He reported that French officers had bought up the entire opium harvest for sale and export from Saigon.

Lansky, Meyer – This Jewish organized crime boss had extensive casinos and other holdings in Havana, Cuba, which were confiscated following the Cuban Revolution of 1959. Lansky and his organization had a good working relationship with the Unione Corse, which dominated the heroin narcotics trade.

Liddy, G. Gordon – One of Nixon's top advisors and lead Watergate "plumber." Liddy was perhaps the most pro–fascist enthusiast in the Nixon White House, regularly sponsoring viewings of the iconic Nazi film, Lena Wertmuller's *Triumph of the Will*, in the movie theater in the White House basement.

Luciano, Lucky – Considered the father of modern organized crime, Luciano created the Commission of Mafia families.

Ludlum, James H. – The CIA liaison to the BNDD from 1969 to 1975.

Malaxa, Nicolae – A wealthy Romanian industrialist, Malaxa funded the Nazi Iron Guard in Romania during the war. Afterward, he moved to Whittier, California, Richard Nixon's hometown, where he became a close friend of Nixon and critical player in Nixon's political strategy to attract ex–Nazis and pro–fascists to his anti–Communist crusade.

Malraux, Andre – This French writer and philosopher was a close personal friend of Paul–Louis Weiller. During the Second World War, Malraux was a pilot with the legendary Normandy Squadron, which escaped France after it was overrun by German forces.

Marshall, George C. – As Secretary of State in the Truman Administration, Marshall approved the Marseille Agreement (or Accord) in February 1947. This agreement enlisted the support of the Unione Corse in opening up the Port of Marseille to U.S. shipping and breaking the labor strikes on the docks. In return, they were promised by France and the U.S. to give the Unione Corse a free hand concerning their worldwide heroin trafficking operations.

Mezey–Feher, Elisabeth–A suspected informer for the German Nazis in Romania during and after World War II. She had an affair with OSS Major Robert Bishop and likely obtained top–secret information from him.

Moore, Robin – The author of *The French Connection*, *The Green Berets*, and other works, Moore became one of William Spector's most influential advocates. He went on record to say that he believed that Spector's allegations should have been more thoroughly investigated by law enforcement agencies.

Cast of Characters · ix

Mudge Rose Guthrie & Alexander – the New York law firm that Richard Nixon joined in 1963 and used as a springboard for his successful presidential campaign in 1968.

Nepote, Jean – Nepote was a Vichy–French collaborator with the Nazis during World War II, who deftly joined the resistance organization "Ajax" at the war's end. He then joined Interpol to become its Secretary General.

Nixon, Richard – The 37th President of the United States, from 1969 until his resignation in 1974, Nixon got his political start with the help of the CIA and ex–Nazi donors to his 1947 campaign for a seat in the U.S. House of Representatives. He helped cover up the close ties between the CIA, ex–Nazis in the U.S., and the Unione Corse. He then established a national reputation as an anti–Communist crusader with the help of all three groups. During his campaign for the presidency in 1968, Nixon received a much–needed infusion of $2 million in cash after a meeting with Patricia Richardson and Paul–Louis Weiller of the Unione Corse at the Côte Basque restaurant in New York. The Watergate break–in ordered by Nixon was precipitated, at least in part, by Nixon's obsession with fear that the Democratic National Committee headquartered in the Watergate complex had information about his ties to the French–Corsican mob.

Nixon, Donald – The brother of President Richard Nixon, Donald Nixon received a $205,000 loan from Howard Hughes. President Nixon worried thart evidence of this loan would be used against him in the 1972 re–election campaign.

Nixon, Jr., Donald – The son of Donald Nixon, "Don–Don" worked for fugitive financier Robert Vesco on various fraudulent and stock manipulation schemes in both the U.S. and Cuba.

O'Brien, Lawrence – Larry O'Brien was the Chairman of the National Democratic Committee during the Nixon administration. O'Brien and former Vice President Hubert Humphrey ran a disinformation campaign against President Nixon during his 1972 presidential re–election. They leaked suggestions they had more "dirt" on Nixon than they really did. This disinformation campaign triggered Nixon's "green–lighting" of the infamous Watergate break–in.

Office of Strategic Services (OSS) – The OSS was a wartime intelligence agency of the United States during World War II and a predecessor to the CIA. The OSS was formed as an agency of the Joint Chiefs of Staff to coordinate espionage activities behind enemy lines for all United States Armed Forces branches. William Spector was one of several wartime officers of the OSS who were asked to stay in Europe to help the process of rebuilding Western Europe. He was also asked to secure control of as many Nazi scientific secrets and scientists as possible before they were grabbed by their Soviet counterparts.

Operation X – This was the code–name for the clandestine opium trafficking from Vietnam and elsewhere in Indochina, involving the Unione Corse and French intelligence officers.

Organisation de l'Armée Secrete (Organization of the Secret Army, or "OAS") – This was a French dissident paramilitary organization during the Algerian War (1952–62). The OAS engaged in a campaign of assassinations and bombings to try to stop the political process that resulted in an independent Algeria in 1962. French President Charles de Gaulle was one of the targets of an OAS assassination attempt. De Gaulle and the French government used the muscle and ruthlessness of the SAC members within the French intelligence services to launch a counter–terrorism campaign against the OAS.

Ottman, Mary Jo – A neighbor of Patricia Richardson in Syracuse, New York, she accompanied Patricia and her children as the children's caregiver on an extended trip that Patricia took to her home island of St. Martin.

Pasztor, Laszlo – One of the Nazis recruited by Richard Nixon for his 1968 presidential campaign, Pasztor was the founding chair of Nixon's Republican Heritage Groups Council. As a diplomat in Berlin during World War II, representing the Arrow Cross government of Nazi Hungary, he supervised the extermination of the Jewish population in Hungary.

Peretti, Achille – A police inspector in Marseille who worked closely with Unione Corse members, he formed a resistance group of police officers during WWII known as "Ajax."

Peroff, Frank – This DEA informant tape-recorded a conversation with Conrad Bouchard, the leading Unione Corse figure in Montreal, Canada. Bouchard told him that fugitive financier Robert Vesco would be financing a major heroin transaction. However, when Peroff told his DEA handlers about this, they abruptly terminated him as an undercover informant. Several Congressional investigations regarding Peroff's allegations of DEA corruption ensued.

Pieds–Noirs – Literally meaning "black feet" in French, these were the people of French and other European origins who were born in Algeria during the period of French rule from 1830 to 1962. The vast majority departed for mainland France or Corsica as soon as Algeria gained independence in 1962. Many became affiliated with the French–Corsican drug syndicate known as the Unione Corse.

Rebozo, Charles Gregory "Bebe" – President Richard Nixon's closest friend and bagman for many years, Rebozo had close ties with Cuban, Italian, and French–Corsican organized crime groups. He was at the 1968 meeting with Nixon, Patricia Richardson, and Paul–Louis Weiller at the Côte Basque Restaurant in New York, where a deal was struck for the $2 million cash payment to the Nixon presidential campaign.

Richardson Martinson, Patricia – A woman of extraordinary beauty and brains, Richardson rose from abject poverty as an orphan on the Island of St. Martin to become a successful international model. She was also the protégé of some of Europe's most influential industrialists and business leaders, including Sir Charles Clore of the U.K. and Commandant Paul–Louis Weiller of France. In partnership with Weiller, Richardson rose in the ranks of the Unione Corse to become the only woman to enter the inner circle of the secret organization's leadership. Along the way, she married William Spector, a former OSS intelligence officer, using Spector's Cadillacs to transport large quantities of heroin from Montreal across the border to Ogdensburg,

New York, and southward to the heroin markets of New York and elsewhere on the East Coast.

Ricord, Auguste – A Unione Corse and SAC member, Ricord developed the *contrabandista* airborne smuggling routes throughout South and Central America for the Unione Corse.

Service d'Action Civique ("SAC") – This was the "dirty tricks" or "hit squad" within the SDECE, the French intelligence services. Its members, known as "barbouzes" or "bearded ones," controlled most of the narcotics trafficking activities of the SDECE and coordinated those activities with the Unione Corse.

Service de Documentation Extérieure et de Contre–Espionnage (SDECE) – This was France's external intelligence agency from November 1944 to April 1982, equivalent to the U.S.'s CIA. The SDECE had a decades–long "working relationship" with the Unione Corse and indirectly shared in the profits of this narcotics trafficking syndicate.

Shackley, Theodore – The CIA's Chief of the Western Hemisphere Division from 1972 to 1974, he was involved with Cuban exile plots to overthrow Castro and the Iran–Contra drug scandal.

Sibert, Edwin – Brig. Gen. Edwin Sibert, the head of G–2 (Army intelligence) of the Twelfth Army in Germany, was the first U.S. intelligence officer to debrief Nazi General Gehlen, who turned himself in to U.S. forces at the end of World War II. Gehlen brought with him a treasure trove of intelligence files on the Russians.

Smith, Phillip R. – As Acting Chief Inspector in the DEA, he was a key player in much of the DEA's internal turmoil.

Société des Moteurs Gnome et Rhône (Gnome–Rhone Motor Works) – Paul–Louis Weiller and his father were majority owners of this French aircraft manufacturer.

Spector, William – After a distinguished career as a U.S. Army intelligence officer during World War II, he married Patricia Richardson, the irresistibly stunning model. They settled in Ogdensburg, New York, where Spector had a Cadillac dealership. After only a few short years, Richardson disappeared, and the marriage was dissolved. Spector's subsequent investigation disclosed that his ex-wife was using his dealership's cars to run heroin across the border from Canada. Spector turned over the substantial amount of information he had collected to federal, state, and local law enforcement agencies. Still, none of them seriously pursued the leads he provided. Undeterred, Spector relentlessly pursued the matter for many years, taking his information and files to several Congressional committees. However, no conclusive evidence was ever developed that led to criminal charges. Richardson, Weiller, and others in the upper echelon of the Unione Corse–the real culprits behind the French Connection case–were never caught. Spector died a frustrated and bitter man, while Richardson remarried and lived happily in a luxurious villa on her home island of St. Martin.

Stillwell, Joseph – U.S. General Joe Stillwell allowed many members of the French armed services to become U.S. citizens after World War II in return for their assistance to the U.S. during the war. Many joined the CIA and established close ties with the Unione Corse.

Tartaglino, Andrew C. – As Acting Deputy Administrator of the DEA, he managed several corruption investigations, including one involving a DEA employee who was a close friend and associate of DEA Administrator John Bartels. The internal dispute led to a Congressional investigation and dismissal of Bartels.

Trafficante, Jr., Santos – One of the most powerful Mafia bosses in the U.S., Trafficante controlled most of the organized crime operations in Florida and Cuba. His organization maintained close links with the Unione Corse.

Truman, Harry S. – Vice President Truman became President in 1944 after the death of President Franklin D. Roosevelt. Determined to save the democracies of Europe after World War II, the Truman Administration directed large quantities of foodstuffs and machinery shipments to Europe. The prime aim was to stave off starvation, economic collapse, and a take-over by pro-Russian Communist parties and their allies in the labor unions. Truman approved the February

1947 "Marseille Agreement," giving the Unione Corse a freehand in narcotics traficking.

Unione Corse – The French–Corsican organized crime syndicate that controlled the manufacture of heroin in Marseille, France, and its distribution in North America and around the globe. Paul–Louis Weiller and Patricia Richardson were in the upper echelons of the organization's leadership.

Vesco, Robert – A 2001 Slate.com article accurately referred to Vesco as "the undisputed king of the fugitive financiers." Vesco fled the U.S. in February 1973 aboard a corporate jet with more than $200 million embezzled funds from a public company called IOS. Shortly before his departure, however, Vesco arranged for some substantial cash contributions to be made to President Richard Nixon through Nixon's nephew, Donald A. Nixon. Vesco was also investigated for a secret $200,000 contribution to the 1972 campaign to re–elect Nixon. Vesco reportedly died of lung cancer in Havana in November 2007, but reports of his death were greatly exaggerated. His associate Frank Terpil disclosed that he had fled to Sierra Leone, with the help of Weiller and Richardson.

Voorhis, Horace Jerimiah "Jerry," – The incumbent Democratic Congressman from California's 12th Congressional District lost to Republican candidate Richard M. Nixon in a bitter and close race in 1946.

Weiller, Paul–Louis – A French pilot and war hero in the First World War, Weiller became one of the wealthiest leading French industrialists both before and after World War II. Less known was that Weiller was the principal financier and one of the leaders of the Unione Corse, which dominated the heroin trade for several decades. Patricia Richardson was Weiller's close associate and paramour.

WIN – A Polish underground group operating during the post–World War II period that supplied the U.S. and its allies with military information on Soviet troop movements.

Wisner, Frank G – The commander of the OSS special unit in Bucharest, Romania, from August 1944 until January 1945, which included Lt. William Spector.

Zyposch, Major General – As the commanding general of the Hungarian 5th Army, General Zyposch surrendered the Crown of St. Stephan to Lt. William Spector and other U.S. officers. The crown was transported to Fort Knox, Kentucky for safekeeping and eventually returned to the Hungarian government in the post–war period.

Introduction

As a young federal prosecutor during the 1970s and 1980s, I played a minor role in the federal government's "War on Drugs," originally launched by the Nixon Administration and continued by both Republican and Democratic administrations. The Drug Enforcement Administration (DEA) was established in 1973 by an executive order signed by then–President Nixon, ostensibly as part of "an all–out war on the global drug menace." It was not until much later that we learned that Nixon's real objective was not so much to stop the trafficking of narcotics but, rather, to criminally prosecute and incarcerate as many inner–city blacks and civil rights leaders as possible on drug charges, as well as their anti–war and "liberal" allies in the white communities.

Nixon considered African–Americans and anti–war liberals to be his two major political enemies. The War on Drugs was designed to neutralize both of them. Well–financed undercover narcotics operations and networks of paid informants led to a blizzard of well–publicized but low–level prosecutions against marijuana users and small–time drug dealers. In the process, a large percentage of young black males were condemned to a life in prison, and both the civil rights and anti–war movements were impeded as they became riddled with undercover agents and paid informants looking to build a case against as many leaders as possible.

Over the span of a decade, billions of dollars in taxpayers' money were spent on increased law enforcement manpower, sophisticated equipment, as well as payments to a vast network of undercover informants and operatives. However, what puzzled me and, no doubt, many other observers was that virtually all of the federal government's efforts in its "War On Drugs" were focused on stopping the flow of narcotics from Mexico and elsewhere in Latin America, with little or no effort to halt the flow of pure white heroin being refined in Marseille,

France and distributed throughout North America and globally by the French–Corsican organized crime group known as the Unione Corse. Indeed, the DEA's near tunnel-vision focus on eliminating the marijuana, cocaine, and brown heroin coming into the U.S. from Latin America seemed to be having the unintended (or perhaps intended) result of eliminating–or at least restricting–the trafficking operations of the Unione Corse's major competitors from South of the Border.

In 1969, a hugely popular book by author Robin Moore, entitled The French Connection, was based on the real-life story of how an investigation by NYPD detectives Jimmy "Popeye" Doyle and Buddy "Cloudy" Russo arrested some low-level French narcotics traffickers who were attempting to bring a large shipment of narcotics into the U.S. hidden in an imported French car. The movie of the same name won five major awards at the 44th Academy Awards, including Best Actor Gene Hackman, Best Director, and Best Movie for the year 1971. However, what intrigued me the most was that none of the higher-ups in the French–Corsican organization that supplied the heroin through the established Marseille channels were ever prosecuted or even publicly identified. The federal indictment in the case made cryptic reference to an unidentified "John Doe" defendant who was identified as the "kingpin" of the operation, but for some unknown reason, he was never arrested, prosecuted, or even identified.

Many years later, after I had left the U.S. Department of Justice to become a civil litigator, I started doing research for a book on the history of U.S. narcotics enforcement. This research led me back to the question of why the Unione Corse seemed to have been given a "free pass" by U.S. and French law enforcement agencies supposedly engaged in an international War on Drugs. It took me several years of research to find the answer, which is that the U.S. and the French government had entered into a "hands-off" agreement in 1947 with the French–Corsican organized crime syndicate based in Marseille in return for the Unione Corse's assistance in breaking the labor strike in Marseille. This strike had closed down the Port of Marseille to shipping, thus crippling U.S. efforts to provide France and the rest of Western Europe with the food and equipment that was desperately needed to stave off the political take-over in those countries by Communist and other pro-Russian political parties. Know as the "Marseille Accord" or "Marseille Agreement" at the time, there was very little, if any, readily available historical evidence of the agreement, which effectively gave the Unione Corse virtual immunity from prosecution and carte blanche to carry out their narcotics trafficking without significant governmental interference.

But why hadn't I heard about this before? After all, I had been a history major in college and an avid reader of almost any book or article dealing with 20th Century U.S. and contemporary history, so why had nothing been written about this highly significant and consequential agreement and its aftermath? Why hadn't I heard about any high-profile Congressional hearings about this, and why hadn't some enterprising investigative journalist latched onto this story to become the next media superstar, just as Woodward and Bernstein had rode their way to fame and fortune by doggedly pursuing the Watergate investigation?

To my amazement, I discovered that there were, in fact, Congressional and state legislative investigations of the Unione Corse and its narcotics trafficking operations in the U.S., but that these investigations had largely fizzled out, like some supernova that lights up the sky for a few fractions of a second and then dies out just as quickly. In a June 1975 article entitled, *The Model, the Drug Ring And the Big Evidence Hunt*, the New York Times reported that "a swarm of local, state, federal and international police agencies, along with a United States Senator and an Albany committee, have been racing each other for more than two months in pursuit of a spurned husband's bizarre tale of an international drug ring." The Times article elaborated: "Spurred by post-Watergate fears of a cover-up and tantalized by an unlikely cast of characters that includes European millionaires, Caribbean jet-setters, the Nixon White House and a gorgeous model, the investigators are about to hold unusual public hearings into the affair...."

The public hearings being referred to were conducted by the New York State Select Committee on Crime, spurred by Senator James Buckley of New York. Buckley and his staff had become fascinated by the tale of international intrigue and corruption reaching the highest levels of the U.S. and French Governments. The primary source of this information was William Spector, a Cadillac dealer from upstate New York who had been an intelligence officer and Lieutenant in the U.S. Army during World War II, and then stayed on in Europe after the war as an OSS/CIA agent to help collect as much Nazi intelligence information on Russia as possible before key Nazi officers and their information fell into the hands of the Russians. Most notably, Spector was one of three U.S. officers who attended a clandestine meeting in Marseille in 1947 to formulate a plan to reopen up the Marseille Port to U.S. shipping. At the meeting, an agreement was reached between the French, U.S., and representatives of the Unione Corse. The Unione Corse would provide the necessary "muscle" to break up the strikes, in return for which the U.S. and French governments would give them a "free hand" with regard to their heroin manufacturing and distribution operations. Known as the "Marseille Accord" or "Marseille Agreement," this unwritten agreement became one of the cornerstones and "dirty little secrets" of U.S. and French law enforcement policy for the next several decades.

What was so electrifying and sensational about Spector's revelations was that he was now ready to blow the whistle on this longstanding corrupt relationship that the U.S. (through the CIA) and France (through its intelligence services) had with the Unione Corse. Spector's ex–wife and ex–international model from the island of St. Martin, Patricia Richardson, had literally destroyed his Cadillac dealership business and his own reputation by using his cars to transport heroin across the U.S.–Canadian border from Montreal, and then siphoning off millions of dollars from his business with an elaborate bank fraud scheme. His own investigation, based in part on various papers and diaries she had left behind, revealed that she herself was a member of the Unione Corse's top leadership, and that along with another leading member of this French–Corsican mob, Paul–Louis Weiller, had provided the critical financial support to Richard Nixon's successful 1968 presidential campaign.

So where were the transcripts of these State Select Committee hearings and the evidence that had been collected? Incredibly, the New York State Senate archives and other public sources in Albany and New York did not have copies of the hearing records or the final report. Nor could these records be found among Senator Buckley's records or anywhere else where we searched. It soon became clear that this was not a case of inadvertence or mistake. Extensive public records like this do not just disappear. Clearly, someone or something did not want these records to be publicly available, so they had been "disappeared" or "deep sixed," to use the parlance popular at the time of the Watergate investigation. The National Archive records relating to Weiller, Richardson and other critical players in this drama had also gone missing, although some of the filing cards on Weiller and others had been overlooked and were still available.

Not to be deterred, I and a few intrepid researchers assisting me were able to piece together the "back story" of the leadership of the Unione Corse that were behind The French Connection case, including the story of how two of the kingpins in this organization–Weiller and Richardson–were the ones who provided Richard Nixon with the $2 million in much-needed cash to win the 1968 presidential election by a razor-thin margin. We also uncovered conclusive evidence that this French-Corsican organization, through its leadership and affiliated ex-Nazis and fascists, gained unrestricted access to the Nixon White House and the entire federal administration. And finally, it was the Nixon team's unholy alliance with the French-Corsican mob and their unsavory cohorts that was the major precipitating factor in Nixon's decision to authorize the Watergate break-in of the Democratic National Committee offices, which Nixon had been led to believe held documents linking him to cash payoffs from the Unione Corse, Howard Hughes, and others.

With the benefit of access to previously unavailable diaries, records, and witnesses, and after years of in-depth research, the Marseille Connection's full story and its previously undisclosed impact on the U.S. can finally be told.

Chapter 1:
The Beginning, 1947

It was Autumn 1947. The war with Germany was over. Yet the emerging Cold War loomed like a massive storm cloud over Europe. Much of the European continent lay in ruins, with the U.S. and Soviet Union maneuvering to control what remained. The Soviet Red Army had already locked down most of Eastern Europe with an iron grip, including the eastern portion of Germany and East Berlin. But its ambitions did not stop there. Stalin and his allies in the Communist parties of Italy, West Germany, and France believed that the time was ripe to expand their hegemony to the shores of the English Channel.

After years of war, upheaval, and misery, Europe was in a state of political instability bordering on chaos. Charles de Gaulle, leader of Free France (France Libre), the government-in-exile throughout World War II, suddenly retired in January 1946. His departure left a power vacuum in French politics. With no fewer than 25 political parties in 1946, France suffered the trauma of over 30 changes of government in less than two years, as talks to form coalition governments stalled.

The U.S. was deeply concerned about the growing power of the Communist parties in Western Europe and their allies in the trade and labor unions. As one of the few political parties with impeccable anti–Nazi credentials solidly intact, the Communists scored impressive political gains across Western Europe. In the 1946 French general election, the Christian Democrats led by Robert Schuman won by the thinnest of margins, with only 28% of the vote. The Parti Communiste Français (PCF) was just behind them, with 26% of the vote in the polls. Italy's 1946 election ended similarly. The Partito Comunista Italiano (PCI) took 21% of the vote and came in second to the Christian Democracy Party led by Alcide De Gasperi.

Using labor strikes as a powerful weapon, Communist-controlled unions in France and Italy were in a position to demand significant concessions from both governments and industries in the ports and cities where they were the most powerful. By November 1947, communist-led labor strikes had already wreaked havoc on the fragile economies of France and Italy, nearly bringing both countries to their knees.

Nowhere was France more vulnerable than in Marseille, its largest port on the Mediterranean. After liberation in 1944, American aid poured into the port through a seemingly endless stream of cargo ships stretching across the Atlantic. The Marshall Plan (officially the European Recovery Program), designed to rebuild Western Europe with an economic stimulus of $13 billion, did not formally start operations until April 1948. However, immediately following the war's end, America began shipping massive amounts of grain, foodstuffs, machinery, and supplies into Marseille. This effort was critical in staving off mass starvation and economic collapse throughout Western Europe. Instead of bullets, bombers, and rifles, America's formidable war machine was rapidly retooled to mass-produce peace products.

The fledgling democratic governments of France and Italy had no chance of surviving without the lifeline thrown to them by the United States. The Soviet Union and the pro-communist labor unions throughout Western Europe were doing everything they could to bring about the collapse of the centrist democratic governments, particularly in France and Italy. American aid was the only thing still propping them up.[1] Even with massive American assistance, France's industrial production sunk by 25–50% by the end of 1947, primarily due to labor stoppages and strikes.[2]

The Cold War was thus well underway by 1947, and the U.S. and Soviet intelligence services were at the center of this struggle.

* * *

Although most American military and intelligence forces in Western Europe had been sent home after the war, some wartime intelligence operatives were asked to stay on in Europe. They were ostensibly there to help with the process of denazification and rebuilding Western Europe. But they also secured control of as many Nazi scientists and secrets as possible before their Soviet counterparts grabbed them.

On September 20, 1945, shortly after V–Day, President Harry S. Truman signed an executive order dissolving the Office of Strategic Services ("OSS"), dividing its functions between the U.S. State Department and the War Department. However, the Truman Administration quickly realized it had made a mistake, and the division lasted only a few months. The OSS, modeled on the British counter–intelligence organization known as MI–6, had been hugely successful during the war. The arbitrary separation of such an effective team of young intelligence officers was highly demoralizing and left the U.S. disadvantaged compared to Britain and Russia's professional covert activities. Realizing his mistake, Truman restored the core OSS elements by establishing the National Intelligence Authority in January 1946. Its field agents were part of the Central Intelligence Group, the direct predecessor of the CIA.

Many intelligence agents traditionally came from elite U.S. colleges such as Yale, Harvard, and Princeton. One of the country's first intelligence officers during the Revolutionary War, Nathan Hale, was a Yale graduate. After him, most U.S. intelligence officers hailed from the "old boy" Ivy League network. These men had often known each other during their undergraduate years and trusted the character of their classmates. For example, Allen Dulles, a Princeton graduate, was a senior OSS officer during and immediately after the war. He went on to become the longest–serving Director of the CIA. Another distinguished OSS/CIA agent was Sherman Kent, a Yale graduate who worked as a history professor before joining the OSS in 1942. Kent is credited with pioneering the art of modern intelligence analysis. In tribute, the CIA named its school for intelligence analysis after him in 2000.

One soldier who agreed to stay in Europe was William H. Spector, a young, Russian–speaking military intelligence officer from Syracuse, New York. He had served with distinction in Romania and elsewhere in Eastern Europe. By the time he entered military service, Spector had already completed his undergraduate degree at Cornell. After distinguishing himself in Officer Candidate's School ("OCS"), he started his active duty in the U.S. Army as a First Lieutenant.

4 · The Marseille Connection

"Newly Commissioned Lieutenant William H. Spector." Newspaperarchive, Syracuse Herald American, 29 Mar. 1942.

Because he had learned the Russian language from his parents, Lieutenant Spector was assigned to the secret intelligence unit of the OSS in Bucharest, the capital of Romania. This OSS special unit was commanded from August 1944 until January 1945 by the dynamic Frank G. Wisner, director of OSS operations for Southeastern Europe, with Major Robert Bishop second in command.[3]

At the start of World War II, Romania was a monarchy that had acquired Transylvania, Bessarabia, and some Hungarian territory after joining the victorious Allies in WWI. However, because of strong anti–Russian sentiment in those newly acquired regions, a Nazi–allied political party known as the "Iron Guard" gained political power in the country. When WWII began, Romania entered the war on the German side. This affiliation with the Nazis ended in 1944 when the Soviet armies reached the Romanian border. King Michael of Romania, installed by the military dictator and Prime Minister Ion Antonescu, switched over to the Allied side, hoping to save his nation's industrial base from Russian annexation.

The U.S. goal in sending an OSS team to Romania had initially been to rescue 2,000 captured airmen held as prisoners of war there and in Bulgaria. As the war ended, their mission changed to preventing Eastern Europe from falling into the Soviet sphere. Lieutenant Spector played a critical role in this heroic–yet ultimately unsuccessful-campaign.

Spector's most notable achievement during the war was that he was the U.S. officer who accepted the surrender of General Zyposch, commanding general of the Hungarian 5th Army.[4] At that time, Russian forces were moving west through the Balkans, and the American troops were moving east through Germany. The Hungarian 5th Army fought a rear-guard action out of Budapest into Austria. Under Major General Zyposch's care was the Crown of St. Stephan, which represented the equivalent of the Declaration of Independence to Hungary. Hungarian history and legend have it that whoever owns that crown or possesses it is the legitimate king of Hungary. It was, therefore, a powerful symbol.

General Zyposch was in Brünnau, located in Bavaria in southern Germany. His entire Army was encamped there. The standing orders to U.S. military personnel were that the Hungarian Army was to be treated as friendly allied forces and not treated as prisoners of war. General Zyposch wisely decided that it was in his best interests and that of his entire Army to surrender to the Americans rather than the Russians. A Russian force tried to penetrate the area to beat the Americans to the Hungarian encampment. Lieutenant Spector and other U.S. officers attached to the U.S. 86th Infantry Division blocked this effort. After frantic consultations between Spector and Admiral Miklos Horthy of Hungary, General Zyposch surrendered his military forces and the Crown Jewels to the American Forces on May 4, 1945.

In addition to being a senior military officer, Admiral Horthy was a politician and statesman between the two world wars, serving as Regent of the Kingdom of Hungary. Although Horthy allied Hungary with Nazi Germany, and Hungarian forces participated in the Soviet Union and Yugoslavia invasion, Horthy's reluctance to contribute any further to the German war effort eventually led the Germans to invade and take control of the country in March 1944. In October 1944, Horthy announced that Hungary would surrender and withdraw from the Axis alliance, but the war continued until the following year.

Like Spector and Hunt, Angleton already had a distinguished record of accomplishments as a wartime intelligence officer. He also had an Ivy League pedigree–a bachelor's degree from Yale and some time at Harvard Law School. His time at Yale and Harvard helped his rapid advance up the chain of command in the U.S. intelligence services. During the war, Angleton served in the counter-intelligence

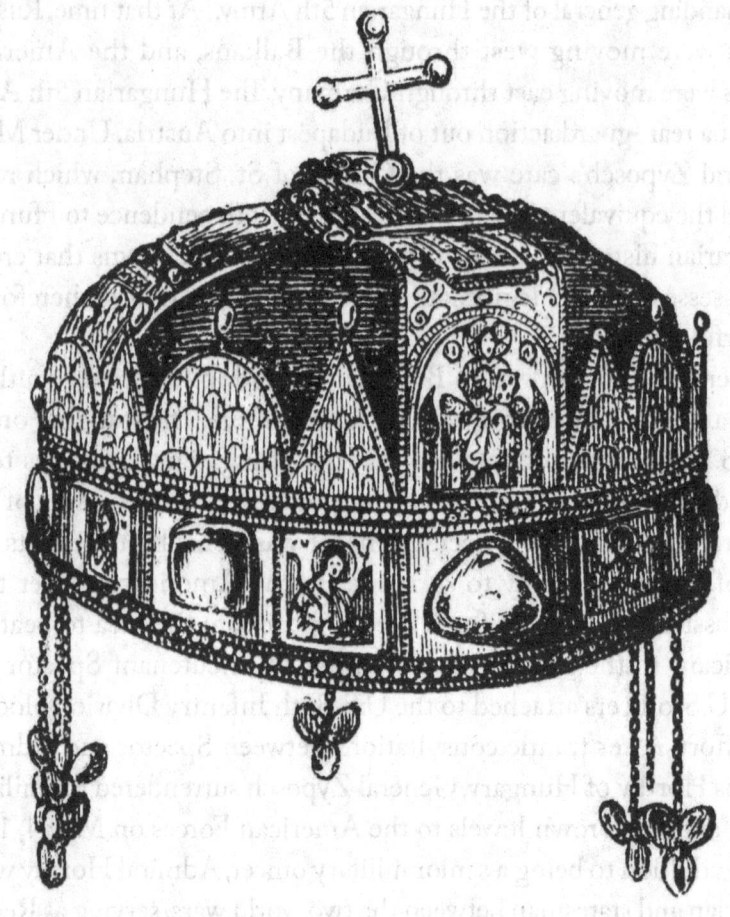

The Crown of St. Stephen. It is said that whoever possesses the Crown is the legitimate ruler of Hungary. Quagga Media/ Alamy Stock Photo.

branch (X–2) of the OSS in London. In 1944, he transferred to Italy as commander of the OSS Secret Counterintelligence (SCI), Unit Z, which handled "Ultra" intelligence based on the British intercepts of German Gestapo radio communications. Immediately after the war, Angleton headed up the U.S. influence campaign to support the right–wing Christian Democrat party in the upcoming Italian general elections. He was given over $1 million to sway public opinion through funding radio broadcasts, posters, and over ten million letters to Italian voters.[5] Later, Angleton became the controversial head of CIA Counterintelligence Operations during the 1950s and 1960s.

Before being assigned to a top-secret mission in the Mediterranean, Angleton visited Lucky Luciano, the Italian-born Mafia chief who had been imprisoned on prostitution charges in 1936. Luciano had already assisted U.S. forces by providing intelligence reports from his Mafia counterparts in Sicily and Southern Italy. The information proved invaluable to the successful U.S. amphibious landings in Sicily and rapid advance up the Italian peninsula. Luciano also used his substantial influence with the New York longshoreman's union to quell labor unrest on the docks during the war. Now Angleton was asking the aging don to help the U.S. once again to solve a critical labor union "problem." In return for his release, the U.S. requested Luciano to contact his Italian Mafia associates to help break the labor strikes at the Port of Marseille and other French and Italian ports on the Mediterranean. Luciano agreed. Shortly after that, he was freed and deported to Sicily.[6]

***

The orders given to Hunt, Angleton, and Spector in November 1947 were simple: keep Marseille's waterfront open to shipping, no matter the cost. President Truman and Secretary of State George Marshall had been fully briefed on the dangers posed by the Communist-led labor unions in Marseille and other French ports. They directed that all available resources be brought to bear to keep the ports open. The U.S. effort to rebuild Europe would be choked off in its infancy if ships could not unload at the docks. Their precious cargo would not be distributed to feed a starving Europe. The fate of the U.S.-backed centrist governments in Italy and France—which had won elections by the skin of their teeth—hung in the balance.

The Soviet Union and its allied Communist parties in Italy, France, and West Germany had other ideas. They saw a golden opportunity to bring Western Europe into the Soviet sphere. They were deeply suspicious of U.S. efforts to economically dominate Western Europe and rebuild West Germany. Russia had watched in horror as Germany had recovered from a devastating First World War by refashioning itself through the 1930s into a Nazi economic and military powerhouse. They vowed they would not stand idly by while West Germany again rebuilt and remilitarized.

The Soviet Union also did not want a robust centrist government to emerge in France. Charles de Gaulle reentered the political arena in early 1947 with his stabilizing new movement, Rally of the French People (RPF). The Communists preferred to keep France in a state of political ferment, hoping that a Communist party–led coalition would have a chance to rise to the top.

Then, in November 1947, a newly-elected conservative mayor in Marseille provoked a new set of severe protests that brought the city to the edge of civil war.[7] As the port became paralyzed by strikes, U.S. cargo ships began stacking up outside the harbor, unable to unload their cargo. The U.S. started to suspect that these Communist labor union–led strikes could metastasize into a full-blown communist uprising. Something had to be done immediately to restart the infusion of essential resources. Angleton and his team of counter-intelligence officers, including Spector, received direct orders from the White House and the U.S. State Department to break the union blockade of the docks "by any means necessary."

Gen. Charles de Gaulle, leader of the Free French movement, c. 1942. Library of Congress, Washington, D.C. (Digital File Number: cph 3b42159).

On the French side, de Gaulle turned to his old friend and comrade in arms with the Free French Forces in London, Commander Paul-Louis Weiller. He asked Weiller to come up with a solution to the union strikes that had shuttered the Marseille waterfront. If anyone could come up with a solution, it was Weiller. He had been the most celebrated pilot in the French Air Force in the First World War. As a wealthy industrialist between the two World Wars, Weiller was financially able to provide much-needed monetary support for the Free French Forces after the fall of France in 1939–1940.

De Gaulle and Weiller knew that the Unione Corse was the only effective force in the Marseille area that could counter the unions' strength. This band of Corsican-French syndicates resembled the Mafia and ran illegal gambling, prostitution, and heroin factories in Marseille.

The Unione Corse had also been used to combat communists before. Following tactics pioneered by Mussolini's dreaded Black Shirts, street violence between Fascist agitators and Communist or Socialist demonstrators spread across Europe in the interwar period. Yet, in Marseille, a bastion of French radical working-class politics, fascism struggled to find a popular base. In 1931 Simon Sabiani, the Corsican mayor of Marseille and committed fascist, struck a deal with two leading Corsican gangsters. In exchange for municipal appointments to underworld figures, the Corsican syndicate led by François Spirito and Paul Bonnaventure Carbone would use their henchmen to harass and intimidate local communist demonstrators.[8] This power-sharing agreement made Carbone and Spirito the de facto leaders of "Le Milieu" (French organized crime) in Marseille.[9]

After Sabiani was voted out of office in 1935, Carbone and Spirito's power faded somewhat. But their fortunes turned with the Nazi invasion of France. Sabiani became an influential Vichy French collaborator. Meanwhile, Carbone and Spirito exchanged information regarding local communists (and resistance forces) to the Nazi occupation forces in exchange for the tacit agreement by the Nazis to give their criminal activities free reign.[10] Carbone was eventually killed in a train bombing planned by the French Resistance in 1943, while Spirito and Sabiani managed to escape to Spain following the Normandy landings in 1944.

It may be hard to accept that Corsican syndicates who served as fascist street brawlers formed an alliance with French Resistance icons like De Gaulle and Weiller. However, unlike the Italian Mafia, the Unione Corse lacked central leadership or structure. Instead, the Unione was composed of cells structured around family and clan associations within Corsica, with each syndicate operating largely independently—sometimes in direct conflict. While Carbone and Spirito's syndicate collaborated with the Nazi occupation, other Unione Corse affiliated groups found it more profitable to support resistance efforts.[11]

Marseille's most critical Corsican Resistance fighters were the syndicate led by the Guérini Brothers, Antoine and Barthélemy. While the Guérinis had fought fascist occupation, they also had a bone to pick with the communist strikers.

Following liberation in 1944, the French Compagnies Républicaines de Sécurité (CRS), paramilitary police, were established to restore public order and round up collaborators. Staffed by many former communist resistance operatives,[12] the CRS came down hard on the black-market operations run by Corsicans. This greatly upset the Unione Corse, who had been largely left alone since the 1930s.

By 1946 and 1947, the Communist and Socialist-controlled unions dominated the Marseille waterfront. Time and time again, they had proven their strength by throwing up picket lines, shutting down the waterfront, and using their strength at the ballot box to elect leftist mayors. In April 1945, a left-wing coalition of Communists and Socialists elected Socialist Gaston Defferre as mayor of Marseille. Following a split in the left-wing alliance, Communist candidate Jean Cristofol won the mayorship the following year. Cristofol ordered the closure of several nightclubs, including Guérini's Parakeet Club. However, by October 1947, the schism between Socialist and Communist voters, combined with de Gaulle's reemergence on the political scene, led to the election of Michel Carlini, a Gaullist conservative, as mayor.

As one of his first acts in office, Carlini decided to raise tram fares to reduce the growing city budget deficit. A seemingly innocuous decision, this infuriated the working-class of Marseille. They were already struggling to purchase basic supplies and make ends meet after the war. Raising the cost of public transport proved to be enough to push hungry, underpaid workers over the edge. Immediately following Carlini's decision, Communist and Socialist unions announced a boycott of the city's tram system.

The situation escalated and reached fever pitch on November 12, 1947. The day began with a massive protest demanding the release of four metalworkers accused of attacking a tram that had dared break the boycott. After mobbing a police station and freeing two of the accused, the protestors received word of violence against their comrades on the city council. After Communist party councilors publicly interrogated the mayor over the fare increases, several audience members—muscle from the Milieu—rushed on stage and began brutalizing the Communists. Demonstrators gathered outside City Hall, only dispersing when former Communist mayor Cristofol arrived to diffuse the situation. Most of the demonstrators left peacefully, but others went on a rampage. They attacked brothels and bars around the Opera House, an area widely known as the seat of the Marseille underworld. Antione and Barthélemy Guérini, the former resistance fighters, appeared in the chaos, firing into the crowd and killing one of the protestors.

The following day, November 13, 1947, La Marseillaise, a communist newspaper, ran the headline "Carlini and De Vernejoul Reinstate Sabiani's Methods in the Mayor's Office of Marseille." The article alleged that it had been Guérini's henchman behind the city council attack the day prior. The conservatives and Corsican criminals were once again allied against the left. That same day, a general strike was called by local labor unions, bringing Marseille and its pivotal harbor to a complete standstill. The next day, November 14, the French General Confederation of Labor called a national strike, sending the French economy into a tailspin.

The Guérini syndicate, both locally powerful and deeply offended by the attacks on their operations, was the obvious first choice by the U.S. agents to combat Communist demonstrators in Marseille. The assistance Angleton had requested of the Italian Mafia was only of marginal usefulness. It soon became clear that the Mafia would have no decisive impact on the outcome of the struggle to break the 1947 Marseille dock strikes. The Unione Corse had been able to gain the upper hand over the Sicilian and Calabrian–based Mafia in Marseille. The French–Corsican syndicate also ruled the narcotics trade with superior access to the most important heroin–producing region of the world—Indochina.

***

French Indochina, the home of the "Golden Triangle," was one of the primary sources of opium for the world. France's grip on the region was slipping as the Viet Minh waged an increasingly successful war on French colonial control of Vietnam. After the outbreak of hostilities in December 1946, the Viet Minh soldiers and French colonial forces quickly found themselves in a stalemate. The French were unable to quell the uprising.[13] The French intelligence services were also desperately underfunded and needed a new source of cash revenue. This is when French intelligence and paramilitaries secretly took over the narcotics trafficking in the region to fund their covert operations against the Communist Viet Minh.[14] The Unione Corse was the obvious partner of choice for this operation, given its experience in drug smuggling and dominance of Marseille, France's "Gateway to the Orient."

In 1953, U.S. Colonel Edward G. Lansdale made a six-week tour of Indochina for the CIA. He reported that French officers had bought up the entire opium harvest on orders of the commander-in-chief of the French Expeditionary Forces for sale and export from Saigon. Lansdale was directed to drop his investigation because it might "embarrass" a U.S. ally.

Dubbed "Operation X," this clandestine opium trafficking operation involving the Unione Corse and French intelligence officers continued virtually uninterrupted. It continued even after French forces exited Indochina and U.S. forces took their place. The former French intelligence officers simply stayed behind in the narcotics trafficking business. They were now full-fledged members of the Unione Corse. They did not have to continue the pretense of working for the French government. This was also a simple extension of French colonial policy, which relied on revenue from importing and selling opium to the Vietnamese since the 19th century.[15]

In addition to their monopoly over Indochina, the Unione Corse also had established close ties with Turkish officials and local poppy producers, the other key source of opium for the international heroin trade. French and Corsican sailors manned much of the maritime trade between Turkey and Mediterranean ports, including Marseille. They could be relied on to discretely carry concealed packages of opium products to Marseille to be refined in the many labs dotting the hillsides there. The French-Corsican syndicates also controlled the organized crime operations in Quebec's "French" areas, including Montreal. Following his escape from Marseille, fascist collaborator and Unione Corse syndicate boss François Spirito fled to Montreal. Once there, he began importing heroin into the U.S. until he was arrested and imprisoned in 1950.

Through Montreal and the Canadian regions immediately across from northern New York State, the Unione Corse had an ideal gateway for heroin transport to markets in New York City and the rest of the East Coast. In the 1960s, when the Ogdensburg Bridge was built over the St. Lawrence Seaway, separating the U.S. and Canada, the transport of narcotics southward into the U.S. became even more accessible. The Ogdensburg Bridge and Tunnel Authority that controlled the bridge also upgraded the Ogdensburg International Airport. The airport made it even easier for private planes to smuggle contraband between Canada and the U.S.

In a stroke of luck, William Spector's father also expanded the reach of his Syracuse–based Cadillac–Oldsmobile dealership to Ogdensburg. He was eager to take advantage of the increase in the Canadian–U.S. car market spurred by the opening of the Ogdensburg Bridge. Cadillacs and Oldsmobiles supplied by the Spector dealership regularly traveled between Canada and New York's North Country, rarely stopped or impeded by U.S. Customs officials at the border.

But we are getting ahead of ourselves here. Let's get back to November 1947.

***

According to Spector, Weiller called for a meeting with the Unione Corse bosses, inviting Angleton and his U.S. team in Marseille to join them. The meeting took place in a nondescript warehouse on the outskirts of Marseille. Security was extremely tight. Only a few of de Gaulle's inner circle members knew of the meeting. Angleton, Spector, and Hunt reported directly to Secretary of State George C. Marshall on the U.S. side. Marshall was in direct contact with the Truman White House.

Weiller and Angleton, as the senior French and U.S. officials at the meeting, laid out a practical and straightforward plan to break the unions' domination of the Marseille waterfront. The Unione Corse was widely feared in Marseille and France for its brutal strong-arm tactics to control all organized crime activities. The Gestapo and the French police took a "live and let live" attitude toward the syndicate and its enforcement tactics.[16] As long as the mangled bodies that turned up in Marseille alleyways were petty criminals or other underworld members, the murder investigations were superficial and rarely led to an arrest.[17] In other words, the French authorities generally gave members of the Unione Corse a wide berth, trying if at all possible to avoid a confrontation.

The Unione Corse leaders at the Marseille meeting in 1947 agreed to provide the "muscle" necessary to break the picket lines thrown up all along the waterfront by the unions. They didn't much like the ideological Communist-leaning union leaders anyway. The unions were filling the heads of their working-class members with dangerous ideas, such as equality and workers' rights, while at the same time warning against the dangers of heroin addiction and prostitution, the two mainstays of the Unione Corse's business model.

The Unione Corse only wanted one small favor in return for their efforts to intimidate the unions. The French and U.S. governments would have to agree not to interfere with their lucrative narcotics smuggling operations throughout Europe and North America.

Weiller and the other French representatives readily agreed to this deal. One brief phone call to de Gaulle confirmed this. After all, Weiller and other higher-ups in the French government already had close ties to the Unione Corse and were benefitting financially from this relationship. The French SDECE, equivalent to the U.S.'s CIA, had a "working relationship" with the Unione Corse.[18] SDECE indirectly shared in the profits of the drug smuggling of opium and morphine paste from Turkey and the Golden Triangle to Marseille and the transport of the refined heroin powder to the American markets.

The close working relationship between the Unione Corse and French officialdom was forged primarily by Weiller and Marcel Francisci who later became the so-called "Heroin King" of France. Francisci, a small-time criminal before the war, was now a highly-decorated veteran of the French resistance. He had taken advantage of General de

Gaulle's wartime offer of immunity in return for wartime service on behalf of Free French forces. After the war, Francisci took a leadership position in expanding the morphine-based smuggling operations into Marseille and exporting the refined heroin to the American markets.

During the early 1960s, Francisci would win the undying support of the Gaullists by organizing groups of Corsican gangsters to fight the right-wing OAS terrorists. OAS was in a virtual civil war with de Gaulle and his forces, attempting to prevent Algerian independence through political assassinations and bombing sprees that left thousands of civilians dead. Known popularly as "barbouzes" or "bearded ones," Francisci's operatives were incorporated into a unit within the SDECE known as "Service d'Action Civique," or SAC. The SAC became the "dirty tricks" and hit squad arm of French intelligence. SAC members were issued unique tri-color identification cards that allowed them free movement and official police protection wherever they went. It was not long before the SAC controlled most of the narcotics trafficking activities of SDECE, which were now closely coordinating with the Unione Corse. Not surprisingly, quite a few of the foreign narcotics traffickers arrested in the U.S. in the early 1970s were SAC members.

However, for the U.S. representatives at the 1947 Marseille conference, the Unione Corse proposal of a quid pro quo presented more of a challenge. Although the Office of Naval Intelligence worked with mob figures like Lucky Luciano during the war, the FBI and U.S. law enforcement agencies did not have any explicit or implicit "agreements" with organized crime. However, U.S. criminal syndicates were the recipients of benign neglect by Federal law enforcement authorities. FBI Director J. Edgar Hoover famously denied the existence of the Mafia until 1957. He had a monomaniacal focus on Communism, leaving little room to fret about domestic organized crime. There were also rumors that Hoover was subject to blackmail and regularly received horse racing tips from underworld characters. Stories were circulating that the Mafia had compromising photographs of him with his protégé and constant companion, FBI deputy director Clyde Tolson.[19]

Hoover also feared the image of incorruptible G-men would be tarnished if agents started investigating narcotics trafficking by the Mafia or the French syndicates in America. Hoover thought these organizations could buy off or otherwise corrupt the more susceptible agents with their virtually unlimited quantities of cash. FBI agents, by contrast, were paid little more than a minimum wage for the prestige of being part of such a widely publicized and celebrated crime-busting organization.

A decision by the U.S. to enter into what, in effect, was a blanket immunity agreement with French-Corsican organized crime was not something that could be taken lightly. It was certainly not a decision that Angelton or any other U.S. intelligence officers at the meeting had the authority to make themselves. Such a decision was far above their pay grade. Therefore, they took a two-hour break to confer with their superiors in Washington, including Secretary of State Marshall. Angelton, Spector, and Hunt went to the U.S. Consulate in Marseille to communicate on a secure line with Marshall about the situation. Marshall told them to stay at the Consulate until he got back to them, which he did within the hour. He gave them the green light to make the deal but emphasized that nothing could be put in writing.

At the time, David Bruce, the U.S. Ambassador to France, and W. Averill Harriman acted as ambassador-at-large to the European continent, focusing on the development and implementation of the Marshall Plan. Angelton, Spector, and Hunt did not speak directly to Bruce or Harriman before receiving orders from Washington to proceed with the proposed deal with the Unione Corse. But they assumed—correctly as it turned out—that Marshall was keeping Bruce and Harriman "in the loop" regarding the ongoing negotiations about the Marseille waterfront "situation."

Angelton and his colleagues returned to the French government warehouse where the meeting was taking place and communicated their agreement. The Unione Corse readily understood why nothing could be put in writing. They had never done so themselves and were more than willing to seal the deal with just a handshake and, of course, a few bottles of Champagne.

The "Marseille Accord," as it was known by the French government, or "the Marseille Deal" to the U.S. intelligence community, had been struck. The rest—as they say—is history. Minister of the Interior Jules Moch ordered CRS forces around France to quickly purge suspected

Communist members. Angleton and CIA agents in Marseille entered into a secret deal to begin funding a new socialist labor union. Force Ouvrière exchanged money and political power for vows to break with the communist strikers. In Marseille, the strikes quickly faltered after CRS officers, along with thugs in the employ of the Guérini syndicate, began attacking the remaining communist picket lines. By November 19, 1947, ships were being unloaded in the Marseille harbor by heavily armed Moroccan soldiers.[20] By December 9, the General Confederation of Labor called an end to the national strike.

The breaking of the Communist grip on the French waterfront was then, in December 1947–and is still now–considered one of the fledgling CIA's greatest triumphs. However, the cost of casualties from heroin overdoses and broken lives is incalculable.

Chapter 2:
Patricia Richardson – The Early Years

Not much is known about Patricia Dolores Amour Richardson's early years. She was born on the French side of the Caribbean island St. Martin on October 8, 1946. Evidence gathered from local records shows that her mother died of a drug overdose when Patricia was seven. She had no other family, so she lived on the beach at St. Martin as part of a large, ragtag community of vagrants. They survived by their wits and ability to relieve unsuspecting tourists of their wallets and pocketbooks. Around the age of 14–like Napoleon's Josephine (herself a creole from Martinique)–Patricia, an enterprising woman with few options, began using a series of wealthy and powerful older men to survive and eventually thrive. Her ambition was to become a rich and independent woman in her own right. Multiple powerful men made the fatal mistake of underestimating her, thinking she was subservient and devoted to them. The reality turned out to be quite different. She may have been committed at times but never subservient.

Ever since Patricia snuck into the local movie theater at the age of eight and saw her first James Bond movie, she was hooked. She made up her mind right away that she would turn herself into a "Bond girl," but with a twist. Not only was she going to be alluring, fashionable, articulate, well-educated, and cosmopolitan, but she was going to acquire the deadly spy skills of James Bond himself. But how could she do this? None of her cohorts living on the beach seemed capable of teaching her these skills. Then she met Raymond Beauharnais.

Beauharnais became her first lover and mentor, perhaps the only genuine relationship she ever had. As the local drug kingpin on the island, his connections reached back through the Corsican organized crime network to Marseille, where the heroin labs and factories turned out the purest heroin in the world. The heroin was distributed throughout Europe and North and South America from these labs. A small part of this network was later popularized in the book and the movie "The French Connection." St. Martin was an ideal transit point for the shipment of heroin from Marseille by boat. Not only was there a common language, but there were virtually no customs inspections conducted on the French side of the island. The Dutch-controlled side was better policed and less attractive for drug smuggling.

But before Richardson could identify and use the men necessary to reach her goals, she needed vocational training. Starting at 14, she became a "runner," moving drugs around the island for Beauharnais. He was handsome and powerful, always living on the edge of danger, yet calm and reassuring. Richardson learned more than the drug business from him. She learned how to use her beauty and sensuality to seduce and conquer men, including ultimately Beauharnais himself. He saw in Patricia the potential for something much more than the small empire he had already built on the island. The combined forces of beauty, brains, and cunning led to a successful partnership that would endure long after she left the island.

During the late 1950s and early 1960s, Beauharnais had served with the notorious French special forces in Algeria. As an intelligence officer, he became highly proficient with sophisticated weapons and explosives, "drop-boxes," and other techniques employed by intelligence officers to communicate secretly with their informants. He also developed a well-deserved reputation as a tireless and, if necessary, brutal interrogator of suspects at the French army headquarters in Algiers. Beauharnais became known for "breaking" down suspects previously considered "unbreakable."

The Algerian War of Independence was extraordinarily violent. It lasted almost a decade before the French forces and the French that had settled there—about 900,000 so-called "pieds noirs" (black-feet)—finally withdrew. This entire experience, which is accurately documented in the legendary documentary film "Battle of Algiers," portrays how this exceptionally "dirty war" hardened and brutalized the participants on both sides of the conflict. But it also provided Beauharnais with invaluable skills, which he readily passed on to his young protégé.

Richardson quickly acquired all the martial arts skills that Raymond offered, plus firearms training. However, she preferred to use knives, concealed more easily than a gun. A concealed knife also had the advantage of not causing any unsightly bulges on her usual tight-fitting clothing. Beauharnais also educated her on basic table manners and etiquette, which he learned by watching French officers and their wives during his tour of duty in North Africa.

Soon, however, Beauharnais and Richardson realized that she needed other mentors to complete her "finishing school" appearance and demeanor. Beauharnais financed a series of dance instructors, clothing consultants, and tutors who rapidly transformed her from an awkward tomboy to a refined and elegant young lady. Richardson underwent a metamorphosis from an illiterate beach urchin to a poised young lady. She could hold her own with most parlor room conversations, at least those taking place on St. Martin.

Patricia was naturally beautiful and brilliant. She was now well-educated, refined, and, most importantly, cunning. She was ready to perform on a larger stage, which for people on the French side of the island of St. Martin meant only one thing: Paris. Beauharnais arranged for Richardson to fly to the French capital. Beauharnais' associates and drug suppliers in France met her and ensured that she was settled into a small but elegant apartment on the Left Bank, overlooking the Seine. She registered at a modeling agency where Beauharnais had close contacts. Several young ladies associated with that agency were couriers in Beauharnais' supply and distribution network. The young models were universally welcomed into the upper-crust salon life of Paris if, for no other reason, they were very pleasing to the eye. Patricia was soon circulating among the Paris elite.

**

One of Richardson's first liaisons in Paris was with Yousef Beidas,[1] a Lebanese financier and founder of Intra Bank, used by Beauharnais and other drug traffickers for money laundering purposes. Before he died in a Swiss prison under mysterious circumstances, Beidas eventually introduced Richardson to the man who became her most illustrious patron.

Enter Paul-Louis Weiller, the internationally renowned French war hero and industrialist. In his 70s, Weiller was known to have a keen eye for the fresh young beauties that arrived in France each season.² He was particularly fond of ladies from the former French colonies in Africa and the Caribbean. He was a commander in the French Legion of Honor, having served with distinction as one of France's ace pilots during World War I. He escaped to Cuba, Mexico, and the United States during World War II. Weiller expanded his fortune by association with J. Paul Getty, who founded the Getty Oil Company in 1942. He also established himself in the banking industry.³ Perhaps most pertinent to Patricia's career and business opportunities was that Weiller also just happened to be the majority owner of Air France.

Both in France and the U.S., Weiller dabbled in politics. He regularly dined with Richard Nixon at La Côte Basque in New York during the 1960s, when Nixon was a partner at the politically connected Mudge Rose law firm. Weiller was later rumored to have provided Nixon with a substantial "off the books" cash campaign contribution for his Presidential campaign in 1968. The only two people who dealt directly with Nixon and his "bagman" Bebe Rebozo in these cash transactions were Weiller and his protégé Patricia Richardson. They never publicly confirmed the "donations," despite countless investigations detailed in this book.

Enchanted by Patricia, Weiller soon let it be known through the Paris rumor mill that Richardson was no longer "available." She was now his exclusive "protégé," a euphemism for "mistress." He showered her with expensive jewelry and an unlimited budget at the finest shops in Paris. Weiller gave her complete access to the vast resources of Air France, which she promptly used to bypass all airport security measures. What Beauharnais was to St. Martin's drug trade, Weiller was to France's. After helping negotiate the Marseille Accord in 1947, Weiller took a role in enabling the transatlantic flow of heroin through his businesses, taking a cut while keeping his hands clean.

Richardson quickly became one of Weiller's agents. She recruited a small army of pilots, flight attendants, and ground personnel to carry "packages" across the Atlantic on regular flights from Paris to Montreal. The innocuous–looking "packages" were delivered to Paris via couriers from Marseille, all arranged for by Beauharnais and his close circle of associates.

Richardson also effectively used one of the Ford modeling agencies in Paris. Weiller promptly bought a controlling interest and directed the agency to employ Richardson. Here she recruited international models to assist her rapidly growing distribution network. She asked young ladies to do "small favors" for her. When they traveled by air to Canada and the U.S., Patricia had them transport "gift packages," which her associates picked up in Montreal, Boston, and New York.

As lax airport security tightened in the U.S. during the late 1960s and early 1970s, Richardson had to increasingly rely on the Paris-to-Montreal flights of Air France to transport the heroin into North America. However, the Canadian drug market was limited. It quickly became over-saturated with heroin, sharply driving down the price even though the increase in drug users reached epidemic proportions.

The big market was south of the border in the U.S. But how could large quantities of heroin be smuggled across the border? To be sure, the Canadian-US border was relatively porous. This had been the smuggler's supply route of preference dating back to the early 1930s when bootleggers ran liquor by truck through the labyrinth of back roads between Canada and the U.S. But by the late 1960s, Canadian and U.S. law enforcement had vastly improved their ability to monitor and hinder the flow of illegal drugs going southward along the border. The "stop-and-search" of suspicious vehicles traveling across the relatively few Canada-U.S. bridge crossings seriously hurt the drug networks ability to move "product" across the border.

So, what was a bright young girl to do? Richardson approached this problem in a coldly logical and analytical fashion, just like she approached everything else in her life. Heroin lent itself well to hiding, as only a few pounds of high-grade product were worth a fortune. Automobiles, made of thousands of parts and shipped en-masse worldwide, were the perfect channel to move large quantities of heroin clandestinely.[4] This was demonstrated by the 1968 seizure of over 200 pounds of heroin imported to the U.S. from France in a Citroen D.S.[5] Richardson's research quickly uncovered a good Cadillac dealership in Ogdensburg, New York, a border town connected to Canada by a bridge over the St. Lawrence River. New and used cars from this dealership were frequently moved back and forth across the border and were rarely searched. It was ideal for Richardson's intended purposes. Better yet, the dealership owner, OSS/CIA–veteran William H. Spector, was single and available.

In Montreal, one of Richardson's operatives visited Spector's dealership, posing as a prospective customer interested in buying several new Cadillacs for resale in Montreal. One thing led to another, and when Richardson's operative was introduced to Spector, an invitation was extended to him to spend a long weekend as a guest at a resort in St. Martin. While Spector was at the resort, he met and promptly fell in love with the irresistible Ms. Richardson. As coincidence would have it, Patricia just happened to be staying at the same resort. They were married a few weeks later, on November 21, 1969. The improbable couple settled in Ogdensburg, which gives new meaning to the term "dull and quiet," especially during the brutally cold winter months. When it blew from the north across the St. Lawrence River, the wind there was known to reach 20 or 30 degrees below zero, not counting the "wind–chill factor."

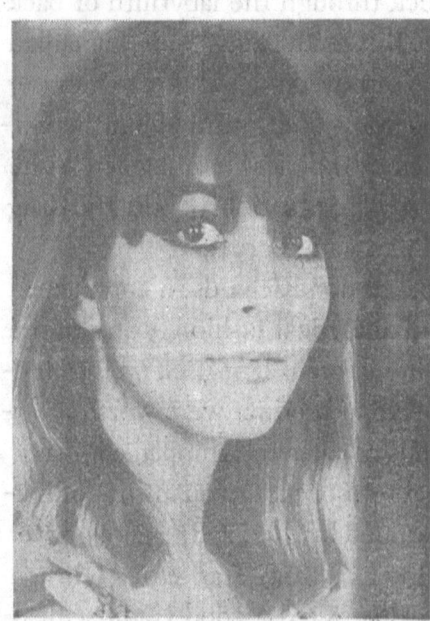

Patricia Richardson Martinson

"The Model, the Drug Ring And the Big Evidence Hunt." The New York Times, 12 June 1975, p. 39. NYTimes.com.

A week before the marriage, Richardson gave birth to a daughter, Tamara Nissa, conceived in a prior relationship. About 18 months later, she and Spector had a child named Tarek Shawn.

Richardson's marriage to Spector reaped immediate business benefits. She instructed two Canadian "mechanics" she introduced to Spector to create custom-designed hidden storage spaces in the used Cadillacs. Very soon, these vehicles were moving back and forth across the border with their hidden cargo. The secret compartments were virtually undetectable. After crossing the border, these vast quantities of illicit drugs were then distributed to the large metropolitan U.S. markets up and down the Eastern seaboard.

Even while pregnant during their marriage, Richardson managed to siphon a couple of million dollars from the dealership itself by persuading her doting husband to take out several fraudulent mortgages and bank financing on the showroom Cadillacs in his dealership. She showed him how to grossly inflate the inventory to get more and more bank financing. Of course, when she vanished from Ogdensburg two years later in 1971, Spector was left holding the bag. The local prosecutor made a name for himself by prosecuting Spector for bank fraud, resulting in a criminal conviction. His life was shattered. Not only had he lost the successful car dealership that had been handed down to him by his father, but he had also lost his beautiful wife, whom he adored. Spector and Richardson formally divorced two years later, in 1973.

The New York Times
William Spector, Mrs. Martinson's ex-husband.

"The Model, the Drug Ring And the Big Evidence Hunt." The New York Times, 12 June 1975, p. 39. NYTimes.com.

* * *

Following her separation from Spector, Richardson laid low for a while in a run-down boardinghouse in Syracuse, New York, owned by a lawyer named Frank Fiore. Despite her lack of any discernable income, she was known to always carry large sums of cash, make expensive international phone calls, and travel a great deal.[6] According to the building manager, Leta Meyers, Richardson was being housed by Fiore in a *quid pro quo* for occasional sexual favors. Meyers and Richardson developed something of a friendship. Richardson recounted stories about "Sir Charles, Hughes, Getty, Ludwig, and Gordon." She confided in her that she had seen "big money" pass between Nixon and Weiller before the 1968 Election.[7] Meyers later signed an affidavit swearing that Richardson had hired a nurse to look after her children full-time. Richardson even asked Meyers to travel with her repeatedly, including to France. But she told her that she would have to "travel light because she might want me to bring back some things."

At this time, Richardson befriended Mary Jo Ottman, a young Syracuse student who lived in the same boarding house. Patricia did not want to remain in self-imposed exile in upstate New York, so in 1972, she booked a holiday trip to St. Martin and rented Les Terres Basses's villa for $2,000 per month.[8] She took Ottman with her to take care of the children since Richardson had a busy itinerary planned. Ottman was frequently locked in her room with the children throughout the trip and warned not to eavesdrop. At the same time, Richardson hosted meetings with many mysterious figures. After Richardson's "guests" departed, leaving stacks of hundred-dollar bills on the living room table, she would release Ottman and the children from her room.[9]

Suspecting that her new friend and boss was "up to no good," Ottman told Richardson that she had to return to the U.S. early. Richardson agreed on the condition she would pack Ottman's suitcase. Desperate to escape, Ottman agreed, falling right into Richardon's plan.

Arriving late at JFK airport in Queens, New York, Ottman was met by a Pan Am service agent named Louis Marcel. After helping carry her bag to her room in a nearby motel, Marcel locked the door behind him and raped Ottman. He then removed a necklace she did not recognize from her bag, and promptly left.[10] Ottman was too terrified to tell the police or Richardson about the assault.[11] When she returned to upstate New York, Ottman's neighbor said that "she was scared to death of Pat …. After her return, she was a nervous wreck." Scarred by her terrifying "holiday" with Richardson and sexual assault by Marcel, Ottman suffered a nervous breakdown and had ongoing mental health issues for the remainder of her life.[12]

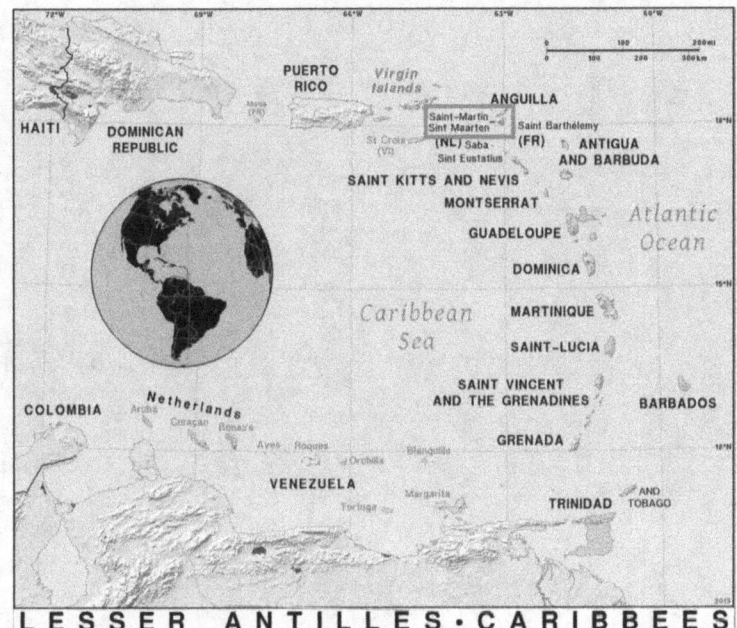

Macky, Ian. 2015. "PAT - Lesser Antilles.gif." Macky.net. 2015. https://ian.macky.net/pat/map/lant/lantblu.gif.

In late November 1972, when Richardson arrived at the St. Martin airport, she bumped into her friend Nicole Frankel. A fellow Weiller "protégé" she was now married to a wealthy St. Martin hotel owner named James Frankel.[13] Frankel accused Richardson of stealing her necklace and further claimed that Richardson was wearing multiple items stolen from her wardrobe. A French gendarme witnessed the confrontation but was unable to intervene due to the airport's location on the Dutch side of the island. Thereafter, Patricia canceled the rental of her villa and returned to the U.S.[14]

The following year or so of her life was spent traveling for Weiller. Then in 1974, after a short romance, Richardson married John R. Martinson, President of the Vedette Oil Company. From 1963 to 1967, John Martinson worked for the Kidder Peabody investment firm, which handled U.S. negotiations for a piece of Yusef Beidas' Intra Bank. Patricia soon lived at a prestigious address in Manhattan's Upper East Side neighborhood, just opposite the Metropolitan Museum of Art on Fifth Avenue.

Like a cat, Patricia had nine lives and always landed on her feet.

Chapter 3:
Paul-Louis Weiller

"We never reached the top. We never really touched the people who supplied all the narcotics, who supplied all the financing for them."

– Statement of NYPD Detective Stephen Balducci, discussing the French Connection case in 1978 before the House Coast Guard Drug Interdiction Hearings

No major narcotics case in the last sixty years captured the American public's imagination as the famous "French Connection" case of 1962. The event was popularized in the book and movie adaptation by Robin Moore. The case involved the recovery by New York City Police Department officers of a significant haul of heroin smuggled into New York in the frame of an imported car. However, though the police eventually seized the heroin and arrested several French nationals, the French Connection case was never closed. Indeed, a sealed "John Doe" indictment was handed down, bringing charges against a man whose identity few knew, yet who was alleged to be the brains and financier behind the deal.

There was only one clue to his identity. Author Robin Moore told Congressional investigators that Detective Eddie Egan described a photograph taken in a Manhattan restaurant. The picture was printed on the cover of a book of matches he saw during the investigation.[1] That picture showed two Frenchmen having dinner. One of them, a French–Corsican named Jean Jehan, was identified. But there was another man at the table in the picture whose identity was known to law enforcement but never publicly identified. He was an elderly, aristocratic–looking gentleman, dressed in a fine suit and appearing to be the group leader, totally in control of the situation.

Detective Egan would not let Moore have this photo. Indeed, he later told the author that he, Egan, had been ordered to "lose" this piece of evidence on orders from higher–ups. Nevertheless, as Moore told a Congressional Committee, the face in that photo bore an amazing resemblance to a certain aristocratic Frenchman named Paul–Louis Weiller.

Until his death in 1993, Paul–Louis Weiller was one of France's best–known and respected public figures. He was one of the major French industrialists, art collectors, and philanthropists of the post–World War II era. However, much about his past was not well known, even by those close to him. Behind his public persona as the *Commandant*, Weiller maintained close ties and longstanding associations with significant underworld figures in the Corsican and French organized crime syndicate known as the Unione Corse. It turns out that he was one of the foremost financiers and leaders of the international narcotics trade.

* * *

What is publicly known about Weiller is that he was born in Paris on September 29, 1893, to a wealthy Jewish family. His father, Lazare Weiller, was born in the eastern French province of Alsace. He became a captain of industry and senator, representing the affluent Charente district for the last decade of his life.[2] His mother, Alice Anna, was born into the illustrious Javal family, another leading family from Alsace.

The Weillers were from Sélesat, eleven miles from the Rhine and Germany. A beautiful medieval city, Sélesat was part of one of the most hotly contested pieces of real estate in European history. Following the annexation of Alsace by Prussia in 1870, the Weiller family moved to Angoulême in Charente. Ownership of the mineral–rich area had shifted back and forth between Germany and France for more than a century. It was one of the trigger points for the Franco–Prussian War and World War I.

Weiller studied engineering at the Ecole Centrale des Arts et Manufactures in Paris and graduated at the outbreak of World War I. His father, Lazare, had an early interest in aviation technology. Paul–Louis followed his lead by joining the fledgling French Air Force, quickly becoming one of France's top aviators. He served as a photographic reconnaissance pilot, making daily low-level flights over enemy lines and exposing himself to deadly ground fire. He was shot down at least five times, sustaining severe injuries. But as soon as he could sufficiently recover, he would be back up in the air, ready for more dangerous action. He became a French war hero for his exploits. He gave the French war correspondents some excellent quotes, often joking about the constant danger and imminence of death around him. When asked whether he was frightened when flying over enemy lines, he laughingly said he was only "worried" when the depleted French Air Force could not even assign a spare gunner to accompany him on his missions. He was the last survivor of France's air aces in that war and one of the few to survive a skirmish with Baron Manfred von Richthofen ("The Red Baron"). His exploits against the Axis powers earned the young flyer the Légion d'Honneur, the Croix de Guerre, and the British Military Cross.

Paul-Louis Weiller photographed for a press release sometime in the 1930s. Source gallica.bnf.fr / Bibliotheque nationale de France

Since flying was his first true love, he and his father entered the young aviation industry after the Great War. With the help of bankers Henry Bauer and Charles Marchal, Weiller took over and reinvigorated the famous Societe Gnome et Rhône motor works in 1922. During the first world war, the company was a major aircraft engine manufacturer that was facing tough times.3 They also acquired the Compagnie Internationale de Navigation Aérienne (CIDNA). During the 1930s, their companies grew to the point where they began scheduling some of the first regular European commercial flights. They later began establishing commercial flight routes into Africa, opening air travel to the French colonies. In 1933, when France nationalized its airlines, Weiller joined the board of directors of Air France. Indeed, Air France's Pegasus emblem is inspired by Weiller's squadron insignia from World War I.

Weiller poses in the gunner seat of an aircraft, sometime during WWI. From a press release by Safran S.A., the corporate descendent of Gnome-Rhône. Espace Patrimoine Safran/fonds PL Weiller Dominique Prot

From a financial viewpoint, it was an auspicious time to be in the fledgling aviation industry, especially in France. Not only was commercial air travel becoming a reality, but French industry had a virtual monopoly on the European continent in the decade after World War I. As a result of the Treaty of Versailles, German industry had been virtually dismantled, especially when it came to any aircraft or other war machinery.[4] As a result, the French aircraft industry dominated the European market. Aircraft engines manufactured by Gnome-Rhône were being exported throughout Europe–from the English Channel to Stalin's Soviet Union.

The elder Weiller traveled to the United States early in the 1920s to arrange licensing with Curtis Aircraft, the forerunner of today's behemoth Boeing Corporation. Meanwhile, his son, Paul–Louis, traveled the length and breadth of Europe selling French aircraft and engine parts. On one of his trips to the Balkans, he stopped in Romania, where he met Princess Alexandra Ghika, a member of the Romanian nobility. In 1922, Weiller and Princess Ghika married, and in 1924 they had a daughter, Marie–Élisabeth. It proved to be a marriage that launched the French industrialist into the top echelon of European royalty, high finance, and international intrigue. Within only a few years, Weiller joined the ranks of the wealthiest men in the world, including Howard Hughes, D.K. Ludwig, J. Paul Getty, and John D. Rockefeller. Ten years later, in 1932, after this "power couple" quietly divorced, Weiller married the world–famous Greek model and Miss Europa 1931, Alika Deplarakou, in a lavish Paris wedding. Weiller and his new wife had a son in 1933, Paul–Annik Weiller.

Weiller and his wife, Aliki Diplarakou, on their wedding day in 1932. Source gallica.bnf.fr / Bibliotheque nationale de France

By the early 1930s, German industry had slowly rebuilt, despite the severe restrictions the Treaty of Versailles imposed. German industrialists combined several interlocking companies into a giant conglomerate. The corporation was large enough to compete on an even footing with the large U.S. trusts, such as Standard Oil and U.S. Steel. The leading members of this German conglomerate included the giant I.G. Farben chemical corporation, Krupp Steel, Theissen, and the Siemens engine works. They also developed some industrial alliances abroad. For example, in 1929, Standard Oil of New Jersey signed an agreement with I.G. Farben, calling for an exchange of research and patents. Still, the underlying unwritten deal was that Standard Oil would stay out of the chemical business if I.G. Farben stayed out of the oil business.[5] Not to be left out, Weiller's Gnome–Rhône Corporation sold aircraft engines to Germany's Siemens Corp., which was building aircraft for Germany's now growing Luftwaffe. The Gnome–Rhône Corporation was, at the same time, building engines for the French Air Force.

As the European continent again drifted into war, Weiller's activities were scrutinized by British intelligence. The files of MI–6 reveal that Weiller was suspected of collaboration with the Axis powers. In 1932, Weiller was accused of conspiring with Emanuel Chaumie of the French air ministry to cede stock in the French Aeropostale company to Deutsche Lufthansa, Germany's flag carrier. Weiller and Chaumie were jailed. However, it was later revealed by police that some evidence against Weiller was, in fact, forged by an opponent, leading to his exoneration.[6]

During the 1930s, Weiller's Gnome–Rhône plant provided engines for the French Bloch bomber, which the French defense ministry had hoped to be a mainstay in the country's air force. Designer Marcel Bloch was a partner with Weiller in Gnome–Rhône. However, things were not going well with the development of the Bloch bomber. Problems of a mysterious nature kept cropping up, and the plane's production was delayed time and time again. French authorities began to question whether these design and manufacturing problems were just bad luck or something more sinister.

In 1939, French police apprehended a Japanese secret agent at the French–Italian border. The agent was carrying confidential documents relating to the manufacture of Gnome–Rhône aircraft engines. Although never mentioned in Weiller's official biographies, the ensuing investigation did not go well for him. French investigators soon discovered that Paul–Louis Weiller had received some $6.5 million in gold Swiss francs deposited in Zurich. It was concluded that he must have received the money in return for the sale of the secrets of his aircraft engines to France's enemies.

After Nazi Germany bypassed the Maginot Line and quickly overran France, the Vichy Government under Philippe Pétain arrested

Weiller in October 1940 and stripped him of his citizenship.[7] Due to their enormous wealth and power in a critical wartime industry, Weiller and his partner Marcel Bloch were obvious scapegoats for the French collaborators in the Vichy Regime to explain how France had been weakened by a "fifth column" from within France itself. Conveniently for the Vichy authorities, Weiller's family origins were Jewish on both his maternal and paternal sides. This made him an easy target for the anti–Semitic vitriol pouring out of the Vichy Regime, often even more venomous than that being spouted by the Nazi propagandists in Berlin. Weiller and Bloch suffered the insult of having their citizenship stripped by the Vichy government.

Weiller's former partner, Bloch, languished in prison for most of the war. He refused to collaborate with the Vichy aviation industry, which led to his deportation from Paris to Buchenwald concentration camp on the last train to leave before American forces liberated the city.[8] Bloch, however, managed to survive the camp and later resumed his position as a leading figure in the French aeronautics industry.

As for Weiller, his fortunes improved dramatically in January 1942, when he managed to escape from prison, fleeing first to Morocco, then to Cuba, Mexico, and Canada. Finally, he made it to London, joining the Free French forces.[9] Some sources report that he also tried, unsuccessfully, to offer his services to the British government.[10]

Brigadier General Charles de Gaulle headed up the Free French forces in London. Though backed by the British and Americans, de Gaulle desperately needed new sources of funds. This was when Weiller stepped in as de Gaulle's financier. He still had access to his cache of gold Swiss francs on deposit in Zurich, and he bet it all on de Gaulle–or at least most of it. Weiller worked with a young French accountant assigned to him by the name of Georges Pompidou, who later became de Gaulle's successor as President of France. Another Free French Finance Ministry member was Valery Giscard D'Estaing, who also rose in the French ranks to serve eventually as the French President.

To circumvent the problem of dealing with a convicted enemy of the French, de Gaulle declared that anyone who joined the cause of the Free French would be exonerated for all crimes–past and present. Naturally, Weiller accepted de Gaulle's terms and became a member of de Gaulle's inner circle. He was honored by being issued "passport No. 1" by the expatriate French government.

Although his slate had been wiped clean with France, Weiller was still viewed suspiciously by his British hosts and their American allies. They continued to keep the Frenchman under watch for suspected espionage for the duration of the war. His "escape" from France was deemed suspect by the O.S.S. They surveilled him in 1942 as he progressed through to Cuba and Mexico, where he stayed at a "favorite Nazi stopping place," the Maria Cristina Hotel.[11] This information came to light in 1944 when Paul–Louis Weiller applied for a visa to enter the United States. British intelligence advised against issuing a visa to Weiller, and U.S. authorities initially denied him.

However, the Frenchman eventually did gain entry to the U.S. in early 1944. The government of the Soviet Union transmitted an official request to grant Weiller's visa. There were close ties between Weiller and the Soviet Government at the time since Weiller's aircraft company had provided the Soviet Air Force with a large percentage of its aircraft engines.

The U.S. Government felt compelled to accede to the explicit request by the Russian government for a U.S. visa to be granted to Weiller. In the meantime, Weiller had been traveling through the Caribbean, spending a great deal of time on the island of Cuba, where he met with such mob leaders as Meyer Lansky, Santos Trafficante, and Carlos Gambino, who also had taken up residency in Havana.

Much of the official U.S. records regarding Weiller have gone mysteriously missing. What still exists can be found on a few F.B.I. index cards at the National Archives in Washington. The files themselves have been destroyed. The index cards refer to Weiller's pre–war conviction, British authorities' surveillance of him, suspected espionage activities, F.B.I. mail intercepts, and telephone taps made while Weiller was in the country.

But what happened to the actual files? One thing is certain: these files were not destroyed by accident. Weiller spent time and money cultivating relationships with the highest levels of the C.I.A. and other government agencies, thus ensuring that his secrets remained–well–secret.

* * *

Within only a few short years, from about 1944 to 1947, Weiller developed a vast commercial enterprise in Europe and the Americas, focused on oil and international banking. He financed oil exploration operations in Venezuela and the Gulf of Mexico, and natural gas exploration in Texas, before concentrating on his international banking activities.

In these post–war years, Weiller was also restored to the good graces of his homeland, becoming, quite simply, one of the great power brokers of Europe. He helped reorganize Air France and sat on its board of directors. He also helped direct companies like Renault, the Michelin Tire Company, Ford Models Inc., and Peugeot.[12] He became a member of the Secretariat of France, an informal but very powerful group of industrialists who had the ear of the government and, to a large extent, pulled the strings from behind the curtain.

As the largest single owner of Air France stock, Weiller and his associates used the airline as their private courier service. Air France staff members were sometimes discretely solicited to carry packages from one continent to the other, avoiding customs checks with no questions asked. The Air France flights to and from Beirut, Montreal, New York, and elsewhere were ideal for transporting heroin, jewels, and other valuable merchandise. They easily circumvented law enforcement and customs personnel. Weiller and his young protégé, Patricia Richardson, along with others associated with the Unione Corse, ran vast quantities of heroin originating from Turkey and the Golden Triangle of Southeast Asia through Marseille to distribution points in North and South America.

Weiller also founded the Stewart Wagner Modeling Agency in the 1950s and 1960s, later becoming the Stewart Modeling Agency, an established affiliate of the Ford Modeling Agency. Weiller's interest in the modeling agency, of course, had something to do with his keen interest in beautiful women. Still, it was also a business opportunity to provide more young models with a chance to travel internationally on Air France. All they were asked to do was to secretly transport small packages from one city to the next without having it inspected. The models were often given Air France ID to make it look like they were part of the crew. But by the time the models/crew went through

Customs, the narcotics packages in their luggage had been removed. The Air France baggage handlers routinely had access to the passenger luggage before it reached Customs. By pre-arrangement, many bags containing narcotics and other contraband were "lost" in the process, having been secretly transferred from the baggage handlers to narcotics couriers. These "missing" bags were then replaced with duplicate bags sent on the next flight, carrying the same identification tags as the "lost" bags. These duplicate bags could then be safely cleared through Customs since they were squeaky clean.

This complex system of trafficking narcotics from France to North America was virtually foolproof—except when the "hostesses" tried to use shortcuts. For example, one Air France female employee was busted when she hid the narcotics package on her person rather than in her luggage as directed.[13]

Over the years, Weiller's fortune continued to grow as he expanded his business interests into shipping, real estate, hotels, and factories worldwide. He was a major investor in the Bahamas Port Authority, in gambling casinos, and even owned New York's iconic Hotel Pierre for a while. He traveled in the rarified circles of the world's wealthiest citizens. In addition to his old industrialist friends, Weiller became close to Sir Charles Clore, one of Great Britain's wealthiest industrialists. He had been another one of Patricia Richardson's "mentors" before Weiller had met her.[14] Clore's holdings included the Ritz Hotel, Selfridge's Department Stores, Bentley Motors, and London casinos.

In 1928, Weiller had a stately home on the French Riviera near Marseille, called Villa La Reine Jeanne, designed by the American architect Barry Dieks. After the war, Weiller's Villa attracted international society, renowned artists, and the business elite for the entire second half of the Twentieth Century. Guests included Juan Carlos I of Spain, Richard Nixon, Charlie Chaplin, and Weiller's old associate, the French President Georges Pompidou.

Weiller also carefully cultivated a reputation as a philanthropist and patron of the arts. He restored the majestic Hôtel des Ambassadeurs de Holland in the Marais area of Paris. He also contributed to the restoration of the Palace of Versailles, founded a ballet company, and set up a foundation for artists and musicians. After his eyesight began to fail, Weiller built a hospital in the Gironde area of France specializing in eye surgery. His goal—which was substantially achieved during his lifetime—was to revive Paris as the capital of world culture. For his efforts, he was unanimously elected to the Academie des Beaux-Arts. In 1989, President Francois Mitterrand awarded him the Grand Croix de la Legion d'Honneur, France's highest honor.

In addition to his connections with the world's business and cultural elite, the Commander, as his retinue called him, also surrounded himself with traditional and contemporary royalty. In Paris, the deposed King Peter of Yugoslavia became a permanent house guest at Weiller's baronial palace on the Rue de la Faisanderie. The home was filled with paintings, furniture, sculpture, and books that could easily rival most museums. One of Weiller's closest friends was the Duc d'Orleans. And no one less than Princess Olympia of Greece would do for a wife for his son, Paul-Annik.

At the same time, however, Weiller was developing close ties with governments behind the Iron Curtain. Beginning in the days when he sold aircraft engines to Soviet Russia, Weiller maintained numerous relationships with various Communist officials. At Weiller's urging, the famous Normandy Squadron of the French Air Force escaped the German occupation of France by flying to Soviet Russia, where they spent the war. One of the squadron members was Andre Malraux, the French writer, philosopher, and close personal friend of Weiller, who was later accused of selling NATO secrets to the Soviets.

Paul-Louis Weiller's millions also attracted the interest of the leaders of France's shadowy underworld. He was approached with the lucrative offer of becoming the primary financier for all narcotics deals in Europe through intermediaries. Not only that, but Weiller's position as a major figure in Air France, with both pilots and pretty young flight attendants to use as couriers, placed him in an ideal position to facilitate international smuggling operations.

Weiller's primary contact in the French and Corsican underworld was Marcel Francisci, a prominent resistance fighter turned politician who came to dominate the Marseille *Milieu*. Another of Weiller's key associates was the Lebanese Eduardo Barroudi. He emerged as one of the world's most successful drug and arms traffickers after working for

Weiller for twenty years as a financial manager of some of Weiller's properties. It was also rumored that he worked as a hitman for Weiller in his spare time.

Weiller also had close ties with several Service d'Action Civique (S.A.C.) team members, primarily composed of de Gaulle's old wartime associates in the Free French forces. French authorities gave the S.A.C. free reign, encouraging them to ruthlessly break up the ultra-right-wing O.A.S. (Organization de L'Armee Secrete). The O.A.S. posed the greatest obstacle to de Gaulle's consolidation of power in post-war France.

One S.A.C. operative, Frederic Christian, was Weiller's primary contact in the Caribbean, with headquarters in St. Martin. Christian worked closely with Patricia Richardson, who had left Paris and returned to St. Martin to expand the syndicate's Western Hemisphere operations. From their base in St. Martin, Richardson and Christian established ties with William Spector, Robert Vesco, and other influential Americans.

Other French S.A.C. members filled out the organization's ranks in the Americas. Christian David, an expert in assassination; Auguste Ricord, a Unione Corse and S.A.C. member, developed the "contra-bandista" smuggling routes throughout Latin America. Henri Helle, who, after a lengthy criminal career in Tangiers and Corsica, settled in St. Martin. Once on the island, he operated a beach resort hotel that served as a narcotics transit hub in which Weiller had an undisclosed interest.

As discussed in chapter one, when the Communist-led unions closed down the docks in Marseille in late 1947, Weiller was the one who came up with the plan to break the strike. This action freed up the tons of wheat rotting on the piers desperately needed to feed the near-starving French citizenry. With the help of his associates in the Unione Corse, Weiller quickly mobilized the combined forces of the Unione Corse and S.A.C. This consolidation broke the ruinous siege the unions maintained on the Port of Marseille. The ordinary working men walking the picket lines were no match for the terror-inspiring seasoned forces that the Unione Corse could assemble in only a few days. In return, they got a free pass from both the French and American governments to pursue their heroin trafficking operations.

Weiller thus walked a tightrope between his image as a respectable financier, war hero, and advisor to top French government officials and his duties as one of the masterminds of the expanding Unione Corse worldwide operations. He was as equally at home in the highest circles of diplomacy and government as he was in the rough-and-tumble world of narcotics trafficking. He and his protégé Patricia Richardson eventually claimed the highest prize of all: "buying" an American president for a mere $2 million in cash.

Weiller and his organization were, in short, untouchable. Based on this 1947 Marseille Accord, neither the French nor the U.S. government interfered significantly with the Unione Corse's narcotics distribution networks, aside from some low-level busts. Weiller and his associates were adept at alerting French and U.S. authorities of the activities of any rogue freelance dealer. A few rogue actors mistakenly thought they could run their own heroin distribution operations without clearance from Weiller or others at the top of the Union Corse. They were quickly disabused of any such illusions. With the help of French and U.S. law enforcement, Weiller and the Unione Corse had these freelancers quickly eradicated, thus solidifying their monopoly on the worldwide heroin trade.

For example, one of Weiller's former associates, Marcel "Flokki" Boucan, was arrested in 1972 off the coast of Marseille in a shrimp boat carrying several hundred pounds of heroin. It was Weiller who gave the go-ahead to French authorities to arrest Boucan after Weiller learned that Boucan was planning to make a "freelance" trip on his shrimp boat from Marseille to the Bahamas with a cargo of pure heroin. He had not gotten prior clearance from Weiller and other syndicate leaders. Boucan naively thought he could make the trip unnoticed, keep all the profits for himself, and then retire. He forgot the simple unwritten rule of French heroin smuggling: "Nothing moves without permission from the top."

Interestingly, Patricia Richardson's name was on papers later seized by French authorities from Boucan's home. They thought this was puzzling since Richardson's association with the Unione Corse had escaped detection by law enforcement. Little did the French authorities know that Richardson–with substantial help from Weiller–had already climbed her way up this organized crime ladder to the highest rungs of the organization. By now, she exerted considerable influence throughout North and South America and the Unione Corse networks.

By the mid to late 1970s, French and U.S. law enforcement belatedly became aware that Weiller and Richardson had seized financial and operational control of the Unione Corse's narcotics trafficking operations. NYPD Detective Balducci later testified at the Congressional Coast Guard hearings: "We were informed through Senator Buckley's office ... that he [Weiller] was considered a major financier of narcotics on an international level."[15] And yet no law enforcement agency came even close to laying a glove on either one of them.

They were untouchable.

Chapter 4:
The Ex-Nazi Connection

As World War II ended, many ex-Nazi officials being relentlessly pursued by Allied Forces were desperately seeking a safe haven. This presented a unique business opportunity for Unione Corse. Many of these high-ranking Nazis had amassed large fortunes by looting artwork and other valuables from the terrorized Jewish population of Europe. Now they needed a way to transport their loot and themselves out of Europe, preferably finding sanctuary in South America or even in the United States.

The French-Corsican members of the Unione Corse were experts in smuggling, particularly from the Mediterranean coast of southern France and Italy to the Americas. The ship captains and crews who regularly transported heroin and other contraband for the syndicate cared little about whether the shipment involved narcotics or ex-Nazis. But they expected to be paid generously for their services.

Most of the French and Corsican members of the Unione Corse were Roman Catholic, and Unione Corse leaders—such as Weiller—had contacts reaching the highest levels of the Vatican. It did not take long for both the Vatican and the Unione Corse to be involved in the mass movement of hundreds of ex-Nazis from war-torn Europe to safe havens in South America. The Franciscan Order and other elements of the Church were keenly interested in protecting the Nazis. After all, both ex-Nazis and the Church shared common ground. They were both committed to fighting the spread of Communism, particularly in Croatia and surrounding regions that were in danger of falling into pro-Communist and Russian hands. In particular, one Franciscan Croatian priest, Father Krunoslav Draganović, led a small but influential group of like-minded priests and the Church hierarchy. The group organized a sophisticated network of churches and monasteries—known as the "Ratline." Through this system, they transported ex-Nazi officials from

Krunoslav Draganović, a Croatian catholic priest and fascist who organized the "ratlines" used to smuggle ex-Nazi's out of Europe at the end of the war. (Wikimedia Commons 2020).

detention centers in Austria and elsewhere to coastal ports such as Genoa and Marseille for transport by ship to Latin America.[1] This group—who were closely aligned with the neo–facist Croatian Ustase—used the Franciscan headquarters and Seminary at San Girolamo in Rome to aid the transportation of anti–Communist war criminals.

Allen Dulles and others in the hierarchy of the OSS quickly realized that these ex–Nazis were an invaluable source of information and intelligence on the struggle by anti–Communist forces in Eastern Europe. Hopefully, they thought, these ex–Nazis could help prevent these countries from falling irretrievably behind the Iron Curtain.[3] Therefore, on a selective basis, U.S. intelligence officers assisted the transport of ex–Nazi war criminals, in return for which U.S. intelligence services benefitted from these ex–Nazis' expertise and contacts in Eastern Europe. U.S. intelligence agents could use this information and, sometimes, the ex–Nazis themselves, to establish contact with the anti–Communist resistance groups in Eastern Europe.

According to a now–declassified U.S. Army Counterintelligence Corps (CIC) report from 1950, U.S. intelligence officers began using the Draganović established network to evacuate its own selective "visitors" to coastal ports. The Unione Corse then arranged to smuggle them aboard ships leaving for Latin America and the U.S.[4] As the report put it,

> there were visitors who had been in the custody of the 430 CIC and completely processed in accordance with current directives and requirements, and whose continued residence

in Austria constituted a security threat as well as a source of possible embarrassment to the Commanding General of USFA, since the Soviet Command had become aware that their presence in U.S. Zone of Austria and in some instances had requested the return of these persons to Soviet custody.[5]

Instead of turning these war criminals over to the Red Army for prosecution or execution, the U.S. intelligence agencies decided to "make a deal with the devil" and, in many cases, transport them to the Americas. They became valuable "assets" for U.S. intelligence and, coincidentally, valuable additions to the Unione Corse's narcotics distribution networks.

The most influential ex–Nazi to legally enter the U.S. was Nazi Lieutenant General Reinhard Gehlen. On August 24, 1945, three months after the German capitulation and two weeks after the end of the war with Japan, General Gehlen arrived by plane at Washington National Airport on board a U.S. Army transport plane. Dressed in a U.S. Army officer's battle uniform to not attract attention, he was hustled into an unmarked van and driven to Fort Hunt in Fairfax County, Virginia. He was considered one of the U.S.'s most prized Nazi assets. U.S. intelligence officers had gone to great lengths to keep him from falling into Russian hands. Russian forces were frantically hunting for him, seeking retribution for the damage that Gehlen and his team of German intelligence officers had inflicted on the Russian war effort. However, when the advancing Russians searched Gehlen's headquarters at Zossen, they found empty file cabinets. When the U.S. Army notified the Soviets of Gehlen's apprehension, he had already been secreted out of Europe.[6] After arriving at Fort Hunt, Gehlen was given a dark-grey business suit, which became his new "uniform" as a U.S. intelligence "asset" in the rapidly developing Cold War.

The most precious commodity Gehlen had to offer was an extensive collection of intelligence files on Eastern Europe and the Soviet Union. He had secretly buried the papers in steel drums in the Bavarian Alps. Gehlen correctly anticipated that the United States and its Allies would turn their attention to an increasingly powerful communist Russia once the war was over. With these files, Gehlen would be in an excellent position to negotiate his freedom and that of hundreds of his

Deutsches Bundesarchiv. 1943. "Reinhard Gehlen." Www.bild.bundesarchiv.de. Deutsches Bundesarchiv. 1943.

key agents strategically scattered throughout Eastern Europe.

One month before Gehlen surrendered to the U.S. Army CIC in Bavaria, he had been fired by Hitler over his discouraging reports on the strength of the Soviet Red Army. At first, his U.S. captors did not recognize Gehlen and classified him as "just another Nazi." Soon, however, his significance was realized, and Brigadier General Edwin Sibert, the chief of G–2 (Army intelligence) of the Twelfth Army in Germany, personally interviewed him. Sibert spent many hours with Gehlen in long debriefing sessions. Gehlen provided vital information on the Russian military and the Soviet political landscape. Gehlen told Silbert, for example, that Stalin had no intention of surrendering Poland to the Western powers. Russia had already decided that Hungary, Romania, Bulgaria, and Czechoslovakia would remain in the Russian political orbit. Gehlen also revealed the names of many OSS officers who were secretly members of the U.S. Communist Party.

Gehlen used his leverage to forge a deal whereby he would turn over all his Russian intelligence files to the Americans in exchange for his freedom. He also wanted freedom for his top military colleagues, who were still in POW camps in Germany. General Sibert immediately contacted his superior, General Walter Bedell Smith, Eisenhower's chief of staff, who told Sibert to continue his talks with Gehlen. General Smith then consulted with William Donovan, the head of the Office of Strategic Services (OSS), and Allen Dulles, the OSS station chief in Bern, Switzerland. Both of them agreed that a deal should be struck with Gehlen. The fact that he had been an enthusiastic supporter of Hitler's "Final Solution" for European Jewry and the subjugation of the Slavic people was of little import to them. "He's on our side, and that's all that matters," commented Allen Dulles. "Besides, one need not ask him to one's club."[7]

After further negotiations, Gehlen was given a leadership position in a newly created clandestine U.S.–German intelligence network, specifically tasked with spying on the Soviet Union. Known simply as "the Gehlen Organization," the new espionage agency was nominally under the control of the United States. However, it was largely given free rein to use whatever methods it deemed necessary to build a network of intelligence assets in the Eastern Bloc.

In July 1946, Gehlen and 350 former German intelligence agents of his choosing relocated to Munich, the organization's new headquarters. Gehlen used a dummy corporation as cover, called the "South German Industrial Development Organization." Over time, his group grew to over 4,000 undercover agents, *Vertrauensmen* or "V–men," as they were called, to serve throughout the Soviet Bloc nations. For years after that, these agents proved to be the CIA's eyes and ears on the ground in areas where American agents couldn't operate.

The Gehlen Organization included hundreds of the most despicable former Gestapo, *Wehrmacht*, and S.S. officers. Among those now working for the U.S. through Gehlen's group were S.S. Captain Alois Brunner, Adolf Eichmann's most trusted aide, and SS Major Emil Augsburg. They oversaw the murder of hundreds of Russians. Another Nazi employed by Gehlen was Franz Six, the exterminator of hundreds of Jews in the Smolensk Ghetto.

S.S. Chief Walter Rauff, the designer of mobile gas trucks used to execute Jewish and disabled people on the Eastern Front, was another beneficiary of protection by the OSS and later the Gehlen Organization. After U.S. forces began closing in on Milan in 1945, Rauff entered negotiations with the OSS. He exchanged promises with Allen Dulles to surrender S.S. forces in Italy in return for immunity from war crime prosecutions.[8] Rauff was kept hidden in a convent in Italy and began working for the Israeli Intelligence Service in Syria in 1947. He made his way to South America in 1949.[9]

The infamous Klaus Barbie was the most notable Nazi "luminary" within the ranks of Gehlen's group. Barbie was known as the "Butcher of Lyon" for having personally tortured prisoners of the Gestapo—primarily Jews and members of the French Resistance—while stationed in Lyon. Gehlen and others in his organization provided Barbie with forged documents to flee to Bolivia, where he lived for years under the alias "Klaus Altman." Decades later, he would be caught and returned to France to stand trial for his crimes there during the German occupation.

Although Allen Dulles and his newly created CIA were aware of the criminal backgrounds of many of Gehlen's agents, they chose to ignore the thorny ethical issues involved. For them, any opportunity to gain a leg-up on their new Soviet foes was worth exploiting. They even went so far as to obstruct legitimate investigations into the whereabouts of some of these Nazi war criminals.[10]

The Gehlen Organization and its agents also had strong support among former French Vichy officials and sympathizers who had worked closely with Nazis during the wartime occupation of France. Gehlen recruited dozens of these officials and agents in the south of France. At the explicit directions of Allen Dulles, he established contact and a good working relationship with the Unione Corse based in Marseille. The French–Corsican mobsters thus joined forces with Gehlen's ex–Nazis and their Vichy French sympathizers to re–open Marseille to American shipping. They helped break the pro–Communist labor unions' stranglehold on the Marseille port. After this success, Gehlen continued his longstanding working relationship with Weiller and other leaders of the Unione Corse. They helped Gehlen secretly arrange for the transit of dozens of ex–Nazis by ship to South America. In return, Gehlen and his organization helped arrange for some heroin shipments by the Unione Corse to North and South America, receiving a generous cut of the profits.

The Gehlen Organization had a few notable successes in carrying out its primary mission in Eastern Europe. For example, Gehlen's agents uncovered the secret Russian assassination unit SMERSH. They also helped in the secret construction of the Berlin Tunnel. Americans used the tunnel to sneak beneath the Berlin Wall and monitor signal intelligence from the Soviet forces in East Germany. They also played a part in snatching a copy of a secret speech given by Soviet Premier Nikita Khrushchev in which he lashed out at the crimes of the Stalin era.

Gehlen repeatedly proved that he had an uncanny ability to supply the Americans with precisely the information they wanted to hear. CIA chief Allen Dulles and his brother, Secretary of State John Foster Dulles, were convinced that the "captive nations" of the Soviet bloc would rise up and throw off the yoke of Communism if given sufficient encouragement. Gehlen wholeheartedly agreed, despite all objective evidence pointing to the contrary.[11]

With the active support of the Dulles brothers and the rest of the U.S. government, Gehlen recruited and trained a mercenary force of about 5,000 exiled Eastern European nationals. They were ready to move in as an anti–Communist liberating force without any overt involvement of American units. Known as "Operation Sunrise," Gehlen's men received espionage training at a camp named Oberammergau in Germany. The groundwork for this operation was initially laid by OSS Chief Allen Dulles. He started secretly negotiating for Nazi support with Karl Wolff, the Waffen S.S. General in Northern Italy, even before Germany's formal surrender. The OSS closely coordinated this effort with the British MI-6, which had its own "Operation Unthinkable," the British contingency plan to fight the USSR, if necessary, after the war's conclusion.

Yet, despite a few successes, the Gehlen Organization had a surprisingly high failure rate. Soviet counterspies effectively infiltrated Western intelligence agencies, including the Gehlen Organization, so they were tipped off whenever a mission was planned. The results were catastrophic. One key double agent who gave advance information to the Russians in the late 1940s and early 1950s about the CIA raids was Adrian "Kim" Philby, the British intelligence liaison with the CIA. While ostensibly working for British intelligence, Philby was a member of the "Cambridge Five" spy ring, acting as an undercover agent for the Soviet Union even before World War II. He leaked information to the Soviet intelligence agencies until he resigned from MI-6 in 1951, later fleeing to Moscow.

One operation that proved to be a disaster was an anti–Communist mission dubbed WIN. The Gehlen Organization contacted WIN, a purported Polish underground group supplying the West with military information on Soviet troop movements. U.S. agents gave WIN members intelligence and military supplies to conduct hit-and-run raids inside Poland. By 1952, many of WIN's agents, including those parachuted into Poland by Britain and the U.S., had been compromised, and the information flowing back to the West was of little use. In the end, the West discovered that Soviet intelligence services had created WIN in the first place.[12]

Eventually, the entire Gehlen Organization was transferred to the West German Government, becoming its first intelligence arm, the BND. With Gehlen's help, Dulles engineered a coup in Iran that toppled Prime Minister Mohammad Mossadegh and reestablished the Shah's Pahlevi family regime. The family patriarch, General Reza Pahlevi, had been banished from the country for his pro-Nazi activities during the war. Now his son, Mohammed Reza Pahlevi, ascended to the Iranian throne. The Shah of Iran thus became one of the CIA's most powerful assets, and the ex-Nazi and fascist influence in Iran grew exponentially.

Gehlen's influence was not limited to Eastern Europe and Soviet Bloc countries. Gehlen set up dummy fronts and cover companies in the U.S. He used Eastern European emigre groups in the U.S. to help keep the U.S. government's focus on the Soviets, not the hunting of ex-Nazi war criminals. The "Tolstoy Foundation" and the "Union of Bishops of the Orthodox Church Outside Russia" were funded by the CIA at Gehlen's urging.

Gehlen's chief agent-in-place in the United States was Otto Albrecht von Bolschwing, a captain in Heinrich Himmler's dreaded S.S. Von Bolschwing worked for the OSS and then the CIA, but he took his orders directly from Gehlen. By the time he entered the U.S. in February 1954, von Bolshwing had erased almost all traces of his Nazi past. He befriended Elmer Bobst of Warner-Lambert Pharmaceutical and was hired to become the Director of International Marketing. Bobst was an early backer and good friend of Richard Nixon. By 1960, von Bolshwing had inserted himself inside Nixon's unsuccessful 1960 campaign for the presidency. Later, he was affiliated with a California high-tech firm TCI that held classified Defense Department contracts. By 1970, von Bolschwing had become the president of TCI after his extensive contacts with German banks enamored him with J. Paul Getty Jr., one of the company's directors.[13] His translator for German projects was Helene von Damme, who later served as Ronald Reagan's appointments secretary while governor of California. Von Damme was later named as U.S. Ambassador to Austria.

Another favorite place for ex–Nazis to hide was Interpol. This international police organization was under the control of the Nazi regime for the duration of World War II. Created in 1924, Interpol was a noble attempt to form an international police organization. In theory, Interpol would serve the same purpose for law enforcement that the League of Nations intended to provide the world's governments. Initially called the International Criminal Police Commission, the organization was headquartered in Vienna, Austria. Acting as a "super police force," its purpose was to fight crime across Europe and worldwide.

By 1935, the most enthusiastic member of Interpol was Nazi Germany. Swastikas began to appear at the annual meetings of Interpol, and a series of Nazi S.S. generals were elected as presidents. In 1938, Germany annexed Austria and Interpol went officially over to the Nazi side. Still, there was not much of a protest from other Interpol members. Nazi Germany, after all, had a police force that was the envy of the world, and Germany was willing to foot most of the bill for the operations and administration of Interpol.

In 1941, Interpol's headquarters was moved to Berlin. Two Gestapo officers, Ernst Kaltenbrunner and Reinhard Heydrich, took over Interpol's administration. The organization continued to operate for the duration of the war. It was given a new space in Berlin's fashionable Wannsee neighborhood, which they shared with the Gestapo.[14]

Interpol's operations came to a temporary halt at the war's end. Kaltenbrunner, the organization's

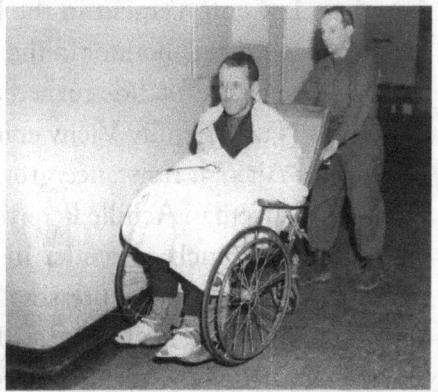

Former Gestapo Commander Ernst Kaltenbrunner in U.S. detention in 1946. He was later hanged after being convicted of War Crimes and Crimes Against Humanity at the Nuremberg Trials. (Harry S. Truman Library & Museum 1946).

president, was hanged as a war criminal at Nuremberg. But the organization did not die with him. In the closing days of the Nazi regime, Gestapo Colonel Carlos Zindel packed up as many Interpol files as he could carry and fled Berlin. Zindel ended up in the French–controlled city of Stuttgart, where he gulped down a cyanide capsule rather than surrender. Thus, the French gained control of the extensive files of the Nazi police and Interpol. These files included the identities of many Nazi and Interpol agents and their informants.[15]

It was not wholly coincidental that France volunteered in 1946 to become the primary sponsor and supporter of a reborn Interpol. France generously offered funding and personnel to rebuild the organization that had served Nazi Germany for nine years. Many personnel hired to rebuild Interpol were ex–Nazis and Nazi sympathizers from Germany and France. Many had either worked for the organization during the years it was under Nazi control or were members of staunchly anti–Communist organizations on the extreme right of the political spectrum.

With help from well–placed connections within the French government, the Unione Corse could also place its people inside the organization. One such person was Jean Nepote, who rose in the ranks of Interpol to become its Secretary–General in 1963. An investigation by American law enforcement in the late 1970s discovered that Nepote had been a Nazi collaborator in the Vichy police forces throughout the war.[16] However, as the tide turned against the Nazis in 1944, Nepote erased his Nazi–friendly Vichy credentials. Instead, he claimed membership in "Ajax," a resistance group of police officers formed by the Corsican policeman Achille Peretti, who worked in the Marseille area.

After the French surrender in 1940, Peretti was charged by the new Vichy regime with repressing Marseille's infamous black market and smuggling rings. Peretti adroitly used this position to accumulate a personal fortune by working closely with Resistance–allied Unione Corse members under Marcel Francisci. Following the Allied invasion of Sicily in 1943, Peretti formed the Ajax network with fellow police officers. Their success in smuggling at–risk resistance fighters out of the country caught the attention of de Gaulle, who brought Peretti on to oversee security for his exiled government in Algiers.

As the U.S. moved through France in 1944, Ajax's membership swelled—at least on paper—from 200 to 2000 operatives. France was on the brink of liberation, and many sympathizers were desperate to legitimize their wartime betrayal. To those collaborators willing to pay, a cottage industry of unscrupulous resistance fighters was ready to sell "proof of membership" in their organizations. Among the massive influx of names in the Ajax membership book was that of Jean Nepote. After paying his dues to Peretti, Nepote could comfortably return to his old ways under the Interpol umbrella. Interpol was exceedingly tolerant of those who had actively worked for the Nazi cause. Interpol even went so far as to refuse to aid in the prosecution or evidence gathering concerning Nazi war criminals until the 1980s.[17]

Over the years, France's support for Interpol continued to build. A new, seven-story headquarters was built in the Parisian suburb of Saint-Cloud in 1969 using French funds, and staffing at the headquarters was 85% French. As the French national police force and intelligence services had a long tradition of avoiding narcotic trafficking investigations, Interpol's narcotics crime-fighting record was virtually nil. In 1976, the U.S. government's General Accounting Office (GAO) spent ten months studying Interpol's files. They could not find evidence that Interpol had on any major international drug smuggling organization, including the Unione Corse. Instead, GAO found that "most narcotics cases handled by Interpol involved young Americans or U.S. servicemen arrested overseas with small quantities of drugs, such as marijuana."[18]

Unfortunately, despite occasional half-hearted attempts to clean house, Interpol's leadership appears to have remained deeply corrupt. In 2008, Interpol President Jackie Selebi was arrested and later convicted of accepting over $150,000 in bribes from a South African drug lord. And in 2020, Meng Hongwei, who served as president of the agency between 2016 and 2018, admitted to taking $2 million in bribes, including from leading drug traffickers.

Old habits die hard.

Chapter 5:
Nixon, The Nazis, and the French Connection

Although he probably did not realize it at the time, a critical event occurred in Richard Nixon's life in 1945 while serving as a young naval officer. He was assigned to review the captured Nazi wartime records of Karl Blessing, former Reichsbank officer and then head of the Nazi oil cartel, Kontinentale Öl A.G.[1] Popularly known as 'Konti,' this oil cartel was in partnership with I.G. Farben, which had close ties with the Dulles brothers from their time as lawyers at Sullivan & Cromwell. The Dulles brothers and their law firm had helped organize bond offerings for I.G. Farben and Krupp in the 1930s.[2]

Allen Dulles had one of his agents personally reach out to Lt. Nixon to enlist his support for their efforts to bury the Konti documents. In return, Dulles' offered a verbal IOU of support if the young, ambitious naval officer wished to pursue a political career in his native state of California. Nixon—already considering a career in politics—took the deal, and the Konti files mysteriously disappeared.

Dulles made good on his promise by arranging for much of Nixon's first congressional campaign financing shortly after the war. While still a navy officer, Nixon was recruited by the local Republican organization in his home congressional district to run against Horace Jerimiah ("Jerry") Voorhis, the incumbent Democrat. When Nixon left the Navy at the start of 1946, he and his wife Pat returned to Whittier, California, where Nixon began a year of intensive campaigning. His campaign painted Voorhis as an ineffective Congressman and suggested that Voorhis's endorsement by a PAC linked to the AFL–CIO labor union tied him to Communists. In other words, Nixon relied on "red–baiting," painting Voorhis as a "radical pinko" and "un–American."

Nixon handily won the election and thus launched a political career that would take him to the U.S. Senate, the Vice Presidency, and

Lieutenant Commander Richard Milhous Nixon, USN. Richard Nixon Foundation, 1945. Courtesy to Richard Nixon Foundation.

the White House. Of course, his political career ultimately ended in disgrace, as the only President in U.S. history to resign from office.

In Congress, Nixon became the informal representative of the Dulles brothers. At this time, Allen Dulles was Director of Central Intelligence, and John Foster Dulles was an advisor to New York Governor Thomas Dewey and U.S. delegate to the United Nations. The Dulles brothers carefully burnished Nixon's credentials as a staunch anti–Communist by sponsoring him on a tour of fascist "freedom fighters" in West Germany. These fighters were preparing for the day when their home countries in Eastern Europe would be liberated from Communist oppression.

In a further effort to show that he was strongly opposed to Communism, Nixon became a member of the House Un–American Activities Committee (HUAC) in February 1947. U.S. Representative Charles J. Kersten introduced him to Father John Francis Cronin, who shared with Nixon his privately circulated paper, "The Problem of American Communism in 1945." This paper contained information about alleged communist infiltration of the U.S. government, Hollywood, and other sectors of the American economy. Father Cronin's paper was primarily based upon information leaked by the FBI's William C. Sullivan, who later headed up the Bureau's domestic intelligence operations under J. Edgar Hoover.

By May 1948, Nixon had co–sponsored a "Mundt–Nixon Bill" to combat "internal communist subversion." The Bill required registration of all Communist Party members and a statement of the source of all printed and broadcast material issued by organizations "that were found to be Communist fronts." On May 19, 1948, the bill passed the

House by 319 to 58 but later failed to pass the Senate after Washington and New York protests.

Nixon gained further national attention in August 1948, when his persistence as a HUAC member helped break the Alger Hiss spy case. Most knowledgeable observers doubted Whittaker Chambers' allegations that Hiss, a former State Department official, had been a Soviet spy. Nevertheless, Nixon pressed for the Committee to continue its investigation. When Hiss filed suit for defamation, Chambers produced documents that were turned over to Nixon and the HUAC, supposedly corroborating his allegations. The most significant of these documents were paper and microfilm copies that Chambers claimed had been hidden overnight in a pumpkin field. Inevitably, they became known as the "Pumpkin Papers." Hiss was convicted of perjury in 1950 for denying under oath he had passed documents to Chambers, and overnight, Nixon became a household name across America.

Later, Senator Joseph McCarthy of Wisconsin started his "Red Scare" crusade against what he described as hundreds (if not thousands) of closet Communists and Communist-sympathizing "pinkos." Public figures, including W.E.B DuBois, Charlie Chaplain, Orson Welles, and Albert Einstein, were subjected to public humiliation under the aegis of McCarthy's anti-Communist crusade. He also went after employees of the U.S. State Department, the U.S. Army, and other organs of government. Nixon served on the Congressional committee to enhance his public image. He also ensured that McCarthy did not go too far "off the rails" and start pointing fingers at the CIA and the rest of the intelligence community. However, by the 1950s, McCarthy began investigating the CIA, much to the chagrin of Allen Dulles. Dulles started a covert operation with James Angleton to feed McCarthy disinformation and discredit his investigations.[3]

The links between the CIA, their allies in Congress (such as Nixon), and the ex-Nazi organizations combatting Soviet consolidation of power in Eastern Europe also had political benefits for the Republicans. For example, in preparation for the 1952 Eisenhower-Nixon campaign, the Republicans formed an "Ethnic Division," which recruited the 'displaced Fascists' who arrived in the United States after World War II.[4] Like similar organizations in Western countries, the Ethnic

Division attracted many Central and Eastern European Nazis recruited by the S.S. and then switched their allegiance to the U.S. and its allies at the war's end.

So, why were Republicans willing to court such unsavory allies?

Senator Joseph R. McCarthy (1908-1957), ca. 1954.
National Archives and Records Administration, Records of the U.S. Information Agency.

Desperation may have been part of their motivation. By the 1950s, the Republican party had spent two decades languishing outside the Oval Office. Roosevelt's New Deal coalition redefined the Democratic constituency by courting progressive intellectuals, immigrants and minorities, rural farmers, and urban labor, leading to smashing victories over the Republicans in 1932. It would take a similarly fundamental shift in the base of the Republican party to unseat Roosevelt's Democratic successors.

This close relationship between the Republican party and ex–Nazis became even closer after the electoral defeat of New York Governor Thomas Dewey, the Republican presidential candidate in 1948, to President Truman. Nixon, Allen Dulles, and other leading Republicans blamed the loss on "the Jewish vote," which was overwhelmingly for Truman. When Nixon became Eisenhower's vice president in 1952, he was determined to build his ethnic base to counter the Democrat's

Jewish solid support. Nixon naturally turned to the German and Eastern European communities, particularly receptive to his staunchly anti–Communist rhetoric, and contained many Nazi and fascist sympathizers within their ranks. The Refugee Relief Act in 1953, intended to give sanctuary to those fleeing Soviet oppression, also opened U.S. borders to many former fascists, including former Waffen S.S. members and Croatian Nazis. Pro–fascist organizations such as the Croatian Ustase soon became an integral part of Republican politics. These fascist Eastern European groups also had an anti–Communist affinity with the Unione Corse and French organized crime groups that dominated the heroin trade. At every step of the way–from the poppy fields of Turkey to the chemical labs outside Marseille, to the distribution networks on the East Coast of the U.S. and elsewhere worldwide–the Unione Corse maintained its iron grip.

One of Nixon's most influential fascist supporters was wealthy Romanian industrialist Nicolae Malaxa. He had maintained a close relationship with Hitler's Nazi regime in Germany until shortly before the end of the war. Afterward, Malaxa sought asylum in the U.S. while on an economic mission for King Michael of Romania. Malaxa eventually settled in New York City, where his family joined him after being expelled by the Groza government.[5]

Malaxa had escaped from Europe with over $200 million in U.S. dollars. Upon arriving in New York in the 1940s, he claimed another $200 million in previously frozen Nazi money transferred through various European accounts to Chase Manhattan Bank. To assist him in his fight to unfreeze the accounts, Malaxa retained the

Romania Insider. 2011. "Famous Romanians: Nicolae Malaxa, the Tycoon Who Built the First Romanian Locomotive and Car." Romania Insider. January 11, 2011.

law firm run by John Pehle, a former attorney for the U.S. Treasury who had determined the funds needed to be frozen during the war.[6] Malaxa's legal path for his entry was smoothed by Sullivan & Cromwell, the Dulles brothers' law firm. Undersecretary of State Adolph Berle, who had helped Nixon and Whittaker Chambers convict Alger Hiss, personally testified on Malaxa's behalf before a congressional subcommittee on immigration. However, Malaxa was widely known to have supported Romania's fascist Iron Guard during the war, and by 1951 Malaxa was forced to leave the U.S. for Canada.

Senator Nixon—determined to ingratiate himself to the wealthy Malaxa—jumped into the middle of the immigration dispute by introducing a private bill to allow Malaxa permanent residence in the U.S. In addition, Nixon helped Malaxa create a corporate front, Western Tube Corp., based in California. One of Nixon's most prominent financial backers for his 1946 Congressional run was Herman L. Perry, who later became president of Western Tube. Malaxa was promptly hired as treasurer of the company. Although Western Tube had no actual operations, its supposed mission to fabricate seamless tubes for the oil industry made it—at least on paper—vital to the country's growing Korean War effort. Nixon personally sponsored Western Tube's application to obtain "wartime priority" for its personnel, including Malaxa.[7]

In a January 1953 CIA report, Malaxa was labeled a "financial shark." The report continued calling him a "slippery fence rider, who plays both ends against the middle for personal reasons," and "the most perfidious man in Romania."[8] In 1955, while Malaxa was visiting Argentina, the U.S. Immigration and Naturalization Service ("INS") briefly revoked his re-entry permit.[9]

Despite Malaxa's unsavory reputation, he was wholeheartedly embraced by Richard Nixon. He established a close financial and business association with Malaxa, who exerted considerable influence in the expatriate Eastern European communities. Nixon and his fellow Republicans were actively trying to woo this group to the Republican camp by taking a solid anti-Communist stand and turning a blind eye to ex-Nazis and fascists such as Malaxa.

The Democrats tried to turn Nixon's relationship with Malaxa against him in his failed 1962 electoral campaign for Governor of

California. Still, a government investigation cleared him of the accusations.[10] Jack Anderson of The Washington Post revisited Malaxa's pro–Nazi past in 1979. He claimed in a story that Nixon and other high–ranking American officials close to Malaxa had been involved in a cover–up of Malaxa's shady past.[11] But by then, Nixon was long gone from public political life. After the Watergate scandal and Nixon's resignation as president, there was virtually nothing that could further damage his already tarnished reputation.

Nixon won the White House in 1968 with substantial help from his new fascist–friendly U.S. base. It was no coincidence that he surrounded himself with a Praetorian Guard of advisers with crew cuts and Germanic–sounding names. Nixon's "German High Command" at the White House included Bob Haldeman, John Ehrlichman, Egil "Bud" Krogh, and Richard Kleindienst, amongst many others.

Nixon also maintained a close friendship with Elmer Bobst of Warner–Lambert Pharmaceutical, a Nazi supporter. Nixon referred to Bobst as his "honorary father," and their families often spent Christmas together. They perhaps bonded over shared antisemitism. Nixon was recorded saying that "the Jews are just a very aggressive and abrasive and obnoxious personality."[12] Bobst went even further. He told his "Dear Dick:" "If this beloved country of ours ever falls apart, the blame rightly should be attributed to the malicious action of Jews in complete control of our communications." He added, "nearly two hundred million of our people will strongly resent the hardships which they now face, mainly because of the Jews."[13]

Nixon actively recruited ex–Nazis and fascist sympathizers for his 1968 presidential campaign. Many came from fascist and anti–communist fraternities and organizations at the University of Southern California and the University of California at Los Angeles. These groups, primarily populated by ethnic Germans, Croatians, and other ethnic Eastern Europeans, were natural recruiting grounds for the Nixon campaign. One of the Nazis recruited by candidate Nixon was Laszlo Pasztor, the founding chair of Nixon's Republican Heritage Groups Council. Pasztor was a diplomat in Berlin during World War II, representing the Arrow Cross government of Nazi Hungary, which supervised the extermination of the Jewish population in that country.[14]

Once elected in 1968, Nixon quickly implemented an "open door" policy for all émigré fascists. Such notables as Ivan Docheff, head of the Bulgarian National Front and chairman of the American Friends of the Anti–Bolshevik Bloc of Nations (ABN), an organization dominated by war criminals and fugitive fascists, got immediate access to the president. Nixon welcomed Docheff and others to the White House for a "prayer meeting" to celebrate "Captive Nations Week."

There were also confirmed rumors that G. Gordon Liddy, one of Nixon's advisors and perhaps the most pro–fascist enthusiast in the White House, regularly sponsored viewings of the iconic Nazi film Lena Wertmuller's *Triumph of the Will* in the White House basement movie theater.[15] Whether Nixon himself attended any of these basement fascist pep rallies is unknown. Still, the fact that they took place in the White House implies that he condoned or tolerated them.

Based upon Nixon's careful maneuvering over more than two decades following the end of World War II, he had effectively consolidated the support of the corporate titans and American uber–rich, traditionally the solid core of the Republican Party base. But he was also able to expand on this base by courting ex–Nazis and neo–fascists for financial and political support. Playing up his fiercely anti–communist rhetoric, Nixon helped bring many Eastern European émigrés into the Republican fold. Nazi support had been a longstanding strain in conservative American politics ever since Charles Lindbergh, the iconic American aviator, publicly expressed his admiration for Adolph Hitler and the Nazi creed during the 1930s. Nixon had also lined up the support of Weiller, Richardson, and the Unione Corse, whose virtually unlimited funds helped finance Nixon's political rise to power.

Chapter 6:
Bebe "The Fixer" Rebozo and Lunch at La Cote Basque

On July 13, 1968–the day before France's annual national celebration known as "Bastille Day"–Nixon's crony, Charles Gregory "Bebe" Rebozo, arranged for a meeting between Nixon, Paul-Louis Weiller, and Patricia Richardson. The luncheon meeting took place at La Côte Basque, the iconic French restaurant on West 55 Street in midtown Manhattan. Rebozo, a sometimes banker and full-time money launderer and political fixer, was well known to Weiller, Richardson, and the rest of Unione Corse's upper echelon. Rebozo had close ties with what was known as "the Corporation," the Cuban-American syndicate led by Juan Miguel Battle. The syndicate operated throughout South Florida and established a foothold in Spanish Harlem in Manhattan and other Spanish-speaking communities on the East Coast. The Corporation and the Unione Corse had formed an informal alliance and symbiotic relationship whereby each group respected the others' "turf." The Corporation stayed away from the Unione Corse's primary source of revenue: the manufacturing and importation of heroin. At the same time, the Unione Corse handled the complex smuggling operation necessary to get the drugs into the country. In return, the Corporation exclusively sourced its heroin from the Unione Corse and restricted its drug operations to the U.S.

Nixon and Weiller first became acquainted at a dinner party hosted by the oil executive John Shaheen, who had served in the OSS during WWII as Chief of OSS Special Projects and head of the Reports Declassification Section. After the war, he made a fortune and became a major Republican Party donor and influencer, giving $100,000 to conservative candidates in the 1968 election. While Nixon had lost the 1960 presidential election to John F. Kennedy, he was still the presumed Republican candidate for the 1968 election.[1] Because of that, he was the center of attention for conservative fundraisers and those seeking to build influence in political circles. Weiller saw great potential in Nixon, who had sufficient moral flexibility to rise to the very top of the political pyramid. Nixon was willing to make almost any deal necessary in exchange for large "off-the-books" campaign funding. Weiller invited him to visit France, where he made a con-

> date -- 3/15/65
>
> Dear Mr. Weiller:
>
> I greatly enjoyed our meeting at John Shaheen's dinner last night.
>
> My present tentative plans are to visit Paris sometime between May 28 and June 7. Within three weeks I should know the exact date and will be in touch with you then.
>
> I greatly appreciate your invitation to visit you in Paris but I hope the date my trip is scheduled will not interfere with any other plans you may have atthat time.
>
> With kindest personal regards,

> A letter sent by Nixon to Paul-Louis Weiller following their introduction in 1965. Weiller would go on to covertly give Nixon $2 million in support of his 1968 Presidential campaign. Courtesy of the Nixon Foundation.

certed effort to cement his relationship with this rising Republican star. For instance, in May 1965, Nixon and Weiller met in a villa owned by Weiller at Versailles to solidify their friendship. That June, Nixon also joined Weiller in Rome for the wedding of his son, Paul-Annik Weiller, to Olimpia Torliona, the granddaughter of King Alfonso XIII and Queen Victoria Eugenia of Spain.[2] Weiller's invitations to these gilded events demonstrated to Nixon precisely the degree of influence and power that could be gained by allying with him and the Unione Corse. These meetings in 1965 were only setting the stage for Weiller's long-range plan for Nixon.

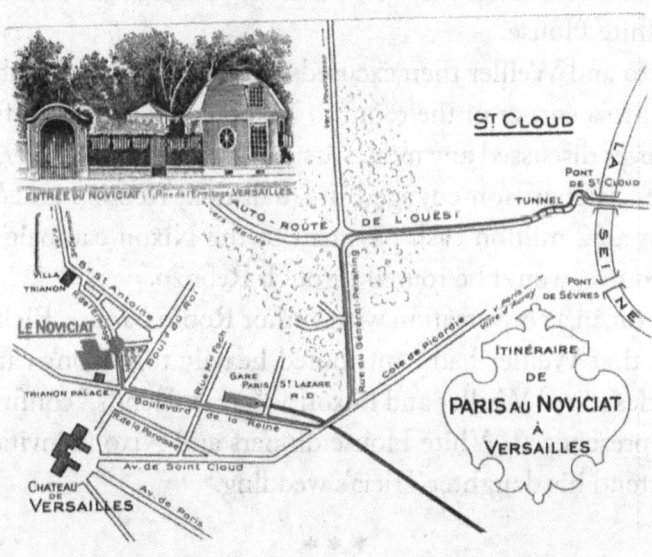

An invitation from Paul-Louis Weiller to his villa at Versailles. Courtesy of the Nixon Foundation.

At the Côte Basque, after the usual pleasantries were taken care of, Nixon and Weiller finally got down to business in one of the restaurant's private rooms. Nixon was well aware of the longstanding working arrangement between the Unione Corse and the CIA and let it be known that he would "respect" that arrangement if elected president. However, he acknowledged that he was in a tight race with the Democratic presidential candidate, Hubert Humphry. His campaign needed a substantial cash infusion to maintain his slight edge in the polls.

In response, Weiller and Richardson made it clear that their organization preferred Nixon to be the election winner. They were "concerned" that Humphrey and the Democrats were not sufficiently respectful of "traditions," such as the unwritten agreement between the U.S. and the Unione Corse forged in 1947. They also made clear that some of Nixon's closest advisors, particularly those with "German connections," were familiar with the Unione Corse. They assured Nixon that their organization had collaborated with the Germans on previous occasions. They were confident that they would continue to have a good working relationship with Nixon's German–Americans in a Nixon White House.

Rebozo and Weiller then excused themselves from the table. The men went to a corner of the room so Nixon could later truthfully say that he never discussed any money issues directly with Weiller. While Nixon and Richardson engaged in small talk, Rebozo and Weiller agreed on a $2 million cash payment to the Nixon campaign.[3] The cash, of course, would be routed through Rebozo.

Later on, in a conversation with author Robin Moore, Richardson admitted that Weiller had contributed heavily to Nixon's campaign. She also described Weiller and Nixon as "good friends," confirmed by Weiller's presence at White House dinners and Nixon's invitation to him to attend his daughter Tricia's wedding.[4]

* * *

Nixon was elected president on November 5, 1968. Bebe Rebozo set up an office in the White House shortly after the First Family moved in following the January 20, 1969 inauguration. After that, he came and went from 1600 Pennsylvania Avenue as he pleased and was considered one of President Nixon's inner circle. Although Rebozo had no official position with the U.S. government, he was exempted from logging in and out with the Secret Service. In addition to a private office, he had a designated bedroom always at his disposal.[5] He was widely known as President Nixon's best friend and, later, as Nixon's bagman.[6] But few knew that he was also Nixon's intermediary with the Cuban mob and the French–Corsican syndicate.

Rebozo's connections with the Italian Mafia were more widely known than his associations with other organized crime groups. The FBI was well aware of Rebozo's affiliations with Godfather Santos Trafficante of Tampa and Alfred "Big Al" Polizzi of the Genovese Crime Family. As Vincent "Jimmy Blue Eyes" Alo–a close associate of Meyer Lansky–told journalist Anthony Summers in 1997, "Rebozo was the one who picked up the money for Nixon."[7] Rebozo picked up money for Nixon from both mob figures and such wealthy Nixon donors as Howard Hughes, one of Nixon's longtime financiers. Rebozo came under investigation during Watergate for accepting a $100,000 bribe from Hughes for Nixon. But without the cooperation of either Rebozo or Hughes, the investigation stalled.

After graduating from high school, Rebozo got his first job as a steward with Pan–American Airways, shuttling between Miami, the Caribbean, and Panama. He quickly learned that he could supplement his modest salary by secretly transporting bags of heroin for the Unione Corse. This was how he originally came to know Patricia Richardson. While based in Miami, Rebozo befriended Bernard Barker and Eugenio Martinez, who later gained notoriety as Watergate burglary team members. Rebozo also served as the liaison between Nixon and his personal Watergate supervisor and master of secrets, E. Howard Hunt. In addition, he coordinated the Nixon team's efforts to energize the ex–Nazis and right–wing ideologues, who were crucial elements of Nixon's "base" and that of the Republican Party.

The relationship between Rebozo and Nixon dates back to 1950, when Democratic Senator George Smathers of Florida, a childhood friend of Rebozo, asked Rebozo to look after his new Congressional colleague. Nixon was celebrating his election to the Senate with a trip to Key Biscayne, Florida, where Rebozo took him deep–sea fishing.[8]

The two immediately hit it off and forged an enduring friendship. The "two amigos," as they came to be known, were also together in Key Biscayne after Nixon narrowly defeated Vice President Hubert Humphrey in the 1968 presidential election.

Known as "Uncle Bebe" to Nixon's two children, Trisha and Julie, Rebozo frequently bought expensive gifts for the girls and Nixon's wife Pat. Rebozo later purchased a $100,000 house in the suburbs for Julie after she married David Eisenhower. Rebozo also paid for the bowling alleys installed in the White House and Camp David. He regularly flew on Air Force One, wearing a blue Navy flight jacket bearing the Presidential Seal with his name stitched onto it. Nixon often infuriated Henry Kissinger by calling his Secretary of State in the middle of the night after long drinking bouts with Rebozo. Based upon Rebozo's alcohol-induced advice and counsel, Nixon often gave Kissinger hair-brained directives on sensitive international diplomatic issues.[9] These calls became so frequent that, before acting on any of Nixon's middle-of-the-night orders, Kissinger usually waited until the following day to see if Nixon had remembered their nocturnal phone conversations. Nixon usually forgot.

President Nixon with Bebe Rebozo. 1960 (circa). State Archives of Florida, Florida Memory. Courtesy of Florida Memory.

Thus, Rebozo became the center of the unholy alliance between the Nixon White House, the CIA, the Unione Corse, the Italian Mafia, and Nixon's ex-Nazi and right-wing supporters. This unlikely partnership chugged along relatively smoothly throughout the Nixon presidency. Barring a minor blip caused by the Watergate scandal, Nixon and Rebozo's friendship remained intact to the grave.

Chapter 7:
Nixon's Phony "War on Drugs"

Most Americans—including the older generation of "Baby Boomers" who came of age in the 1960s and 1970s—have little or no memory of when the U.S. was not supposedly engaged in a "War on Drugs." However, it was not until the early 20th Century that most "hard" drugs were declared illegal. Until 1912, products such as heroin were sold over-the-counter in cough syrup. Doctors also regularly prescribed opiate-based products to treat irritable babies, bronchitis, insomnia, "nervous conditions" such as hysteria, menstrual cramps, and "vapors." In addition, laudanum, an opioid, was a common item in home medicine cabinets.[1] Benjamin Franklin himself came to rely on opium to soothe chronic pain late in his life.[2]

Some local laws restricted the distribution and use of drugs as early as 1860. The first national U.S. law banning the distribution and use of certain drugs was the Harrison Narcotics Tax Act of 1914.[3] The Federal Bureau of Narcotics was established within the United States Department of the Treasury by an act of Congress dated June 14, 1930. Soon, the Marihuana Tax Act of 1937 was enacted, effectively outlawing the sale of marijuana.

During the Nixon presidency in the late 1960s and early 1970s, widespread news reports of a growing heroin epidemic among U.S. service members in Vietnam began circulating.[4] These reports triggered calls for Congress and the federal government to take a more aggressive law enforcement approach to prevent the rapidly rising distribution and use of narcotics.[5] On October 27, 1970, Congress passed the Comprehensive Drug Abuse Prevention and Control Act of 1970. The act classified drugs according to their medical and industrial potential and set out strict requirements for securing and preventing the sale of narcotics.[6]

Much has been written about how the Nixon Administration's anti-drug crusade was motivated less by a concern for public health than calculated and cynical power politics. Essentially, Nixon thought a draconian drug policy could be effectively used as a weapon against two segments of U.S. society that he viewed as his greatest threats: African–Americans and anti–war activists, particularly those within the Jewish community. In a 1994 interview by journalist Dan Baum, Nixon's domestic policy adviser, John Ehrlichman, explained: "The Nixon campaign in 1968, and the Nixon White House after that had two enemies: the antiwar left and black people.... We knew we couldn't make it illegal to be either against the war or black, but by getting the public to associate the hippies with marijuana and blacks with heroin, and then criminalizing both heavily, we could disrupt those communities."[7]

Considering the years he spent in federal prison due to his association with the Nixon White House, bitterness may have tainted Ehrlichman's remarks about Nixon.[8] Nevertheless, his post–Watergate statements still had the ring of truth about them. It is well acknowledged–and evidenced in tape recordings–that Nixon held strong racist and anti–Semitic prejudices. His drug policies also reflected these prejudices.[9] The result had a highly disruptive effect on African American communities, leading to the incarceration of an extraordinarily high percentage of young black men.[10]

Portrait of John D. Ehrlichman, Assistant to the President for Domestic Affairs; Nixon White House Photographs. Oliver F., A. (1969, May 13). National archives nextgen catalog [NARA]. Courtesy of the National Archives and Records Administration.

Much less is known, however, about Nixon's third–but equally important–motivation: to combat the growing competition of drug suppliers from Mexico, Colombia, and Southeast Asia to the heroin being distributed up and down the East Coast by the Unione Corse and its affiliates. Nixon's political career had greatly benefitted from the Marseille Accord struck by the Truman Administration and the Dulles brothers in 1947. He had personally received bags of cash in the run-up to the 1968 presidential election from Weiller and Richardson on behalf of the Marseille-based Unione Corse.

The supreme hypocrisy of Nixon–who accepted significant cash contributions from the leaders of the Unione Corse for his presidential campaigns and then declared a "War on Drugs"–has only come into clear focus in recent years. We now know the whole story of how Weiller, Richardson, and their organization helped bankroll Nixon's rise to the Presidency. We have also seen how the highest levels of Interpol, the French police, intelligence services, and politicians profited from the Unione Corse's success. On the U.S. side of "the pond," the CIA played a crucial role in preventing the BNDD and, later, the DEA from conducting any effective investigation of Unione Corse drug smuggling operations that had the secret CIA stamp of approval on them.

Ironically, Nixon's formidable rhetorical powers were most evident when he castigated international drug peddlers. At the same time, he relied on their covert financial support. In one rousing speech in 1971, Nixon emphatically declared:

> We are going to keep the heat on until the despicable profiters in human misery are driven out of their hiding places and are put in prison where they belong. The men and women who operate the global heroin trade are a menace not to Americans alone, but to all mankind. These people are literally the slave traders of our time. They are traffickers in living death. They must be hunted to the end of the earth. They must be left no base in any nation for their operations. They must be permitted not a single hiding place or refuge from justice anywhere in the world, and that is why we have established an aggressive international narcotics control program in cooperation with the governments of more than 50 countries around the world. That is why I have ordered the Central Intelligence Agency, early in this Administration, to mobilize its full resources to fight the international drug trade, a task, incidentally, in which it has performed superbly. Let me interject here a word for that much maligned agency.

As I have often said, in the field of intelligence we always find that the failures are those that are publicized. Its successes, by definition, must always be secret, and in this area there are many successes and particularly ones for which this agency can be very proud. The key priority here is to target on the traffickers wherever they are, to immobilize and destroy them through our law enforcement and intelligence efforts. And I commend all of you on the fine initial progress which has been made in these programs.[11]

Even if the Nixon Administration and law enforcement agencies seriously wanted to dismantle the Unione Corse drug distribution network in the U.S., they would have found it a herculean struggle. The discipline and secrecy surrounding this syndicate were even more rigorous than that of the better-known Italian Mafia, with its infamous "Omerta," or code of silence.

The Unione Corse's secrecy was exemplified by a case involving *Milieu* member Antoine Rinieri.[12] On June 12, 1962, Rinieri, posing as an art broker, arrived in New York City from Paris, France, carrying $247,000 in hard cash. When his contact in New York was a "no-show," Rinieri decided to visit a friend living in Asheville, North Carolina. While in Asheville, Rinieri stored the cash in a safe deposit box at a Wachovia Bank branch. On June 18, Rinieri left Asheville, flew to Chicago, and boarded a plane to fly to Zürich via Montréal. However, based upon a tip received by law enforcement, the flight was rerouted to New York, where Rinieri was arrested and questioned.[13] When required to appear before a grand jury, Rinieri refused to answer any questions based upon what he described as a "code of ethics" and "confidentiality." He declined to invoke the Fifth Amendment of the U.S. Constitution's anti-self-incrimination provisions. He was sentenced to six months in prison for contempt of court, after which he was put on a plane back to Paris. Since authorities discovered no evidence of a link between Rinieri's money and any drug dealing, it was returned to him, with interest.[14]

Rinieri's story is indicative of the Unione Corse's steely silence. Due in considerable measure to this extraordinarily high degree of secrecy and discipline, there was relatively little public scrutiny in the

U.S. of the Unione Corse's drug smuggling operations. The lack of media portrayals depicting the Unione Corse kept them far below the level of attention lavished on the Italian mob, most notably in Mario Puzo's 1969 hit novel *The Godfather*.

In contrast to the Unione Corse's discretion, the Mexican drug cartels specializing in marijuana and smuggling across the southern border drew a great deal of attention in the late 1960s by leaving a messy trail of gun battles, violence, and dead bodies. Also, due to its bulk and pungent odor, marijuana is far more difficult to smuggle than heroin. Thus, the Nixon administration's focus on combatting the Mexican drug cartels picked an easy target. The effort generated substantial political support from Nixon's base while simultaneously putting the Unione Corse's competitors in the crosshairs of U.S. law enforcement.

Thus, the "War on Drugs" was focused, from its outset, on assisting the Unione Corse in eliminating—or at least substantially degrading—the ability of its competitors to continue to smuggle drugs across the U.S.'s southern border.

***

The U.S. government had been regulating the import and sale of various drugs since before Prohibition. For some, the War on Drugs' origins can be traced to a June 1971 press conference. There was also a message to Congress by then–President Nixon, who declared drug abuse "public enemy number one."[15] But Nixon's War on Drugs started even before then.

To prove that he was serious about his intention to restore "law and order" to America, President Nixon launched his 1969 "Operation Intercept" along the Mexican border.[16] This massive "stop and search" operation was designed to slow traffic from Mexico into the U.S. and interrupt the increasing inward flow of narcotics sent by the Mexican drug cartels. Multiple government agencies warned that a focus on Mexican marijuana had a "high risk of making the Administration appear inept by playing into the hands of organized crime and creating more hard drug addicts." Nonetheless, Nixon gave the go–ahead to Operation Intercept.[17] Minimal quantities of drugs were seized, but

Nixon's primary goal was achieved. He showed his so-called "Silent Majority" that he was willing to be tough on crime (even though it was all a charade).

Operation Intercept, however, caused a diplomatic crisis with the Mexican government, which was outraged by the massive interference with the free flow of trade across the U.S.–Mexican border. It so severely damaged relations with Mexico that National Security Advisor Henry Kissinger formed the Ad Hoc Committee on Narcotics (dubbed "the Heroin Committee") to control and coordinate federal drug enforcement policy and prevent further diplomatic disasters.[18]

The Heroin Committee was composed of Cabinet members, including representatives of the CIA and the Federal Bureau of Narcotics (FBN), the predecessor to the Bureau of Narcotics and Dangerous Drugs (BNDD) and the Drug Enforcement Administration (DEA). James Ludlum, a member of the CIA's Counter-Intelligence staff and CIA liaison officer with the FBN since 1962, represented CIA Director Richard Helms.

By this point, the CIA was as much a drug-smuggling organization as it was an intelligence agency. For many years, the CIA controlled the heroin traffic from the Golden Triangle region of Burma, Thailand, and Laos into South Vietnam to maintain a substantial "off the books" source of income for the agency.[19] This money was then used to pay off top government officials in those countries for supporting U.S. policies. Heroin had also been the primary funding source for the CIA's activities in training Hmong troops from Laos to fight as a proxy army in the region, dating back as far as 1959.[20] This reality, however, presented the Nixon White House with a dilemma. The drug addiction rates among U.S. troops in Vietnam were soaring out of control. Increasing quantities of Southeast Asian heroin were being smuggled into the U.S. This presented a public health crisis. It also constituted a breach of the CIA's longstanding agreement with the Marseille-based Unione Corse that it would be given a monopoly on U.S. heroin distribution.

Nixon passed the word to CIA Director Helms that the CIA's heroin trade in Southeast Asia would have to end. The CIA did so reluctantly since the heroin trade in that part of the world had bought the U.S. a great deal of influence among corrupt government leaders. It was feared that if the money spigot were suddenly turned off, there would be severe adverse consequences to U.S. interests in Vietnam and throughout the region. As Helms told Ludlum in his usual colorful language: "We're going to break their rice bowls."[21]

The U.S. Ambassador to Vietnam, Ellsworth Bunker, called an emergency meeting in Saigon. He told the CIA Station Chief Ted Shackley that the orders from the White House to terminate the CIA's drug operations in Southeast Asia had to be executed. However, the corrupt South Vietnamese officials would have to be slowly weaned off their reliance on the CIA "money tree." If these corrupt leaders suddenly went "cold turkey," the US–backed government in South Vietnam would be thrown into a diplomatic and military crisis due to a lack of funds.

Meanwhile, to protect its global network of drug trafficking assets, the CIA intensified its infiltration of the BNDD. CIA officers were placed in critical positions in the BNDD and every other federal agency concerned with drug law enforcement. For example, CIA agent Paul Van Marx was assigned to the U.S. Embassy in Paris as the narcotics chief.[22] From this position, Van Marx monitored BNDD investigations that dealt with the Unione Corse so that they did not present any substantial threat to that organization's operations.

The Nixon administration also dramatically increased funding for the BNDD and hired hundreds of new agents to be posted abroad. Many of these new BNDD agents had previously worked for the CIA and continued covertly to do so. For example, ex–CIA agents assigned to the BNDD started working with an anti–Castro group of Cuban exiles participating in a CIA–financed drug operation known as "Operation Eagle." When it was disclosed that this group imported narcotics from Latin America into the Miami area, BNDD controlled the scandal by announcing a "reorganization" of the agency to prevent it from happening again.[23] However, many Cuban exiles who were arrested and then released for their participation in the drug smuggling operation went on to be hired by the BNDD as agents or "assets." They were then assigned to various strategic locations in Latin America. While on the BNDD payroll, they secretly reported to the CIA to avoid the

Bureau being embarrassed again by having one of its drug trafficking operations blown wide open.

In 1972, BNDD's inspection unit started expressing concerns about the Bureau's involvement in the CIA–sponsored drug operations in Latin America, BNDD Director John E. Ingersoll brought this problem to the attention of CIA Director Helms. They concocted a scheme whereby BNDD's inspection unit was disbanded. It was then replaced by a new "counter–intelligence" unit within BNDD called BUNCIN (Bureau of Narcotics Covert Intelligence Network). The department would be staffed by 19 CIA officers who would officially be sworn in as BNDD agents but would continue working for and reporting to the CIA. Under the guise of "investigating" corrupt BNDD agents, the new unit's function was to prevent any internal scrutiny of BNDD's links with the CIA–run drug operations in Latin America and South Florida.

The CIA's infiltration of the BNDD was now complete. It was with good reason that many BNDD agents began jokingly saying that the acronym "CIA" actually stood for "Cocaine Importing Agency." The ties between the CIA and the Unione Corse drug smuggling operations in Latin America had become inextricably intertwined. It was impossible to unravel this intricate web, even if they had wanted to.

The most notable CIA officer to be assigned to BNDD was Lucien Conein, who started his legendary career as a member of the OSS during World War II. Conein was born in France but was raised in Kansas City, Kansas, by an aunt who had married a U.S. soldier. During World War II, he parachuted into France to help form resistance cells that

Fussell, James A. "Conein... Lucien Conein." Kansas City Star [Kansas City, Miss.] (Sep. 20, 1998), pp. G-3, G-8.

included members of the Unione Corse, also known as the "Corsican Brotherhood."

Conein infiltrated spies and saboteurs into the Eastern European Warsaw Pact countries during the Cold War. In 1951, he helped the CIA establish a base in Nuremberg, Germany, assisted by Ted Shackley. In November 1963, during the CIA–arranged coup against South Vietnamese President Ngô Đình Diệm, resulting in Diệm's assassination, he served as Henry Cabot Lodge, Jr.'s liaison officer. He delivered $42,000 in cash to the leaders of the coup.[24] Due to his track record of successful covert operations, President Nixon appointed Conein as chief of covert operations for the DEA in 1972.[25] His former CIA colleague, E. Howard Hunt, also considered recruiting Conein to join the team that undertook the 1972 Watergate burglary of the Democratic National Committee. It was later reported by The Washington Post that Conein quipped: "If I'd been involved, we'd have done it right."[26]

In 1965, according to historian Alfred McCoy, Conein helped the CIA reach an agreement with the Unione Corse in Saigon. The Unione was given free rein to move the Southeast Asian morphine base out of Vietnam to the Marseille heroin labs while continuing to serve as CIA informants worldwide.[27]

Conein was initially assigned to his CIA duties in Southeast Asia by E. Howard Hunt, the CIA operative, who would later play a prominent role in the Watergate scandal. Following WWII, the Unione Corse had diversified their sources of opium and morphine raw products needed for heroin manufacturing, purchasing material from Indochina to not be solely dependent on the Turkish poppy fields. It turned out to be a prescient move. In 1971, the Nixon Administration obtained a temporary agreement with the Turkish government to curtail the cultivation of poppies, thus restricting the Turkey–Marseille supply routes of the raw material needed for heroin production.

Having survived various Congressional investigations relatively unscathed, the BNDD and the U.S. Department of Justice's formidable investigative and prosecutorial tools were primarily directed against the Mexican and Colombian cartels. They also targeted the Italian Mafia, which concentrated on illegal gambling, prostitution, labor racketeering, and other traditional illegal revenue sources. Meanwhile, with its close ties with the CIA, the Unione Corse and its Latin American affiliates–which had a virtual stranglehold on heroin shipments coming into the East Coast of the U.S.–continued to be largely ignored by U.S. law enforcement.

Nixon's War on Drugs was also motivated partly by America's desire to distract public attention from the Southeast Asian quagmire that the country was stuck in. The debacle of the Vietnam War proved the futility of U.S. efforts to prevent the rise of national liberation movements in Southeast Asia and Africa, especially after generations of oppressive colonial rule by France and other European colonial powers. On the advice of Kissinger, Nixon shifted his rhetoric from fiery anti–communism to a more subtle détente politics aimed at relaxing tensions with the USSR and China. Easing up on Communism, however, meant that the U.S. needed a new "enemy." Nixon, after all, was most comfortable rallying public support by channeling animosity. The drug cartels from Mexico and other locales south of the border made for easy targets, both rhetorically and strategically. In addition to helping his allies in the Unione Corse, Nixon's War on Drugs thus gave the public a new "threat" to focus on, just as public support for the Manichaean "War on Communism" was wearing thin.

* * *

Announcing a "War on Drugs" was the easy part for Nixon. The hard part was finding an agency willing and able to do Nixon's bidding without question. Before being infiltrated by the CIA, the BNDD was a relatively ineffective agency that had failed to prevent drug trafficking from sources other than the Unione Corse. The U.S. Military's reputation had also been tarnished by reports of rampant drug use and a failed, costly war in Southeast Asia. The selective service draft imposed on citizens during the war was widely considered an exercise in political folly rather than a military necessity.

Then there was the publication of excerpts from "The Pentagon Papers" in June 1971 by Time Magazine, leaked by Daniel Ellsberg. The "Papers" graphically revealed the illegal CIA and military operations in Southeast Asia to the American public, including those in Laos and Cambodia. Time Magazine's cover, "Pentagon Papers: A

Secret War," electrified the entire country. The detailed story behind it undermined the American public's confidence in their military for more than a generation. Also damaging the Pentagon's reputation was the January 1970 revelation by Christopher Pyle that the U.S. Army spied on U.S. citizens who attended anti-war protests.

Nor could Nixon turn to the CIA for overt leadership in his newly declared War on Drugs. In September 1971, Nixon's CIA-affiliated "White House Plumbers" had broken into Ellsberg's psychiatrist's office looking for information that could be used to discredit him. However, despite suspicions, no one could pin this break-in on the President. An even larger fiasco developed following the June 17, 1972, break-in at the Democratic Party headquarters in the Watergate complex by the White House Plumbers. A few days later, The Washington Post was already reporting the connections that former CIA Agent E. Howard Hunt and Nixon's Special Counsel Charles Colson had to the Watergate break-in.

CIA-employee. (1966). CIA-director en:Richard Helms. https://www.cia.gov/csi/studies/vol46no4/art6_1.jpg. https://commons.wikimedia.org/wiki/File:Richard_M_Helms.jpg.

CIA Director Helms took proactive steps behind the scenes to cover the CIA's tracks, leading to the illegal domestic operations code-named MH–CHAOS and MH–MERRIMAC. These were domestic spying operations of "counter-cultural" groups operating in the U.S., including black civil rights groups, women's liberation activists, and Vietnam War protesters. Teams of CIA provocateurs were strategically embedded within these groups. The mission was to push these groups to more violent and illegal activities so that they could be labeled as terrorist organizations and shut down.

By mid-1973, there was growing public and congressional unrest over the continuation of the U.S. war in Southeast Asia, even after the signing of the Paris Peace Accords. Public anger over the illegal covert actions by the Executive Branch resulted in the veto-proof passage of the Case-Church Amendment. This effectively defunded the war effort by prohibiting further military activity in Laos, Cambodia, and Vietnam that Congress had not approved in advance. The legislation passed with a greater-than-two-thirds supermajority in the Senate and the House of Representatives, despite Nixon's and Secretary of State Kissinger's repeated requests for more time to wind down military operations in Southeast Asia. Nixon had no choice but to sign the war-ending legislation into law on July 1, 1973.

The same day that Nixon was forced to endure the humiliation of ending the U.S. involvement in Vietnam, he issued an Executive Order that created the DEA without Congressional authorization. The timing of the Order was no coincidence. The signing of the legislation formally marked the end of Nixon's foreign and domestic anti-communist crusade spearheaded by the CIA and its auxiliary ex-Nazi (and pro-fascist) cadre of black ops teams. By signing "Reorganization Plan No. 2" on July 1, 1973, Nixon-with the stroke of a pen-created a brand-new law enforcement apparatus empowered by the executive branch to operate domestically and overseas without the legal restrictions associated with military action.

The DEA was a classic example of Nixonian overkill, but Congress and the public seemed to love his idea. "Right now," Nixon pointed out, "the federal government is fighting the war on drug abuse under a distinct handicap, for its efforts are those of a loosely confederated alliance facing a resourceful, elusive, worldwide enemy. Certainly, the cold-blooded underworld networks that funnel narcotics from suppliers worldwide are no respecters of the bureaucratic dividing lines that now complicate our anti-drug efforts."[28]

Following the formation of the new agency, some CIA and BNDD covert operations in Latin America were consolidated into what the DEA called the "Clandestine Operations Network." The network was known as "DEACON 1." Many expatriate Cubans who participated in the disastrous 1961 Bay of Pigs invasion were now recruited into these covert operations teams. They spent most of their time facilitating the CIA-sanctioned drug smuggling operations in Central and South America. Members of this motley crew of miscreants later went to work for Marine Lt. Col. Oliver North, a key National Security Council aide under President Ronald Reagan who had close connections with the the Iran-Contra drug and terror network. One of the DEACON 1 assets, Francisco Chanes, owned two seafood companies. They came to serve as fronts in Oliver North's Contra supply network, receiving and distributing tons of Contra cocaine.[29]

In the spring and summer of 1973, the U.S. House of Representatives and the U.S. Senate heard months of testimony on President Nixon's Reorganization Plan Number 2. It called for creating a single federal agency–the DEA–to consolidate and coordinate the government's drug control activities. At that time, the BNDD was responsible for enforcing the federal drug laws within the Department of Justice. However, the U.S. Customs Service and several other federal entities (ODALE and the Office of National Narcotics Intelligence) were also responsible for various aspects of federal drug law enforcement at the border and overseas. They had come under criticism for their lack of coordination and cooperation between the U.S. Customs Service and the BNDD. There were also public calls for better intelligence collection on drug trafficking organizations.

The final report from the Senate Committee on Government Operations, issued on October 16, 1973, gave full support to the creation of the DEA. The Committee felt that creating such a super-agency would end the interagency rivalries. The conflict had undermined federal drug law enforcement, especially the rivalry between the BNDD and the U.S. Customs Service.

By forming the DEA and essentially letting the CIA secretly pull the strings inside his new agency, Nixon kept the alliance between the CIA and the Unione Corse intact. His highly touted "War on Drugs" could focus on eliminating their enemies and competition.

However, in February 1974, the CIA's operational control of the DEA became a public scandal. It was discovered that the CIA had directed DEA agents in Mexico to "eliminate" Aviles Perez, a Mexican drug dealer competing with the Unione Corse.[30] An informant arranged for a DEA operative by the name of Chavez to pose as a drug buyer and meet with Perez. A deal was struck, but DEA Director John Bartels Jr. made the mistake of instructing the DEA's regional director in Mexico City to be briefed on the operation beforehand. At a meeting with the DEA regional director, the subject of "neutralizing" Perez came up, and a DEA analyst, Joan Bannister, took this to mean that the operational plan included the assassination of Perez. When Bannister reported her concerns to DEA headquarters, an anti–CIA faction within the DEA leaked her report to Washington Post columnist Jack Anderson. The Washington Post then printed a story by Anderson alleging that the DEA provided cover for a CIA assassination unit in Mexico.

Anderson's article also disclosed that a Senate Committee had investigated Conein for shopping around for assassination devices, like exploding ashtrays and telephones. It became known that Conein's longstanding CIA colleague, Mitchell WerBell, had arranged to sell several thousand silenced machine pistols to Robert Vesco.[31] WerBell lived in Costa Rica and worked with a "death squad" of drug trafficking Cuban exiles associated with the Tampa–based Trafficante organized crime syndicate.

At the time, Santos Trafficante Jr. was also living in Costa Rica as a "guest" of President Figueres, whose son had purchased weapons from WerBell and used them to arm a death squad.[32] Whenever things became too "hot" for Trafficante in the U.S., he retreated to his estate in Costa Rica. This is what he did in the early 1970s while a Congressional Committee was trying to serve him with a subpoena requiring him to testify. The investigation however, never seriously threatened the alliance between the CIA, DEA, and the Unione Corse. But it did scare those two federal agencies into scaling back on their assassination program. They now restricted their targets to "independent" (i.e., non–CIA-sanctioned) drug dealers in Latin America.

About a decade later, on December 20, 1985, the dirty little secret of linkage between the CIA and the DEA exploded into full public view. An Associated Press article was published detailing the results of an extensive investigation of the drug smuggling operations by the CIA and other federal agencies. The research concluded that the CIA and the DEA were assisting the Nicaraguan Contra rebels with their cocaine smuggling operations on the West Coast of the U.S.[33] As explained by David MacMichael, a former CIA contract employee, the CIA's involvement in the Contra drug smuggling operations was almost inevitable once the CIA decided to provide aircraft and other logistical support to the rebels in the Nicaraguan civil war.[34] "Once you set up a covert operation to supply arms and money, it's very difficult to separate it from the kind of people who are involved in other forms of trade, and especially drugs," MacMichael commented.[35] "There is a limited number of planes, pilots, and landing strips. By developing a system to supply the Contras, the U.S. built a pathway for drug supply into the U.S."[36]

Five American Contra supporters who worked with the rebels confirmed the charges, noting that "two Cuban–Americans used armed rebel troops to guard cocaine at clandestine airfields in northern Costa Rica."[37] They identified the Cuban–Americans as members of "Brigade 2506," an anti–Castro group that participated in Cuba's 1961 Bay of Pigs invasion.[38] Brigade 2506 was one of the Cuban exile groups that were wholly–owned front organizations financed by the CIA. An American involved in the Contra operation explained, "the cocaine is unloaded from planes at rebel airstrips and taken to an Atlantic coast port where it is concealed on shrimp boats that are later unloaded in the Miami area."[39]

Throughout the 1970s, the CIA and DEA were spending much of their resources financing anti–Castro and Nicaraguan Contra political and drug operations. At the same time, they were degrading the Mexican and "independent" Latin American cartels that were not CIA–sanctioned. This gave the Unione Corse a free hand to expand its lucrative heroin distribution network in North and South America. As the Unione Corse's fortunes rose in the Americas, so did those of Weiller and Richardson. By then, they firmly established themselves as the de facto leaders of the Unione Corse distribution networks in North and South America, as well as in the Caribbean.

Chapter 8:
Robert Vesco, Nixon, and The Unione Corse

In February 1973, U.S. financier Robert Vesco fled the country to avoid arrest on stock fraud charges. He was accused of looting hundreds of millions of dollars from Investors Overseas Service, Ltd. (IOS), a mutual fund investment company with holdings of $1.5 billion.[1] Among the accusations against Vesco was that he parked funds belonging to IOS investors in a series of dummy corporations, one of which was the Amsterdam address of Prince Bernhard of the Netherlands. He also allegedly broke into a Swiss bank vault to obtain shares. However, this allegation was never fully established after he fled the country. Vesco spent the next fifteen years on the run, moving from one Central American country to the next. The only criteria were that these countries lacked extradition treaties with the United States.

Shortly before he fled the country in 1973, Vesco made a series of substantial cash contributions to President Nixon through Nixon's nephew, Donald A. Nixon.[2] In Spring 1972, fearing an investigation, Vesco paid off John Kelly, Assistant Regional Director for the BNDD office in Los Angeles. In return, two DEA electronic surveillance agents swept his house for surveillance devices.[3] His goal was to get the Nixon administration to quash the S.E.C. investigation. Still, the sheer scope of his financial fraud at IOS made it politically impossible for the Nixon White House to now act overtly on Vesco's behalf. Instead, both Nixon and Vesco were soon facing an investigation of the secret $200,000 "contribution" that Vesco had made to Nixon's 1972 re–election campaign. New Jersey lawyer Harry L. Sears had delivered the contribution at Vesco's direction to Maurice Stans, finance chairman for the Committee to Re–elect the President (CREEP). When Vesco fled the country, Stans, Sears, and John Mitchell, Nixon's

Attorney General, were indicted for obstruction of justice. However, the charges against all three were later dismissed.⁴

Once the investigation was announced, Vesco's first move was to use IOC's corporate jet to flee to Costa Rica along with about $200 million worth of company assets. During his exile, Vesco attempted to buy a Caribbean Island from Antigua to create an independent country. Failing that, he persuaded Costa Rica (with plenty of strategically placed cash payments) to enact a national law called "the Vesco Law" that prohibited his extradition from the country.⁵ Among other payments, Vesco donated $2.1 million to Sociedad Agricola Industrial San Cristobal, S.A., a company linked to Costa Rican President José Figueres. Vesco also lived in Nicaragua while the Sandinista government was in power. His high-profile escapades running from the law eventually led to him being termed "the undisputed king of the fugitive financiers."⁶

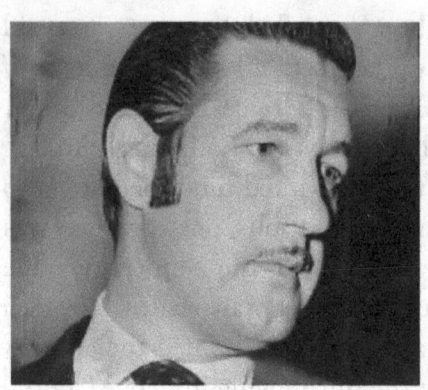

Robert Vesco in the 1970s. Courtesy of the Toronto Star.

While living on the island of Nassau during the 1970s, Vesco established close business ties with the two most powerful men in the Bahamas: Lynden Pindling and Carlos Lehder Rivas. Pindling, who was regarded as the "Father of the Nation" of the Bahamas, led it to majority rule on January 10, 1967, and independence on July 10, 1973. The first black premier of the Colony of the Bahama Islands (1967–1969), he served as Prime Minister of the Bahamas from 1969 to 1992.

Vesco's other principal associate in the Bahamas was Carlos Enrique Lehder Rivas, a German–Colombian former drug lord, neo–Nazi, and co–founder of the Medellín Cartel.⁷ Lehder eventually ran his cocaine transport empire from Norman's Cay, an island 210 miles off the Florida coast in the central Bahamas.⁸

Vesco's ties with Pindling and Lehder became the subject of an investigation by Bill Fairclough (a/k/a Edward Burlington). As an undercover C.I.A. agent, he was using his ostensible working relationship with the accounting firm of Coopers & Lybrand to investigate Vesco and his activities on the island. Vesco maintained a golden gated mansion protected by armed guards situated North East of Nassau, close to Paradise Island, where one of his yachts was moored. On Vesco's orders, Fairclough was drugged and kidnapped at The Pink Pussycat Club on Delancy Street in downtown Nassau. He awoke on Vesco's yacht but managed to force the ship back to shore and escaped after stealing a revolver from one of Vesco's guards.

Vesco and the Unione Corse Join Forces

Sometime in 1973, Patricia Richardson and Weiller met Vesco through an introduction by Lehder. They met on Lehder's private island and headquarters at Norman's Cay. At the time, the Medellin Cartel's cocaine distribution focused on the upscale market of wealthy business owners, young Wall Street investors, and the Hollywood crowd. The typical heroin junkie was the opposite end of the drug consumer market, primarily poor minorities in the inner cities on the East Coast. The cocaine and heroin markets were expanding exponentially, with no apparent end in sight. So, there was no reason why the Unione Corse and Medellín Cartel could not have a professional working relationship in the Caribbean islands. Both groups used Caribbean transit points for their product. In fact, Lehder offered to let Richardson and Weiller's organization use Norman Key as a transit point for some of their heroin shipments from Marseille. Of course, he wanted a small cut of the profits in return.

While the use of Norman Key in the Bahamas as a transport point was helpful to the Unione Corse, Weiller and Richardson decided that Vesco could also aid in their planned expansion of the heroin distribution network from Montreal to the East Coast of the United States. They put Vesco and his right-hand man, Norman LeBlanc, in touch with Conrad Bouchard and Giuseppe Cotroni. The men were two of the leading figures in Montreal organized crime and were of Corsican heritage and, of course, closely associated with the Unione Corse. In an affidavit by Leta Meyers, Patricia Richardson's landlady after she left Spector, Meyers stated that Richardson "made numerous trips to Montreal and referred to a man by the name of Bouchard who apparently was in Montreal."⁹ Weiller and Richardson authorized the Montreal organization to work with Vesco on a trial basis. They wanted to see if Vesco could back up his promises to provide a new source of financing for the heroin shipments that were moving from Montreal across the U.S.'s northern border.

To prove his "bona fides" as a financier for Unione Corse narcotics transactions, Vesco agreed to provide financing for 100 to 150 kilograms of heroin shipped into Montreal from Marseille. The Montreal organization paid $3,000 a kilogram to Weiller/Richardson and their Marseille associates. Once the heroin was moved south, the street sales value would be many multiples of the wholesale cost Vesco was financing.

One of the benefits of Vesco's affiliation with the Unione Corse was that he now had the political and diplomatic support of the C.I.A. and the DEA behind him. The Unione Corse's power over these agencies came in very handy for Vesco. In July of 1973, smuggler–turned–informant Frank Peroff recorded a phone conversation with a Canadian mobster. The mobster told Peroff that Vesco was the financial backer for a big heroin deal that Peroff was working on.

The Frank Peroff Affair

In early July 1973, Conrad Bouchard and Pepe Cotroni, influential members of the Montreal mob, explored the possibility of diversifying their means of transporting heroin southward. Bouchard had just been released on bail after a heroin smuggling charge in 1971 and looked to get back into the business. Richardson's strategy of using Spector's dealership's cars to move the heroin across the Canadian–U.S. border had worked brilliantly. But with Spector's Oldsmobile–Cadillac dealership out of business since 1971, new cross–border routes were constantly being developed. Even better than ground transport would be enterprising pilots who could move the product southward on private planes since they could efficiently carry much larger quantities of heroin.

In 1973, one such opportunity seemed to appear. Frank Peroff, a small air charter company pilot and the owner, had previously worked for Bouchard transporting Patricia Richardson and other heroin couriers back and forth between Montreal and the Syracuse or Watertown airports in Upstate New York.[10] Bouchard eventually hired him to fly a large sum of counterfeit U.S. cash from Canada into Europe. Unbeknownst to his employers in the French–Corsican–Montreal syndicate, Peroff got cold feet at the last minute. Instead of handing off his illicit cargo, Peroff had gone to the U.S. embassy in Rome. He confessed to U.S. agents his participation in the scheme and handed over the counterfeit cash. The U.S. agents suspected the money was for drugs. After speaking with their drug enforcement colleagues in Paris, they persuaded Peroff to continue the transaction to maintain his credibility with the mob members he was dealing with.[11] After that, Peroff became a highly valuable confidential informant for the Bureau of Customs Narcotics Intelligence Branch. His work with Customs on the counterfeit money case eventually led French police to arrest eight drug smugglers and seize 25 kilos of heroin.[12]

Peroff then was asked to help Customs agents penetrate the Bouchard operation. When he agreed, Peroff appeared in Montreal posing as a private Lear jet pilot who could quickly and covertly transport heroin. His family was relocated to Puerto Rico for their safety. By June, Bouchard had struck a deal with Peroff to pick up the needed bags of cash from Vesco in Costa Rica. However, on July 1, 1973, global drug enforcement came under Nixon's relatively new DEA. Peroff was turned over to a new DEA handler with this administrative change.

On July 3, 1973, Peroff recorded a phone call with Bouchard. Through his employee Norman LeBlanc, Bouchard specifically identified Vesco as the financial source for the heroin transaction they were planning.[13] Peroff dutifully turned over this tape recording to the U.S. agents. He then spoke by phone with DEA Group Supervisor John J. O'Neill. They discussed the plans of fugitive financier Vesco to front the $300,000 for just one narcotics transaction, with the implication that he had the financial capability to finance a string of similar transactions.

Peroff naively thought that the DEA, like his former contacts at Customs, were acting in good faith and would be interested in this information. The truth of the matter was that few in the Nixon White House, the Justice Department, or other federal agencies really wanted Robert Vesco back in U.S. custody. They feared what Vesco might disclose in return for immunity or a reduced sentence.

Later, on July 8, 1973, Bouchard directed Peroff to fly his Lear jet to Costa Rica and pick up the $300,000 cash from Vesco's associate, Norman LeBlanc. Peroff reported these calls to his DEA control agent, Richard Dos Santos. Then he flew with his family from San Juan to New York City, seeking better protection for them given the risky operation he was now embarked on.

However, when Peroff, Dos Santos, and Supervisor O'Neill spoke by phone the following day, O'Neill inexplicably directed Peroff to travel to Costa Rica by commercial airline. He was not to use the government Lear jet that Peroff supposedly owned. Peroff protested, telling them the only reason he was involved in the drug transaction was the belief by the traffickers that he had a jet. They thought he was ready, willing, and able to move the drugs and the money as required. Bouchard had told Peroff that Cotroni and LeBlanc were close friends and associates. They would immediately cease dealing with him–and probably kill him–if he showed up in Costa Rica on a commercial flight.

Now worried that his work was being sabotaged by the DEA, Peroff attempted to reach out to Watergate Special Prosecutor Archibald Cox on July 18. However, his call went unanswered.

On July 20, 1973, Peroff received his "final instructions" for the Costa Rica trip while staying at the Hilton Inn at Kennedy Airport in Queens, New York. Peroff reluctantly agreed to take a commercial flight to Costa Rica. However, he still told the DEA that by doing so, he would "spook" LeBlanc and Vesco, and the deal would probably be canceled. The plan called for Peroff to fly to San Jose, Costa Rica, pick up the money for the heroin deal, then fly to Europe to meet Bouchard, pick up the heroin, and fly back to North America.

In a sudden turn of events on July 22, Peroff was arrested just before leaving for Costa Rica on some old arrest warrants pending with the Orange County Sheriff's office in Orlando, Florida. New York police arrested Peroff at his room in the Hilton Inn and transported him to the Queens County House of Detention. Three days later, DEA agent Dos Santos arranged with the Queens County District Attorney's office to release Peroff, but not until after Peroff agreed, under duress, to "cooperate" with the agency and "do what he was told."

The DEA reversed its earlier decision to send Peroff to Costa Rica via a commercial flight. They sent him back to Canada to meet Bouchard and provided him with information about a Lear jet so that he could complete the smuggling deal. However, the DEA then inexplicably told Peroff to make changes to Bouchard's plan, hoping that this would scuttle the deal. When Bouchard agreed, the DEA directed Peroff to tell him that his jet was no longer available. The excuse was it had been repossessed by the leasing company. Peroff was picked up by the Royal Canadian Mounted Police (RCMP) and transported back to the U.S. In a recorded conversation, Bouchard told Peroff that the heroin deal was now off and if Peroff returned to Montreal, he would be killed.[14]

At the beginning of October 1973, Peroff contacted Senator Henry M. Jackson of Washington, a member of the Senate Committee on Government Operations and chair of the Permanent Subcommittee on Investigations. He relayed to the Senator the bizarre treatment he received from the DEA. Peroff sensed that Vesco's involvement and the potential fallout it might have for Nixon led to the DEA running their investigation aground. Concerned by Peroff's allegations, Senator Jackson arranged for a hearing to be held.

Later that October, agents of the RCMP asked Peroff to return to Canada to help them establish that Bouchard had possession of counterfeit Canadian $100 bills. After some understandable hesitancy, Peroff agreed on November 2, 1973, and flew back to Montreal so that he could introduce an undercover officer to the Bouchard group. Two days later, on November 4, Bouchard was arrested. However, in December 1973, an RCMP constable identified Peroff as a police informant in a subsequent court hearing. This effectively ended his career as an undercover operator and jeopardized his life. The DEA provided Peroff with protection until November 13, after which they offered him a mere $500 and told him to relocate his family if he was concerned about their safety.

At the Senate Permanent Committee on Investigation's hearing chaired by Senator Jackson, Peroff alleged that the DEA had mishandled him as an undercover operative. Peroff testified that the DEA dropped him as an asset after he informed them of Vesco's involvement in the drug transaction under investigation. The DEA did not deny having dropped Peroff like a hot potato. However, they tried to justify it by assuming that they "could not be expected to guard a man who had made charges against us to the Senate subcommittee."[15]

Senator Henry Martin "Scoop" Jackson. Courtesy of the US Senate Historical Office.

As discussed in more detail in the next chapter, the Jackson Committee report on the Peroff Affair was highly critical of the unprofessional way that the DEA handled Peroff's information. The report specifically mentioned the DEA's failure to adequately protect Peroff and his family after the Montreal mob began to suspect that he was an informant. Even worse, the Committee found that the DEA's deliberate refusal to put Vesco's name in any written record of the investigation was unforgivable, since he had been implicated directly by suspects. Peroff's reward for connecting Vesco (and Nixon) with the financing of one of the biggest drug conspiracies in history was to be frozen out of the DEA investigation. He was also detained on stale arrest warrants and then hung out to dry.

Although his allegations against Vesco were nipped in the bud by the DEA, Peroff provided valuable information to Senator Jackson and his Permanent Committee. This information led to the resignation of the first DEA Director, John R. Bartels Jr. In addition to the information provided by Peroff, DEA agents reporting to the CIA raised questions as to Bartels' conduct. It was decided that Bartels "had to go" since he was not acting like a "team player" with the CIA. It was feared that he might refuse to respect the U.S. government's tacit agreement with the Unione Corse that their "CIA–approved" drug operations could not be investigated.[16]

Primarily based on the CIA's obstruction of the various investigations of Vesco, including those related to his financing of drug transactions involving the Unione Corse, Vesco was never extradited or prosecuted in a U.S. court. He never felt sufficent pressure to enter into a cooperation agreement with the U.S. Justice Department that would require him to surrender himself to U.S. authorities. He must have also known that if he entered the U.S. prison system for even a short period, it would probably be a "death sentence" for him. He knew that he would be murdered on orders from the Unione Corse or another organized crime group. They feared he would provide incriminating evidence about them to government prosecutors.

Vesco and Donald Nixon in Cuba

After years of gallivanting around the Caribbean, Vesco moved to Cuba in 1982 to obtain medical treatment for his painful urinary tract infections. The Cuban authorities agreed not to extradite him. In return, he agreed to steer clear of any financial dealings there and avoid any drug smuggling involvement. He married Lidia Alfonso Llauger and appeared to be settling into quiet retirement.[17] This did not last long.

Donald "Don–Don" Nixon, nephew of the President. Hutchison, Robert A. 1974. Vesco. Praeger Publishers.

Chaos and controversy had followed him his entire life, and his period of exile in Cuba proved to be no exception.

Vesco induced his former employee Donald A. "Don–Don" Nixon, son of the President's brother, Donald, to visit him in Cuba. The two of them cooked up an ingenious "immunotherapy cure" scheme that they peddled to unwary investors.

Vesco and Nixon persuaded the Cuban government to back the "research" they supposedly conducted in Cuba involving clinical trials on a substance called trixolan, or TX, which supposedly boosted the immune system. Vesco went so far as to introduce Donald Nixon to Fidel and Raúl Castro. The Cuban government agreed to provide laboratory facilities and doctors to conduct the clinical trials. Inevitably, Vesco claimed that the results from the studies were positive. When it became clear Vesco had falsified the test results, the Cuban authorities arrested Vesco, his wife, and one of their associates, rogue CIA agent Frank Terpil.[18]

At Vesco's arrest, the Cuban Foreign Ministry said he had been taken into custody "under suspicion of being a provocateur and an agent of foreign special services." This was an oblique reference to Vesco's CIA connections. However, he was formally charged with "fraud and illicit economic activity" and "acts prejudicial to the economic plans and contracts of the state."[19] The Cuban government sentenced Vesco to 13 years in prison on charges resulting from the scandal, but he only served a relatively short part of his sentence. He persuaded the Cuban authorities that he had turned over a new leaf and promised to live quietly in Cuba without causing any further scandals.[20]

The "immunotherapy cure" for cancer that Vesco and Donald A. Nixon were peddling to investors was a disaster for Vesco. In 1995,

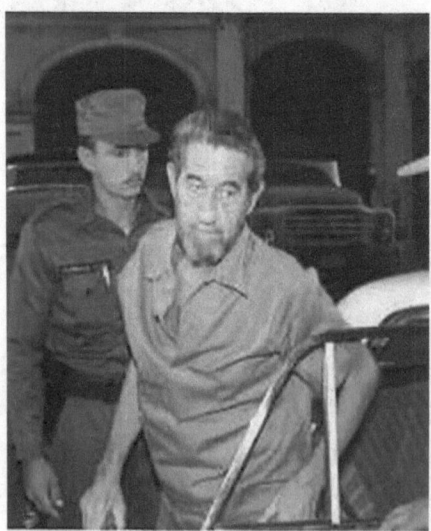

Financier Robert Vesco died in november, document says | the spokesman-review. (1996, August 2). The Spokesman-Review.

Donald A. Nixon barely avoided having criminal charges brought against him by the Cuban government for his participation in Vesco's fraud scheme involving a "miracle cure" for cancer. He wisely broke off his relationship with Vesco, thus avoiding any fall-out from Vesco's desperate attempt to recoup his losses via a few narcotics transactions and stock scams.

***

"Donald" was something of a cursed name in the Nixon family. Even before Donald A. Nixon's debacle with Vesco, his father, Donald Nixon, was a constant source of embarrassment and a thorn in Richard Nixon's side. In January 1957, Howard Hughes lent Donald Nixon $205,000 to bail him out of his "Nixon's drive-in restaurant" venture in Whittier, California.[21] The restaurant went bankrupt less than a year later. Questions as to whether Hughes had lent Donald the money as a political favor to his brother dogged Nixon's unsuccessful presidential bid in 1960 and his failed campaign for the governorship of California in 1962.[22]

Hughes had his fingers in numerous industries—from film to aerospace defense—and was known for his extremely secretive and eccentric lifestyle. He had undiagnosed O.C.D. and, after years of personally testing his new aircraft, suffered from severe brain injuries from multiple plane crashes. His personal behavior made him a constant feature in tabloids, while his aerospace engineering and defense work made him a powerful man in Washington.

Hughes and Donald Nixon's relationship also played a vital role in the events that culminated in the disastrous 1972 Watergate burglary. One of President Nixon's motivations for ordering the break-in to the Democratic national headquarters at the Watergate complex was his obsession with the idea that then-Democratic National Committee chairman Larry O'Brien was secretly working for Howard Hughes. Nixon desperately wanted to obtain a "smoking gun" document establishing the connection between O'Brien and Hughes to help neutralize the negative political fall-out over Donald Nixon having taken money from Hughes.[23] Rumors circulated that Nixon's buddy, Bebe Rebozo, had diverted some of the Nixon campaign funds to two of his brothers,

Donald and Edward. Hence, President Nixon was desperate to create a diversion that would throw the press off his tracks by making a counter-scandal for the Democrats.[24]

The Democrats had done an excellent job of exploiting President Nixon's paranoia about the connections between his brothers and Hughes. In collaboration with former vice president Hubert Humphrey, John H. Meier, one of Hughes' former business advisors, used Donald Nixon to feed misinformation to his brother, the President. Meier told Donald that he was "sure" the Democrats would win the election. He said that Larry O'Brien had information on Richard Nixon's illicit dealings with Howard Hughes which had never been released.[25] Once President Nixon heard this, he felt he had to take whatever necessary steps—no matter the risk—to get hold of the information. When Nixon gave his "plumbers" the go-ahead to break into and search the D.N.C. headquarters at the Watergate, his paranoia set in motion a series of events that culminated in his resignation and departure on the Marine 1 helicopter from the White House lawn.

Interestingly, while O'Brien appears to have been bluffing, Hughes had really been attempting to bribe more than just Nixon. During the 1960s, Hughes became concerned about the underground nuclear testing conducted in the desert not far from where he was holed up in Las Vegas. Hughes, a known germophobe, constantly concerned with his health, was worried that radioactive fallout from the testing could leach into the Las Vegas area. In the late 60s, Hughes offered both Nixon and Lyndon B. Johnson multimillion-dollar bribes through his #2 bagman, former C.I.A. agent Robert Maheu, if they could stop the tests from being carried out.[26]

Vesco's Twilight Years

Although Vesco kept his deal with the Cuban authorities for a time, he soon reverted back to his old ways. These activities inevitably involved financial fraud schemes and drug smuggling. Vesco was charged by Cuban authorities with drug smuggling in 1989. It was discovered that he had started his own freelance distribution network for heroin without clearing it with the Unione Corse. Since Weiller and Richardson had a good working relationship with the Castro government in Cuba, it only took one phone call to get the Cuban authorities to shut down Vesco's operations there and bring criminal charges against him.

Having learned his lesson, Vesco reached an agreement with the Unione Corse whereby Vesco could keep 50% of the profits of the narcotics transactions he financed. The other 50% would "disappear" into the labyrinth of offshore bank accounts that the Unione Corse maintained in the Caribbean, Panama, and other locales worldwide.

Since Vesco had generally kept his end of the bargain with the Unione Corse over the course of many years, Weiller and Richardson felt that they owed him some assistance when he fell ill in Cuba. Perhaps there truly is a sense of honor amongst thieves, at least where the Unione Corse was concerned. Vesco was living under house arrest by Cuban authorities as punishment for several fraudulent schemes. This is a prime example of the truth of the adage that you can't teach an old dog new tricks.

To throw the U.S. and Cuban authorities off track, information was "leaked" by the Unione Corse to The New York Times in November 2007. The Times erroneously reported that Vesco had died five months earlier of lung cancer in a hospital in Havana, Cuba.[27] However, reports of his death were greatly exaggerated since it had been faked. The Unione Corse paid off the right people in Cuba and obtained the

Hutchinson, Robert. n.d. Vesco. Praeger Publisher, Inc.

necessary documentation from the authorities that permitted Vesco to escape from the island in a private jet in early 2007. Vesco's associate, Frank Terpil, also living discretely in Cuba, later disclosed that Vesco had fled to Sierra Leone.[28] With no death certificate forthcoming from Cuban authorities, Vesco successfully escaped the long arm of U.S. law enforcement and cheated death, at least for the time being.

Chapter 9:
The Watergate Special Prosecutor, Spector and the Saturday Night Massacre

On Saturday, October 20, 1973, President Richard Nixon ordered U.S. Attorney General Elliot Richardson to fire Special Prosecutor Archibald Cox. The Watergate scandal had cast a pall over the nation since June. Nixon rightly feared that Cox was closing in on the Oval Office tapes that would prove him complicit with the Democratic National Convention Headquarters break-in. Upon receiving Nixon's order, Attorney General Richardson refused to fire Cox and resigned immediately. Nixon then ordered Deputy Attorney General William Ruckelshaus to fire Cox. Ruckelshaus too refused, then resigned. Nixon then ordered the third-most-senior official at the Justice Department, Solicitor General Robert Bork, to fire Cox. Bork carried out the dismissal as Nixon had directed.

As it became known, the Saturday Night Massacre triggered a firestorm of protest across the country. What happened next is well known. The impeachment process against Nixon began ten

Leffler, W. K. (1973). [Watergate special prosecutor Archibald Cox, half-length portrait, standing, facing left, at a press conference at the Justice Department on June 4, 1973] [Still image]. Courtesy of the Library of Congress.

days later, on October 30, 1973. Leon Jaworski was appointed as the new special prosecutor on November 1, 1973. On November 14, United States District Judge Gerhard Gesell ruled that the dismissal had been illegal. This marked the turning point for public opinion as to the Watergate scandal. While the true extent of Nixon's knowledge and approval of the break-in at the Democratic National Committee's headquarters was still unknown, there was a near-universal outcry from the public and the press. Nixon's heavy-handed attempt to end the Watergate probe outraged even Republicans. Congress took the opportunity to initiate impeachment proceedings against Nixon, ending with Nixon's resignation.

***

How did William Spector factor into the Watergate investigation? We have seen how Nixon was affiliated with the Unione Corse. Still, they were not clearly involved in the Watergate break-in. We must go back to 1971—just after Patricia Richardson left Spector—to get to the root of this connection.

After Richardson abandoned Spector, she left a set of "diaries" behind in their Ogdensburg home. These notebooks were replete with names—including Yusef Beidas, Paul-Louis Weiller, Marcel Boucan, Auguste Ricord, and more—that Spector would soon connect with smuggling activities. In October 1971, Spector traveled to St. Martin to seek evidence for his divorce from Patricia. Several locals there confirmed that she was involved in smuggling operations, while living a double life as a model.

When Spector returned to New York, he immediately contacted local Customs officers and the New York State Police Bureau of Criminal Investigation. He tipped them off about his wife's suspected smuggling activities and an investigator with State Police named Larry Manor was assigned to the case. Manor was skeptical from the outset, given Spector's tempestuous marital and financial issues. Rather than adequately investigating his claims, he wrote Spector off as a jilted lover in dire financial straits who was seeking public attention. Manor met with and interviewed Patricia Richardson but soon concluded that she was nothing more than a destitute divorcee running from an unhappy marriage. Never mind that Richardson's landlady simultaneously reported she had a "fantastic wardrobe," and went on spending sprees at numerous department stores. The case stalled under Manor's direction for a year since he failed to perform even the most rudimentary investigation.

Frustrated by this experience, Spector turned next to the Syracuse Police Department, which assigned Inspector Andrew Peltz to the case. At first, Peltz was eager to help Spector and reported on the allegations up the chain of command. In December 1972, a new police officer, Sgt. David Jewell, was brought in to investigate the case since Spector was losing faith in the willingness of Larry Manor and the State Police to investigate. Inspector Peltz even went so far as to bring the BNDD into the investigation. A BNDD agent named Stephen McClintic, who was both a former Foreign Service and CIA officer with experience in Francophone countries, began to work the case. McClintic was now working as a BNDD liaison at the White House and requested that Spector come to Washington with his files so that they could thoroughly discuss his case.

Spector was in near–daily conversations with McClintic and Peltz throughout 1972, although he pursued his own parallel investigation. In November 1972, he met with Mary Jo Ottman, who provided Spector with a bundle of Patricia Richardson's letters. These letters helped him connect the dots to the smuggling routes the Unione Corse used from Marseille, through St. Martin, and then into the U.S. Spector also met with Richardson's former building manager, Leta Meyer, who told him how Richardson bragged of seeing Weiller make an illegal campaign contribution to Nixon in 1968. From his own investigation, Spector was able to provide Peltz and McClintic with flight numbers for planes that would be trafficking drugs into New York.

When Spector's case began solidifying, Peltz and McClintic inexplicity stalled the investigation, refusing to follow up on Spector's leads any further. In all likelihood, they had been given orders from their superiors to back off so as to protect the alliance of the Unione Corse and CIA to traffic heroin without having BNDD agents sticking their noses in it. By the end of 1972, Spector was again left out in the cold by the very officials supposedly dedicated to investigating drug trafficking.

Although Spector was largely written off by other authorities at this time, he did manage to testify to the Senate Government Operations Permanent Investigations Subcommittee about the possible involvement that Patricia Richardson and Paul-Louis Weiller had with Robert Vesco. In addition, Syracuse Police Sgt. Jewell apparently did not get the memo directing law enforcement officers to steer clear of Spector. Jewell felt that the substance of Spector's case had been improperly ignored, so he continued to pursue it.

Since Richardson, Weiller, and Vesco had all been suspected of offering bribes to Richard Nixon, Jewell began meeting up with Spector again. However, he soon realized that his meetings with Spector were being surveilled by other law enforcement officers.[1] Feeling the need for additional support, Jewell and Spector got back in touch with McClintic, asking him to find someone at the DEA who would reopen the investigation into Patricia Richardson.

At this point, McClintic—in an uncharacteristic moment of candor—revealed to Jewell and Spector that the DEA was not just a "mess," but was also corrupt. He pointedly asked Spector, "Did you ever stop to think that maybe the names were too big—what did you expect when [the names of] Nixon, Weiller, and Vesco surfaced."[2] He finished by telling Jewell and Spector that "if the names of Nixon, Vesco or Weiller surfaced in any investigation… DEA would have nothing to do with the case." McClintic then advised Spector there was only one way to bypass the DEA's jurisdiction over drug cases: to go directly to the Watergate Special Prosecutor, who could investigate Nixon's connections with the Unione Corse.

* * *

This was how William Spector became caught up in the Watergate whirlwind leading to the Saturday Night Massacre. After McClintic made the necessary calls, Spector provided the Special Prosecutor's Office with information about Nixon's associations with Unione Corse and Nixon's cash contributions from international organized crime. When Spector found a receptive audience, his meetings with the

Special Prosecutor's Office staff were abruptly canceled since the future of the office, and the entire Watergate investigation, became engulfed in uncertainty.

The morning after the Saturday Night Massacre, Spector called Henry Ruth, Archibald Cox's chief assistant, and was told by Ruth: "We are locked out of our offices, and we can't get in." Ruth advised Spector to call Carl Feldbaum, another lawyer working with the Special Prosecutor's Office, and to follow his instructions. Ruth assured Spector that they "wanted to work with him" and investigate his allegations. Still, they did not know what would happen with the Watergate investigation.

When Spector called Feldbaum, he was told that the Nixon White House was trying to cover up or destroy any documentary evidence that could incriminate President Nixon. This included Spector's information on the cash payoffs made to the 1968 and 1972 presidential campaigns and the links that Nixon and Rebozo had to organized crime and ex–Nazis. Feldman strongly suggested that Spector "lie low" for the time being and, if possible, leave the country until things "sorted themselves out in Washington."

Spector had associates in Venezuela whom he had not seen for quite some time, so he bought a ticket to Caracas, paying in cash to hopefully avoid detection. At that time, a U.S. citizen did not need a passport to travel to Venezuela. All that was required was a 30–day tourist visa. During this era, he flew on VIASA airline, Venezuela's flag carrier.

Spector did not realize at the time that the NCIS computer interlocks monitored all reservations made through U.S.–based airlines. As soon as he had made his reservation, it was immediately relayed by computer to the F.B.I., the Washington D.C. police, and other law enforcement agencies.

Spector checked into the Abiela Hotel upon his arrival in Caracas, which had an old Spanish elegance. This was the hotel where the Venezuelan authorities preferred that foreign government officials and businesspeople stay so they could be more easily watched. The other hotels in Caracas, such as the Sheraton and the Hilton, were considered strictly for the tourist trade.

After checking into the hotel, Spector proceeded to the offices of the Creole Petroleum Company to meet his good friend, Dr. Carlos Lander. Dr. Lander was the chief of the Venezuelan Economic Commission and the Venezuelan delegate to the South American Economic Development Commission. Dr. Lander exercised considerable influence in Venezuela and was rumored to have turned down the country's presidency at one point, preferring to wield power from behind the scenes.

As Dr. Lander was shaking Spector's hand in greetings, he warned him: "Bill, Washington knows why you are here, so please do not ask me any questions. The walls have ears." They went to the outside patio of Dr. Lander's office, where they felt their conversation would not be overheard. Spector brought Lander up to speed on his tumultuous marriage to Patricia Richardson and the results of his investigation into her ties to the French–Corsican organized crime group dominating the world heroin trade. They also reminisced about Spector's last visit to Caracas, where he had been at Lander's office on November 22, 1963, the fateful day when President John Kennedy had been killed in Dallas, Texas.

After spending several hours with Dr. Lander, Spector returned to his hotel, where he found an "urgent" telephone message from the U.S. embassy in Caracas. When Spector called the embassy, he was told that he should return to the U.S. as soon as possible. The request came from Senator Henry Jackson, the Senate Governmental Operations Committee chairman. Senator Jackson wanted him to testify about the Frank Peroff affair. Specifically, the Committee wanted Spector to testify about the identity of the person who had hired Peroff as a DEA informant and undercover operative.

This urgent request for Spector to return to Washington came the day before Christmas of 1973. Spector dutifully flew back to the U.S. on Christmas so that he could be in Washington on the following day. After checking in at the Quality Motor Inn close to Capitol Hill, Spector called the Senate Governmental Operations Committee offices to notify them of his arrival and confirm the time for a meeting there at 10 a.m. the following day.

Spector met with investigators William Gallinaro and Bill Manuel of Senator Jackson's Committee staff the next morning. Gallinaro was a short, stocky bulldog of a man, while Manuel was his exact opposite: thin, more reserved, and thoughtful. Spector immediately asked them if they had gotten the Weiller file from the DEA. When they said "No," Spector expressed his frustration. He was convinced the BNDD/DEA files would corroborate much of the information he had been providing to them about his ex-wife and her colleagues in the Unione Corse.

Spector also believed that the Watergate Special Prosecutor's Office was back on track since, by late 1973, Leon Jaworski had been appointed as Special Prosecutor to replace Archibald Cox. Jaworski was already making optimistic public statements that the Special Prosecutor's Watergate investigation was moving "full speed ahead."

Gallinaro and Manuel then dropped a bombshell on Spector. When they called the White House to ask for Steve McClintic, they were told they had no record of him being on the White House staff. Spector had previously told the Committee staff that he had been extensively debriefed by McClintic when Spector had been meeting with him in Washington. McClintic assured Spector that he worked out of the White House and was the liaison between President Nixon's administration and the DEA. In fact, Spector had told Gallinaro and Manuel in detail that McClintic expressed enthusiasm about the urgency of investigating Spector's allegations. In Spector's presence, McClintic had even called Kevin Gallagher, the BNDD lead agent in Montreal, ordering him to take charge of the investigation of the information that Spector had provided.

Somewhat disheartened and disoriented by their inability to confirm McClintic's pivotal role in the Nixon administration, Spector cut the meeting short, saying: "Gentlemen, it's been a long trip. I think I need to break it off." Returning to the Quality Motor Inn, Spector called his friend and reporter, Everett Clark, who had written the blockbuster Newsweek article suggesting that Nixon had ties with organized crime. Spector told Clark that Senator Jackson's Committee was investigating the matter and asked Clark to join him for his next session the following morning at the Senate Office Building. Clark agreed and met Spector downstairs at 9:30 a.m., so they could go to the Senate office meeting together. When they arrived, however, Manuel and Gallinaro "threw a fit," according to Spector, objecting to the presence of any reporter while they were questioning him.

Spector countered that he wanted a witness to be present. Clark was agreeable to the ground rule that everything they discussed would be "off the record." Spector also raised the issue of expenses, saying that he had incurred considerable expense to come rushing back to Washington to meet with them and that he wanted to be reimbursed. However, when Manuel and Gallinaro balked at making any firm promise of reimbursement, Spector, now incensed, told them to "Go F**k yourselves," storming out of the office with Clark in tow.

When Spector walked into his hotel room, the phone was ringing. It was Gallinaro, trying to smooth things over. He assured Spector that they wanted to work with him and were serious about investigating the leads he had provided. He then asked Spector where he was storing the originals of his files, to which Spector vaguely replied that they were in "a secure place" in Florida. Gallinaro asked to go down there to see them with Spector but was still equivocal about whether the government would reimburse Spector for his expenses. Spector abruptly hung up on him after shouting a couple of choice expletives. Everett Clark, who was with Spector, said that he couldn't believe it since it was an open secret at that point that Senator Jackson wanted to be President. This investigation could well have launched his campaign.

Bartels, jr., J. R. (n.d.). John R. Bartels, jr., Of counsel. Bartels & Feureisen LLP. Courtesy of Bartels & Feureisen LLP.

* * *

Despite Gallinaro and Manuel's dismissive behavior towards Spector, the Jackson Committee did come to important conclusions about the ineffectiveness—or unwillingness—of the DEA to investigate Vesco's connections to drug trafficking. The hearings showed that the DEA inexplicably failed to put Peroff's or Bouchard's tips about Vesco into writing and then offered conflicting testimony to the senatorial investigation. The report characterized the DEA's handling of the Vesco connection as contributing "significantly to the failure" of their investigation into heroin trafficking, declaring that "DEA officials have shown themselves deserving of responsible criticism."[3] Specifically, the Jackson Committee's report concluded that an internal DEA report into the Peroff affair omitted critical facts regarding the dispute between Peroff and DEA supervisor O'Neill. Facts omitted concerned private or commercial air travel to Costa Rica to pick up cash for a heroin deal.[4]

John Bartels Jr., the DEA administrator, replied to the Jackson Committee with a categorical denial, stating that "there never was a big heroin conspiracy."[5]

The Jackson Committee's final memorandum on the Peroff affair completely rejected the DEA's denials, concluding that "the DEA was responsible for the failure of the Bouchard heroin inquiry. It also concluded that it was DEA personnel who ... precluded the professionally sound resolution of the Vesco–LeBlanc undeveloped lead."[6]

***

After returning home to Ogdensburg from his less than satisfying dealings with the Jackson Committee staff, Spector called Carl Feldbaum of the Special Prosecutor's office. Feldbaum told Spector to be "patient" and wait until they could move their investigation ahead another few steps. Shortly thereafter, on March 23, 1974, Feldbaum called Spector, telling him the Special Prosecutor's office was "bogged down in the Supreme Court thing." He was referring to the legal battle over the disclosure of the Watergate tapes that the Nixon White House was refusing to turn over. Feldbaum told Spector that the U.S. Attorney's Office for the Southern District of New York was taking over part of the responsibility to investigate Spector's allegations. He gave Spector the contact information for the U.S. Attorney's Office.

Spector went to Manhattan the following week to meet with Assistant U.S. Attorney John "Rusty" Wing, lead attorney on the Mitchell, Stans, and Vesco case. Wing told Spector they would need to take his testimony before the grand jury investigating the matter and that

Spector needed to be prepared for his grand jury appearance. The U.S. Attorney's Office gave him a receipt for some of his most important and sensitive documents, and served him with a grand jury subpoena for them. The understanding was that they were still Spector's documents and that he could get them whenever he wished. These included some critical tape recordings with McClintic and others. Spector also presented them with a world map where he had pinpointed and identified every bank and flight route used by the Unione Corse.

At about the same time, Spector got a call from Frank Peroff, who confirmed to Spector that Weiller had flown by plane to the Grand Cayman Islands to meet with Nixon and Vesco. When Spector asked him, "Who hired you," Peroff responded by giving Spector the whole story about how he had gone to Rome with counterfeit currency, and that when he realized this was not something he wanted to get into, he went to the U.S. Embassy in Rome. Peroff further told Spector that he was eventually recruited to work as an undercover informant on both the counterfeit currency and narcotics cases. However, Peroff confirmed to Spector that, when Peroff was told by the Montreal mob about the involvement of Robert Vesco, the newly established DEA immediately cooled off on the case. Thereafter, the DEA agents also made it difficult–if not impossible–for Peroff to maintain his credibility by not supplying him with a jet to facilitate the drug transaction as promised.

On Memorial Day 1974, Spector decided to track down Steve McClintic to find out what, if anything, the DEA and Watergate Special Prosecutors were doing with the information he had provided. Spector called DEA headquarters and discovered that McClintic had retired several months earlier. But Spector still had a phone number for a summer home that McClintic had on Nantucket Island, off the coast of Massachusetts. Spector reached him at his Nantucket phone number and, after some small talk, McClintic agreed to meet with him.

Spector drove from his home in upstate New York to Hyannis, Cape Cod, and then, the following morning, took a ferry to Nantucket. McClintic was waiting for him. Over lunch at the Oyster Bar close to the harbor, McClintic recounted that John Bartels Jr., the DEA Administrator, asked him to write an answer to Archibald Cox's letter requesting Spector's DEA files. But after he had drafted it and circulated it for approval, it was never sent to the Special Prosecutor's Office. McClintic said that, as far as he knew, the DEA file on Spector's allegations had never been turned over to the Watergate Special Prosecutor. In fact, McClintic told Spector that the DEA file relating to Spector could not be turned over because it had been "lost, misplaced, or destroyed." In any event, it was "no longer available."

McClintic also recalled that he had drafted portions of Nixon's speeches at various narcotics conferences, taking a tough stance on the "War on Drugs." However, McClintic admitted to Spector that the BNDD and the DEA considered any investigation involving the French–Corsican syndicate a "very low priority" since they got little or no cooperation from the French authorities. The CIA also had let it be known to the DEA that the Unione Corse drug operations were "off–limits for national security reasons."

At this point, shocked by his apathetic responses, Spector asked McClintic point blank whether he was working for the CIA. McClintic admitted that when he was supposedly working for the U.S. State Department, his position as a consular officer was really just a "cover." His actual employer was the CIA. This made sense to Spector since he already knew that McClintic had worked closely with James Angleton and Frank Carlucci, both known CIA agents.[7]

Once McClintic informed Spector that the DEA files on the supposed investigation into Spector's allegations had "gone missing," he became increasingly uncomfortable with McClintic's repeated questioning about the location of Spector's original documents. He kept asking, "Where are the rest of your files?" McClintic told Spector that he needed to ensure that Spector's files were "secure." His allegations, according to McClintic, had "triggered national security buttons all the way up to the White House." Was McClintic on Spector's side or attempting to destroy his evidence? Spector couldn't be sure.

Spector also found it odd that McClintic became alarmed when Spector informed him that he and his records had been subpoenaed by the U.S. Attorney's Office. McClintic told him he "had to be very careful" in dealing with the U.S. Attorney's Office in Manhattan but did not explain the reasons behind this warning.

Spector returned to Ogdensburg, rather deflated and depressed by what McClintic had told him. The supposed "investigations" of his allegations by the DEA, the Special Prosecutor's Office, and the various Congressional committees were going nowhere. Spector needed someone in a powerful position who would vigorously champion his cause. He needed someone who didn't care how high up the food chain the investigation reached, no matter how many egos and reputations were bruised. The information Spector had collected appeared evident and compelling. He had still not given up hope that there must be someone in Washington who would follow the evidence, wherever it led. He was firmly convinced that, in the end, "the truth will out."

Chapter 10:
The Big Evidence Hunt

In search of retribution, William Spector had doggedly gone from one law enforcement agency to another since 1971. At each agency, he told anyone who would listen about his beautiful yet diabolical ex-wife, who had cast a powerful spell over him and then used his Cadillac dealerships to move large quantities of heroin across the border from Canada. Over several months, Spector had filed complaints with the police departments of New York City, Syracuse, Ogdensburg, New York, and the New York State Police. He also met with agents and prosecutors of the U.S. Attorney's Office for the Southern District of New York, and had testified before a federal grand jury in Manhattan.

In a June 1975 article entitled, *The Model, the Drug Ring And the Big Evidence Hunt*, the New York Times reported that "a swarm of local, state, federal and international police agencies, along with a United States Senator and an Albany committee, have been racing each other for more than two months in pursuit of a spurned husband's bizarre tale of an international drug ring."[1] The Times article elaborated: "Spurred by post-Watergate fears of a cover-up and tantalized by an unlikely cast of characters that includes European millionaires, Caribbean jet-setters, the Nixon White House and a gorgeous model, the investigators are about to hold unusual public hearings into the affair...."

The public hearings being referred to were conducted by the New York State Senate Select Committee on Crime, spurred by Senator James Buckley of New York. Buckley and his staff became fascinated by Spector's tale of international intrigue and corruption reaching the highest levels of the U.S. and French governments.

The Senator's interest in Spector's claims was not entirely without self-interest. Senator Buckley and his chief of staff, Leonard Saffir, saw the investigation of Spector's spectacular allegations as a platform for Buckley to gain national attention. It might even serve as a possible springboard to a presidential run. They calculated that the investigation would change the prevailing public view of Buckley as an accidental Senator. Buckley's election was something of a fluke, since he had won in a three-way race as a Conservative Party candidate with far less than 50% of the votes. Buckley then proceeded to alienate many conservative allies in the Republican Party by becoming the first significant conservative in the country to call on Richard Nixon to resign following the Watergate Scandal in 1974.

Despite his political isolation, Senator Buckley seized on Spector's allegations as an opportunity to redeem his political credibility and even possibly grasp the biggest political brass ring of all—the U.S. Presidency. All he had to do was to uncover evidence proving that President Nixon was even more corrupt than previously known, and had financed his election campaign with bags of dirty money from drug dealers. If he could do this, then he would even be able to vindicate himself with conservative Republicans, who were already starting to have second thoughts about their support for Nixon.

***

U. S. Senate: James buckley(C-ny). (n.d.). U.S. Senate Historical Office. Courtesy of U. S Congress.

James Buckley spent much of his life in the shadow of his older brother, William F. "Bill" Buckley, Jr. Bill was the most influential conservative thinker, author, commentator, and personality of the post–war era. Both brothers received their undergraduate degrees from Yale, and both served in the armed services during World War II. James enlisted in the U.S. Navy in 1942 and was discharged with the rank of lieutenant. Bill served as an officer in the U.S. Army, and after the war, he worked as a CIA agent in Mexico City. The infamous E. Howard Hunt, later of

Watergate fame, had been his immediate superior. After leaving the CIA, Bill Buckley founded the *National Review*, the magazine that energized American conservativism in the late 20th century. He was also the host of *Firing Line*, a public affairs television show from 1966 to 1999, the longest-running public affairs show in American television history with a single host.

In 1968, James Buckley stepped into the limelight by running on the Conservative Party line against the incumbent liberal Republican U.S. Senator Jacob K. Javits of New York. Javits easily won, but Buckley made a respectable enough showing among disaffected conservative Republicans to keep the possibility alive of another run for that office. In 1970, Buckley ran for the U.S. Senate on the Conservative Party line. This time he faced Republican incumbent Charles Goodell and Democratic candidate Richard Ottinger. Goodell had been appointed to the Senate seat by Governor Nelson Rockefeller following the assassination of Senator Robert F. Kennedy of New York.

After coming out in opposition to the Vietnam War, Goodell was considered politically vulnerable. With Goodell and Ottinger splitting the liberal vote, Buckley received 39% of the vote, enough to win the election. James Buckley was sworn in as a U.S. Senator in January 1971, but only served a six-year term. He was displaced by the Democratic candidate in the 1976 election: U.S. Ambassador to the U.N. Daniel Patrick Moynihan.

In the spring of 1974, Buckley had surprised many of his Republican allies in Congress when he called upon the embattled Richard M. Nixon to voluntarily resign the presidency.[2] At the same time, Buckley denounced those "in and out of the media who have been exploiting the Watergate affair so recklessly." He accused the media of trying "to subvert the decisive mandate of the 1972 election."[3] Buckley warned that the Watergate scandal and the resulting impeachment process would tear the country apart, declaring: "There is one way and one way only by which the crisis can be resolved, and the country pulled out of the Watergate swamp. I propose an extraordinary act of statesmanship and courage—an act at once noble and heartbreaking; at once serving the greater interests of the nation, the institution of the Presidency, and the stated goals for which he so successfully campaigned." Nixon did not resign at that time, but eventually did so on August 9, 1974.[4]

Buckley's call for Nixon's resignation may have bolstered his credentials as an honest politician, but, at the same time, it alienated many of his Republican allies. To survive politically, Buckley knew that he had to raise his national profile and build on his law–and–order reputation. A high–profile investigation of an international narcotics trafficking ring was just the ticket.

In March of 1974, it was fortuitous that Buckley and his aide, Leonard Saffir, received a telephone call from State Senator Tarky Lombardi Jr. of Syracuse. Lombardi asked the Senator if he would meet with a constituent named William Spector, who claimed to have certain information on a drug trafficking ring. After Lombardi filled Buckley in on the details of Spector's claims concerning an international drug smuggling operation, Buckley agreed to meet Lombardi over dinner. One week later, Saffir met with Spector for an eight–hour briefing, where Spector presented his case. Considering the detail and documentation Spector provided throughout their day–long meeting, Saffir was perplexed by the lack of attention paid to Spector by both the police and the BNDD/DEA. This mystery left Saffir hooked. He would spend most of the next year or two investigating Spector's tantalizing allegations.

Saffir's first course of action was to meet with Stephen McClintic, the former Foreign Service, CIA, and BNDD agent who had previously worked with Spector. McClintic opened the conversation by telling Saffir that there was "a great deal there" regarding Spector's allegations, and shared his view that the DEA had doctored their files relating to the Spector investigation. McClintic told Saffir that the French police had warned the BNDD as early as 1969 that Patricia Richardson was involved in narcotics smuggling. McClintic also advised Saffir that Christian David, a Corsican heroin smuggler recently arrested in Brazil, was mentioned by name in her diaries.[5]

Following his meeting with McClintic and having learned of the potentially explosive allegations of DEA corruption, Saffir quickly went to Syracuse to meet with Spector. The similarities between Spector's claims and the evidence of the DEA's manipulation of the documentary record in the Peroff–Vesco case were too close to be coincidental. It seemed to establish a pattern and practice of DEA corruption that could no longer be ignored.

After Saffir filled Buckley in on his conversations with McClintic and Spector, they agreed that a full-bore investigation was necessary. Buckley wrote a sharply worded letter to DEA Director John Bartels Jr. concerning the "serious charges reflecting on the efficiency of your Agency." He suggested the "DEA would be in some trouble" if Spector's allegations proved to be true.[6] Buckley asked the DEA to answer several detailed questions about their investigation so that he could better assess whether they had adequately pursued their investigation.

Bartels responded by meeting with Buckley in person and reading him a lengthy letter in the hope of discrediting Spector. Specifically, Bartels stated that his agents spent a "disproportionate" amount of time investigating Spector's claims and that they amounted to nothing.[7] This, however, left Buckley and Saffir unimpressed, considering that Bartels had brought no documents, files, or other hard evidence to demonstrate that they had investigated Spector's claims.[8]

Saffir insisted on meeting with other DEA agents to personally review their case files on Spector after the meeting. The agents refused to show Saffir more than a few brief documents on the case, but they did admit that they had never bothered speaking with Patricia Richardson. Indeed, the agents revealed that they had not interviewed a single person about Spector's claims.[9] As Saffir later told the State Senate Select Committee on Crime, he concluded that "something was terribly wrong" with how the DEA was supposedly investigating Spector's claims.

A follow-up meeting between McClintic and Saffir only made the situation worse. McClintic, now retired and feeling he had nothing to lose, supplied Saffir and Buckley with files on the Spector case that he had taken with him. Among other things, McClintic gave them a letter from Bartels to Watergate Special Prosecutor Leon Jaworski, proving that DEA Director Bartels lied when, in response to Senator Buckley's inquiries, he swore that he had no contact with the Watergate prosecutors about Spector's allegations.[10] McClintic's evidence clearly contradicted Bartel's sworn statements by showing that Bartels had written to Watergate Special Prosecutor Jaworski, stating his opinion that "further exploration" of Spector's case was "not worthwhile."[11]

Buckley and Saffir followed up directly with Jaworski to confirm whether Bartels had lied about his lack of contact with the Special Prosecutor's office regarding Spector's allegations. In response, Jaworski told them, "We had a great deal of difficulty" getting a report from the DEA on Spector. He added: "We had a helluva time; we made many requests and quite belatedly received a brief report which by its contents we viewed as a brush–off. It was rather unsatisfying to us, particularly after Henry Ruth [of the Watergate Special Prosecutor's Office] and I showed our great concern regarding Spector."

Despite the growing evidence of a cover–up at the DEA,[12] Buckley did not have enough seniority in the Senate to launch a Congressional investigation of Spector's charges on his own. Luckily, however, he did have considerable sway with the Republican leadership in the New York State Senate. Buckley used this leverage to get a state legislative investigation underway. He persuaded Ralph J. Marino, the Chairman of the State Select Committee on Crime, to hold hearings on the matter, promising that Buckley and his staff would assume much of the responsibility and cost of the investigation. Buckley directed Saffir to coordinate the investigation through the New York Police Department. Saffir also arranged a meeting with Patricia Richardson to personally grill her about her connections to several known gun runners and drug smugglers. On April 18, 1975, Saffir met with Richardson, which he described as follows:

> She told me at that time that she had met and known Marcel [Boucan] another convicted drug trafficker, though she said she had not been in contact with him for years. I asked her if she knew Eduardo Baroudi. She replied, yes. Baroudi has been in jail for bank fraud in Europe and is referred to by police officials and several countries as a major gun smuggler and drug trafficker. I asked her if she knew Yusef Beidas. She said yes, and said that she had lived with him. Beidas was the founder of the Intra Bank of Beirut, Lebanon, who was indicted for bank fraud…. The former Mrs. Spector has told persons that she knows Beidas was murdered so I asked her about this. She denied any knowledge…. However, later

in a conversation with her present husband, Mr. Martinson, he admitted that his wife did suspect Beidas was murdered by one of her friends. CIA reports today list Beidas' death as a possible murder.[13]

Saffir also contacted John Stevenhagen, who lived with Richardson in 1971 after she left Spector and upstate New York for St. Martin. Saffir had been told by a New York Times reporter that Stevenhagen was a "key individual in this case."[14] When Stevenhagen denied having any involvement with Richardson, Saffir met with Spector to see what he knew about Stevenhagen. At this meeting with Spector, it became clear to Saffir and the NYPD officers assigned to work with him that Spector was being surveilled and followed by BNDD/DEA agents. The actions of these federal agents clearly indicated that federal law enforcement and intelligence agencies had already made the decision that they were not going to cooperate with Buckley, Saffir, or the NYPD, and that they were going to do everything in their power to "stonewall" and impede the investigation.

***

Senator Buckley's investigation had gathered significant circumstantial evidence, but not enough to convict Richardson or Weiller "beyond a reasonable doubt." Buckley and Saffir knew that they needed more proof. They needed something akin to Alexander Butterfield's bombshell testimony at the Watergate hearings about the existence of an Oval Office taping system that recorded all of Nixon's conversations. Buckley and Saffir knew that the post–Watergate public now expected there to be a "smoking gun" in every major investigation. After talking it over, Buckley and Saffir agreed Saffir should go to France to look for some magic key to unlock the irrefutable evidence they needed to prove the truth of Spector's allegations.

When Saffir arrived in France, he met with Paul Knight, head of the Paris DEA branch. Knight made available to Saffir two recently obtained French police reports from 1971 and 1973. These reports detailed investigations into Richardson conducted by French police at the behest of the DEA, which led to a recommendation that U.S. law enforcement agencies conduct a surveillance of Richardson. These

French reports clearly connected Richardson with Henri Helle, Marcel Boucan, and others who were known narcotics traffickers. Assuming the DEA was serious about catching drug traffickers—which was something of a big assumption—these French reports were inexplicably missing from the DEA files. Indeed, Paul Knight, as chief of the Paris DEA office, said he had never seen them until that month.[15]

***

Another part of France that received several visits from Saffir and other federal investigators was the tiny, picturesque village of Mimet, just outside Marseille. Near a hillside on our Lady of the Angels road, just beyond the town, was an ordinary-looking cream-colored villa with orange shutters. On October 9, 1969, this villa achieved international notoriety when the French police seized a heroin-conversion laboratory there, only the third such lab they had uncovered in 20 years.[16] The extraordinary thing about this raid was not that it confirmed that Marseille was a worldwide center for heroin production. This fact has been well known since the end of World War II. What was startling was that the French felt compelled to conduct this token raid at all.

According to the BNDD, by 1969, these makeshift laboratories in the Marseille region produced 80 to 90 percent of the 10 to 14 tons of heroin entering the United States annually.[17] In these labs, thousands of pounds of morphine base—a powder with the texture of talcum and the color of milk chocolate—were converted into heroin each year. U.S. investigators took a hard look below the surface to find out how Marseille came by its role as the international center of heroin trafficking. They had a reasonably easy job tracing it back to the control by local organized crime groups who had run the black market for American cigarettes during and after World War II. When the profitability of the cigarette trade declined, the Unione Corse and other related groups turned to drugs for a new source of income. Marseille's location made it a natural stopover. The city was midway between the poppy fields of Turkey and the most lucrative markets for the product, the East Coast of the U.S. Every year, hundreds of Turkish, Greek, and Arab freighters carried cargo from the Eastern Mediterranean to the Port of Marseille. The hilly region around Marseille—known as Provence—was ideal for heroin laboratories to remain undetected. Within a 15-mile radius of the city, it was estimated that there are 30,000 villas suitable for hiding a drug lab.

One notable Corsican of the post–war era was Marcel Francisci, a Unione Corse member in Marseille and a prominent supporter of Charles de Gaulle's "Rally of the French People" party. Francisci was a wartime resistance hero and winner of several medals. After the war, he focused on his political career and legitimate business interests. But as Francisci's influence grew, so did his ambition. Between 1963 and 1967, Francisci and his clan waged war against the Guerini syndicate in control of Marseille's heroin labs since their deal with de Gaulle, Weiller, and the CIA in 1947.

After the Guerinis sanctioned a hit on SDECE agent Robert Blémant in 1965, they lost the tacit support of the French authorities.[18] Francisci saw this as the perfect opportunity to unseat the Guerini brothers, eventually assassinating Antoine Guerini in 1967. Having won the gang war and forced the Guerini clan into submission, Francisci became the most powerful *pacieri*–peacemaker, the Corsican equivalent of a Godfather–in Marseille's heroin industry. He supplied the heroin for Weiller and Richardson's network of smugglers to transport into the U.S. He also entered politics and was elected as the Gaullist conservative representative for southern Corsica. As a former member of the Resistance and elected official, Francisci's political activities provided him sufficient armor against claims in the 1970s that he was the chief coordinator of the "French Connection" heroin traffic into the New York City area. When accused in 1973 by Time Magazine and Politique–Hebdo, a French magazine, of being a drug lord, Francisci responded with defamation lawsuits, which he quickly lost.[19] However, he was never arrested or criminally charged, and he continued to represent Southern Corsica in the French National Assembly until he was assassinated outside his Paris apartment in 1984.[20]

Marseille also had a ready and willing workforce in the narcotics trade. Generations of young Corsicans, fleeing the poverty of their underdeveloped island, flocked to the city until they constituted a major part of its population. Many of them went into legitimate businesses, and some became nuns or priests serving the numerous Catholic churches throughout Marseille. However, the most financially successful of them ended up making small fortunes (by Corsican standards) working for the crime syndicates. As Antoine Rinieri's tale demonstrated, the code of silence among Corsican criminals was virtually unbreakable. Moreover, the French police had no serious interest in penetrating the near–impenetrable wall surrounding the narcotics operations there.

***

Given Marseille's history as a drug import–export center, it was not very difficult for U.S. law enforcement agents to establish where the heroin must have come from that was being distributed by Patricia Richardson and her cohorts. The connection between Marseille and the world heroin trade was virtually impossible to circumvent, at least during the 1960s and 1970s. However, gathering evidence of Richardson's direct involvement in the heroin distribution network was the more challenging part of the puzzle. Senator Buckley's State Senate Select Committee ultimately failed–like every other investigation–in achieving that objective. But it was not for lack of effort.

Upon his return from France, Saffir arranged for the State Senate Select Committee on Crime to issue dozens of subpoenas to individuals identified by Spector. He hoped to get solid testimony to corroborate Spector's story about the Unione Corse drug ring.

The New York State Senate Select Committee on Crime Hearings Begin

On July 28, 1975, the long–awaited hearing before the State Senate Select Committee on Crime finally got underway. Spector was the lead–off witness. In his testimony, Spector recounted how he spent the last four years gathering a great deal of information and sharing it with state and federal law enforcement agencies. Spector accused these agencies of being grossly negligent, and possibly corrupt. In particular, he claimed that these agencies failed to follow up on his allegations of "known and suspected drug–smugglers" making illegal cash contributions to the campaign of former President Nixon.

In his testimony on the first day of the hearings, Spector specifically alleged that his ex–wife had smuggled large quantities of illegal narcotics across the Canadian border. He claimed that the drugs were hidden in Cadillacs and Oldsmobiles from his upstate car dealership, as well as in toy dolls filled with heroin smuggled across the border. Spector further testified that, on at least two occasions, his car had been tampered with, and someone tried to kill him. As a result, Spector testified, State Police Sergeant Dave Jewell had been assigned as a bodyguard for him during the duration of the hearings.

In response to questioning by Committee members, Spector testified that his former wife had been "involved with," "associated with," and "suspected of" narcotics traffic. He discussed her notebooks, which he said he saw but did not have copies of. According to Spector, these notebooks contained the names of significant narcotics traffickers, evidence of her alleged possession of heroin, and her widespread travel as a leading member of the Unione Corse.

In answer to a question from State Senator Abraham Bernstein, a Bronx Democrat, as to whether he was alleging his former wife was an international drug trafficker, Spector answered with an unqualified, "Yes." However, when Senator Bernstein pressed Spector for specifics, he was interrupted by Chairman of the Committee State Senator Ralph J. Marino, a Republican from Long Island, who said the question might not be "fair" to the witness.

Spector responded anyway, saying that the answer might take him "several hours." Still, the details he could provide were the names of several known narcotics smugglers he said he saw in his ex–wife's diaries. He also claimed to have "direct information from St. Martin [and] having talked to certain witnesses." The Committee members had obviously hoped for more. "I, for one, would like to have a little more basis for the reasons for Mr. Spector's conclusions," State Senator Bernstein grumbled.

At another point in the hearings, Spector testified to what he described as his personal knowledge of the longstanding ties between his former wife, Paul-Louis Weiller, and Richard Nixon. "I was told by her and by Weiller personally that Weiller was on his way to Washington to visit his personal friend Richard Nixon, to whose campaign he had contributed heavily," Spector testified. "How heavily?" Senator Marino asked. "A $2-million cash contribution," Spector replied.

Spector's credibility, however, took a bruising when State Police Investigator Larry Manor testified. He told the committee that a suspicious white powder supplied by Spector had been tested and turned green. Manor said that this indicated that the powder was *not* heroin. According to Manor, if it had been heroin, it would have turned purple.

The French categorically denied the allegations against Mrs. Richardson and "the Frenchman" Paul–Louis Weiller of international heroin trafficking. The director of the DEA's Paris Bureau, Paul Knight, testified there was "no truth" to the claims. He testified the French police gave him a report–just before the hearings–stating that Spector's allegations "were without foundation, and were based on Spector's desire for revenge." This report directly contradicted previous reports by French police that Richardson warranted surveillance due to the likelihood of her involvement in drug smuggling. In response to questioning, Mr. Knight was also forced to concede that the French had never interviewed Spector and that they never conducted a thorough investigation of the charges.

Also introduced into the record by the DEA was a letter from the head of the French Narcotics Division, Francois Mouel, attempting to downplay the earlier French police reports that backed–up Spector's charges of his ex–wife's drug smuggling operations in St. Martin and elsewhere in Latin America.

News photo by Frank Russo
William Spector as he testified at hearing yesterday.

A photo of William Spector. From "Probe Told of Model's Big-Name Dope Diaries," New York Daily News, July 29, 1975. (Fallon and Russo 1973).

On the same day, a neighbor of Spector, John Maynard Langford, testified that, in 1971, Patricia Richardson approached him and asked how to hire someone to kill Spector. She suggested drugging Spector with LSD and asked if Langford could supply the hallucinogen. According to Langford, Richardson offered to split the life insurance proceeds with him if he could kill Spector.

The DEA official who testified at the hearings was John Coleman, based in Marseille. He spent most of his testimony attempting to boast about the DEA's "thorough investigation" of Spector's claims. Coleman's testimony, however, left many questions unanswered, such as why the name "Richardson" was found in the personal possessions of Marcel Boucan. His shrimp boat was picked up in Marseille in 1972 with over 400 kilos of heroin, approximately 900 pounds.

Boucan had moved to St. Martin in the early 1960s after he met Georges Helle, a/k/a "Henri," an established smuggler of cigarettes and narcotics. He had been run out of his operation in North Africa. Boucan had been the captain of the boat Helle traveled on to St. Martin for the first time. During that voyage, Helle recruited Boucan for his smuggling operation. Helle was known to French authorities as having lived with Patricia Richardson before she left St. Martin. This fact was relayed to the DEA in 1971 in a report that was mysteriously "lost" until Buckley and Saffir began their questioning of the DEA in 1975.[21] Coleman claimed in his testimony that he only "very recently" heard Helle's name for the first time. But French police had mentioned it multiple times in their reports to the DEA on Spector's claims.

After Boucan had been arrested aboard his ship by French authorities, he escaped from the cabin where he was confined and jumped into the Marseille harbor. He attempted to swim across the bay but was dragged aboard a luxury yacht owned by a wealthy couple with a pet monkey that spied Boucan in the water and began screeching at him. Boucan, half-drowned by then, was rushed to the hospital, where the French police arrived to arrest and interrogate him.

Shockingly for a Unione Corse member, Boucan confessed to his crime. He even implicated Alexandre Orsatelli, a fellow Corsican who had contracted the ship used to transport the heroin shipment. This confession was strange for another reason: French law at the time made

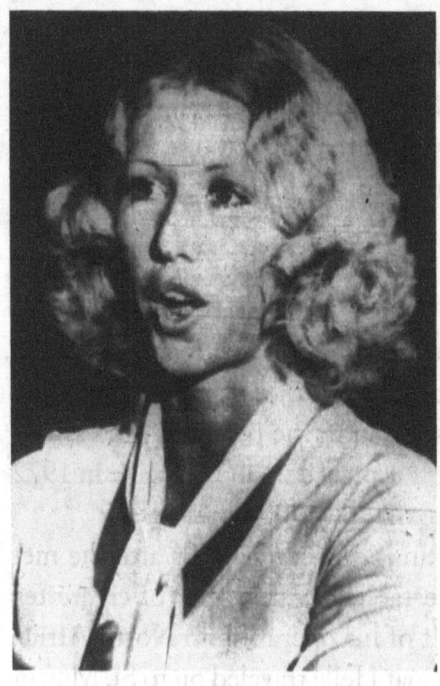

Mary Jo Ottman in 1975. The McAllen Monitor, July 31, 1975.

no accommodation for confessions, leaving Boucan's possible motivations to confess suspect. The strangeness of his confession was noted by DEA agent Coleman in his testimony. Coleman couldn't stop wondering why Boucan might have readily confessed, even though he stood to gain nothing. An obvious possibility was that Boucan's confession, an apparent contravention of the code of silence, was a ruse to protect his actual superiors. Coleman also testified that Boucan said the name "Richardson" meant nothing to him, even though Richardson admitted that she had known Boucan from St. Martin.

Two persons who knew Patricia fairly well made sworn declarations concerning her drug involvement. However, they did not testify in person. Her half-brother, Claude Fleming, who lived on St. Martin, signed a declaration at Spector's urging, discussing "the effect of drugs regarding my sister, Patricia Spector." When interviewed by The New York Times, however, he denied any knowledge of drug use or trafficking by her. John Stevenhagen, who lived briefly with Patricia on St. Martin, and now worked at the JG Melon's bar on the Upper East Side of Manhattan, gave a sworn declaration implicating Richardson in narcotics trafficking. However, Stevenhagen later recanted his testimony by telling his attorney, Richard F. Gibson, that he did not, in fact, "have knowledge" of a narcotics scheme involving her and "the Frenchman." When questioned by the Times, Mr. Stevenhagen said he had made the sworn statement implicating Richardson solely because Spector had been "badgering" him.[22]

Another key witness, Mary Jo Ottman, never testified before the State Senate Select Committee. As discussed in chapter two of this book, Ottman had gone with Richardson to St. Martin in 1972 as a nursemaid for her two small children. She spent much of the trip locked in a room while Patricia met with underworld figures in the living room. When Ottman returned to New York, she was met and assaulted by a Pan Am agent who was subsequently fired by Pan Am for smuggling. Ms. Ottman told investigators that Patricia had insisted on packing her bags for her as they were planning to return to New York. Ottman believed Patricia planted an expensive necklace in her luggage, as well as some drugs, which were recovered by the Pan Am agent working for Richardson at JFK Airport.

Richardson dismissed Ottman's story as "absurd." However, Richardson was not specifically confronted with any testimony on this point since Ottman ultimately failed to appear to testify at the State Senate hearings. According to her lawyer, she was having a "nervous breakdown."

Trying not to be upstaged by Spector or unduly tarnished by testimony about her attempts to recruit a "hit man" to kill her ex-husband, Patricia Richardson told the press she was asking for "protection" before she would agree to testify before the Select Committee. However, she was unusually vague about who or what she believed posed a threat to her. She also told the New York Times: "Bill Spector is trying to ruin my life. He absolutely hates me. I don't know anything about heroin. I've never taken drugs of any kind. I don't even take aspirin."[23]

Richardson tried to avoid giving public testimony by meeting for four hours behind closed doors in a closed committee hearing. However, Senator Buckley and the Select Committee members insisted that she give at least some limited public testimony, which was scheduled for the last day of the hearings.

Finally, on July 30, 1975, the third day of the hearings, Patricia Richardson Martinson took the stand. She claimed that her former husband had made several attempts on her life. She also disputed the testimony that she wanted to murder her former husband.[24] Specifically, she alleged that Spector had tried to kill her by attempting to throw her into the St. Lawrence River, which bordered the town of Ogdensburg.

In her sworn testimony, Richardson also vehemently denied that she had ever been involved in drug trafficking. "I've never been involved in any way with narcotics, in any manner whatsoever. I know nothing

Patricia Richardson Martinson arrives to testify at drug hearing Wednesday in New York City.

Denies Involvement In Narcotics Traffic

Patricia Richardson Martinson before taking the stand at the New York State Senate Committee hearings. From "Denies Involvement in Narcotics Traffic" The Ithaca Journal, July 31, 1975.

of narcotics, I know nothing of any smuggling, I know nothing of any people involved in narcotics smuggling or people who may even know about other people involved in narcotics smuggling."[25]

Richardson categorically denied the testimony of the previous witness, John Langford, in whose home she briefly lived in Ogdensburg, New York, after being separated from Spector. Langford testified that she had asked him to obtain LSD to give to Spector and ultimately offered him $50,000 to kill her then–estranged husband. According to Langford, a third person, William Gohke, who had worked as the bookkeeper at Spector's dealership, was brought into their conspiratorial discussions with Richardson on the subject. But Gohke had been arrested for writing a fraudulent multimillion–dollar cheque to buy a yacht in Miami. He had been impersonating James Durham III, the scion of the Durham tobacco fortune.[26] Already serving jail time for unrelated crimes, Gohke refused to testify or acknowledge any connection to Richardson.

In her testimony, Richardson elaborated on her ex–husband's attempts to kill her. She said he "tried to push me into the river and tried to run me over on several occasions with his car." She denied specific knowledge of narcotics traffic or traffickers. Still, she could not wholly explain the allegations made by other witnesses concerning her suspicious behavior and admitted association with known narcotics traffickers.

Described in press reports as "a slim, husky-voiced blonde," Richardson told members of the Committee that she believed that Spector was accusing her of drug trafficking out of malice.[27] "The only reason that he is making these allegations is that he is vengeful and spiteful to the fact that I divorced him, and he can't live with that," she told the packed hearing room. Ms. Richardson also testified that she had, in fact, traveled the world but that she had done it as a professional model, not as a drug trafficker. In a bombshell admission, she conceded under questioning that she had met former President Nixon "in a New York restaurant" when he was running for office in 1968. But she was vague about the details of the meeting. The New York Times investigation of this matter confirmed Richardson and "a French financier" met with Richard M. Nixon at La Côte Basque restaurant in New York during the 1960s. The Times article did not identify the "financier" by name. Still, it was clear to knowledgeable readers that the report referred to Weiller.[28] Spector testified that the "sizable campaign contribution" Weiller made to Nixon in 1968 was $2 million.[29] Richardson, of course, denied any knowledge about the transfer of cash or Nixon's promise to honor the U.S.'s longstanding "hands off" policy regarding the Unione Corse in return for the $2 million cash contribution to his election campaign.

As to her future plans, Richardson testified that she and her current husband, John R. Martinson, were planning to purchase a "modest" home on her native island of St. Martin. It was later reported, however, that the spacious villa they bought was far from "modest" and was estimated to be worth $10.7 million in 1970s dollars.

Although the State Select Committee did not have Ms. Richardson's notebooks available at the time of the hearings, a copy of her diaries surfaced later. They contained detailed information regarding her dealings with known narcotics traffickers. For example, the name Marcel Boucan appears at least several times. This is not surprising since, as of the time of the State Select Committee hearings in 1975, Boucan's arrest was the largest heroin bust to date. He was still serving a 20-year prison sentence. Boucan's boat had been spotted by Dutch police off St. Martin two weeks before it was seized, although the DEA disputed that fact in the hearing.[30] Patricia explained this away by saying she knew Boucan when she lived on the island but had no knowledge of his criminal activities. However, the numerous diary entries referencing him suggested otherwise.

Post Hearing Developments

Following Richardson's testimony, Leonard Saffir firmly pushed back against her protestations of innocence. "This is a gal who knows about international drug traffic, the most important in the world, and no agency really investigated her," he told the Times. Saffir had to admit, however, that Senator Buckley's office and the State Senate Select Committee had failed to come up with enough hard evidence against Richardson to bring criminal charges against her.

While Richardson denied any knowledge of Weiller's involvement in drug trafficking, she did write in her voluminous notebooks: "I love him, respect him, and need him." She further wrote: "Maybe, at last, we can be together again, and this time I'll be able to love him enough for a lifetime."

***

The State Senate Select Committee investigations were closely monitored by the White House of President Gerald Ford. He succeeded Nixon as president following his resignation on August 18, 1974. The White House senior advisor assigned to monitor the investigation was Lee W. Gladden, then an assistant to Egil Krogh. Gladden met weekly with Stephen H. McClintic, who had close ties with the CIA and the White House. McClintic was understandably concerned that the information he had provided to Senator Buckley and his chief aide, Leonard Saffir, would come back to haunt him. Therefore, he sought to divert attention away from Spector's most incendiary allegations of CIA and BNDD/DEA complicity with the French–Corsican mob by seeking to discredit Spector. McClintic described Spector in his testimony at the hearings as "unstable," "threatening," and solely motivated by a quest to get paid as a government informant and to get a book published about his allegations.

It was later discovered that the DEA and the CIA had copies of Patricia Richardson's diaries and other documents that corroborated and supported the allegations that Spector was making. However, these critical documents were not provided to Senator Buckley or the State Special Committee on Crime. As a result, the Special Committee hearings ended inconclusively, with sharply conflicting testimony between Spector and his ex-wife, Patricia Richardson. The documentary evidence available at the time could not resolve the critical issues one way or the other. This was precisely where the CIA and the part of the DEA under heavy CIA influence (which was most of it) wanted the investigation to end. It would be a "he said, she said" dispute over almost every material fact and left no way to get to the bottom of Spector's allegations.

Curiously, the formal written record of the hearing mysteriously disappeared from the New York State Archives. Despite an exhaustive search by the author, researchers, and archivists at the New York State Library and State Senate, no record of the hearings was ever found. The testimony and evidence presented during the three days of the 1975 hearings had to be pieced together from newspaper articles about the hearings, notes left by Spector, and some excerpts quoted in a later 1978 congressional drug trafficking investigation report. However, none of the sworn testimony of the multiple witnesses who testified at the hearings is now available. The identity of the person or persons responsible for erasing this critical part of the historical record is unknown. The only thing that is known for sure is the identities of those who would have benefitted from the eradication of this evidence: Richardson, Weiller, others associated with the Unione Corse, and the U.S. and French officials who successfully undermined and suppressed any legitimate investigation into one of the best kept secrets in U.S. and French history–the Marseille Accord.

As one investigation after another fizzled out, Spector became increasingly erratic. He was eventually written off as "unbalanced," which, sadly, is what he had become. Meanwhile, Richardson got away unscathed and "Scot free," because she had mastered all the skills necessary to survive and thrive both in the criminal underworld, as well as in the political world and in the media. She used her three significant assets–unbridled ambition, a sharp intellect, and exquisite good looks–to clear the road to success.

Due to some combination of ingenuity, connections, and just plain luck, investigations into Richardson and the leadership of the Unione Corse ended inconclusively, and there were no prosecutions following the 1975 hearings. The old Corsican saying, "The big fish always get away," seemed to hold true, at least in Weiller's and Richardson's case.

Chapter 11:
Jerry Barsha, Robin Moore, and "The Real French Connection"

When Patricia Richardson disappeared in 1971 and Spector realized that she had duped him, she was already ten steps ahead of him. He spent the rest of his life trying to convince law enforcement of something that could never be definitively proven: that his ex-wife was one of the kingpins of an international crime syndicate that was supplying most of the heroin illegally distributed in the U.S. It was as close as it gets to the perfect crime.

Although Spector was not without his own skills, acquired as an OSS and CIA operative in Eastern Europe during and after the war, he was no match for his ex-wife. Nevertheless, he still had contacts within and outside the Government, so he embarked on a tireless campaign to vindicate himself and redeem his tarnished reputation. Even better if he could put the woman who had destroyed his life behind bars.

After a heated argument in 1971, Richardson left their house with only a few belongings. Spector rifled through what she left behind and soon discovered some of her diaries. Reading through them, he realized that Richardson was a smuggler and had used his Cadillacs to transport narcotics across the border. He also discovered that her employer, the Stewart Model Agency, was an international drug smuggling front. He then had his dealership's Cadillacs carefully inspected, which revealed secret compartments in several of them, although they were empty.

Convinced that his wife and her cohorts were still smuggling narcotics across the border, Spector persuaded the local police to set up a roadblock to search vehicles coming across the bridge from Canada. His suspicions seem to have been confirmed when three used Cadillacs were seen crossing the border in a convoy. However, when the police searched the three vehicles for secret compartments, none were found. The police officers dismantled the roadblock and returned to their usual business: hanging out in a local diner, drinking coffee, munching on doughnuts, and trading (mostly apocryphal) war stories.

Dispirited and embarrassed, Spector returned home. About one hour later, a Cadillac crossed the border at the same spot with a fortune worth of heroin powder safely stashed in a secret compartment. The car was not stopped and safely made its way south towards New York and warmer climes.

In addition to triggering criminal investigations by the local and Canadian police, Spector went on to file complaints with the New York State Police, the Special Watergate Prosecutor in Washington, D.C., and the federal prosecutor in Manhattan (who opened a federal grand jury investigation), the FBI, the DEA, the CIA, the U.S. Customs Bureau, the French Surete, the Dutch police, and Interpol, to mention just a few. These authorities primarily wrote Spector off, and his complaints were ignored. The DEA, who made only a token effort to investigate his claims, quickly dropped the investigation once the connections to Nixon, Vesco, and Weiller surfaced.

Spector did, however, find a willing audience in the media. He contacted the New York Times, Time and Newsweek magazines, The Washington Post, the New Republic, and NBC News, who conducted generally futile investigations throughout 1974–1975. However, it took a local upstate newsman to finally break Spector's story and bring it to the attention of the national media.

* * *

In 1974, Jerry Barsha, one of the anchor newscasters at WSTM–TV, Channel 3, the NBC affiliate for Syracuse and Central New York, took a keen interest in the Spector–Richardson story and continued to run with it for most of 1974 and 1975. He continued to pursue the story after most national media lost interest or followed the signals from their CIA and other government contacts to "steer clear" of Spector. The penalty for going against the wishes of these powerful government "sources" was severe. Any reporter or news outlet could be disciplined by being cut off from government leaks of breaking news stories, which was the media's lifeblood.

Barsha was what every news reporter hopes to be, but few achieve. He was fearless and uncompromising when reporting on a story he thought important. In the "Real French Connection," as he referred to Spector's information, he was not afraid to expose some of the most powerful people in the country and the world.

A Brooklyn native who came to Syracuse to attend college at Syracuse University, Barsha started working at the Syracuse radio station WSYR in 1957. He spent the next 32 years behind the radio microphone and in front of T.V. news cameras. Over the years, Barsha—who had a flair for the dramatic—broke several important local news stories. Still, none of them could hold a candle to what he and author Robin Moore believed was the real story behind The French Connection.

Spector's electrifying tale of international drug smuggling, plus a cover-up by U.S. law enforcement agencies, was the kind of story Barsha hoped would catapult him from a regional newscaster onto the national stage.

Jerry Barsha (right foreground) c.1975. Courtesy of RadioTimeline.com "WSYR Syracuse Tribute."

On August 10, 1974, Jerry Barsha and T.V. 3 news broke the story that Spector's ex-wife had used Spector's Cadillac-Oldsmobile dealership in Ogdensburg to smuggle vast quantities of drugs into the U.S. from Canada.[1] Barsha reported that Spector had "compiled a huge amount of material," which had already been turned over to law enforcement authorities. Barsha further reported that Spector had already appeared before the Senate Watergate Committee, the Committee on Governmental Operations, and was cooperating with the staff of Special Prosecutor Leon Jaworski.

As part of this "breaking news story," Barsha conducted an on-air interview with Spector. In response to Barsha's questioning, Spector explained that he was in "practically daily contact with Inspector Peltz" of the Syracuse Police Department about the transport of narcotics from Canada to Syracuse. Spector claimed to have specific flight, plane, and baggage claim numbers that should be checked at the Syracuse Airport. He explained that the Syracuse Airport was the primary air transit point for flights transporting narcotics from Canada into Northern New York.

Spector further explained during his on-air appearance with Barsha that he had also traveled to Washington to brief Special Agent Tom Coll, the assistant to FBI Director Pat Gray. However, Spector stated that he never heard from the FBI again, ominously suggesting that the FBI itself had been compromised and was now part of a massive conspiracy to silence him.

Robin Moore Gives Spector His Endorsement

During Barsha's August 10, 1974, breaking news story, he pulled off a journalistic tour de force by being the first reporter to interview Robin Moore, the author of *The French Connection*, about Spector's allegations. Moore fully endorsed Spector and his revelations about the Unione Corse and its corrupt relationships reaching the highest levels of the U.S. government.

Moore was one the most successful writers of his generation, authoring the hugely popular *The Green Berets*, in addition to *The French Connection* and other famous works. *The French Connection* was based on a low-level drug case in New York City in 1961. The bust was largely unheard of until Moore dusted off the story in 1969 and produced the book, which was then developed into a film of the same name. The movie, starring Gene Hackman as Jimmy "Popeye" Doyle, a rough and tenacious police detective, swept the Academy Awards in April 1972.

Moore had served in the Army Air Corps during World War II as a nose gunner on a B-17 bomber. After the war, he went to Harvard, graduating in 1949. Moore's first book, *The Devil To Pay–The True Story of an American Soldier of Fortune in Castro's Revolution*, was published in 1961. Moore's life then took a detour back into military service as the Vietnam War escalated. At the ripe old age of 37 (at least for a man re-enlisting in the military), Moore graduated from the U.S. Army's airborne school and the Special Warfare Center. On January 6, 1964, he arrived in Vietnam and spent six months there with the Green Berets. At the end of that Special Forces training mission, Moore wrote *The Green Berets*, which he followed up with the equally popular *The French Connection*.

The French Connection was loosely based on a narcotics investigation by New York City detectives Eddie Egan and Sonny Grosso. These men uncovered some lower-level participants in a narcotics trafficking operation from Marseille to New York. Acting on a hunch, the detectives began surveillance on Pasquale "Patsy" Fuca, a lower-level New York drug dealer. They soon uncovered the involvement of two Frenchmen, Jean Jehan ("The Giant"), one of the people responsible for importing a heroin shipment into the U.S., and Jacques Angelvin, a French television personality. The plan was to smuggle $32 million worth of heroin by hiding it in the body of a car imported into the U.S. After a lengthy stakeout, the detectives impounded the suspected car, and in a police garage they and their team tore the car apart piece by piece. The hidden packages of heroin were found in the rocker panels.

On-air with Jerry Barsha, Robin Moore gave Spector his unqualified endorsement: "Everything that Bill has turned up has turned up prior to his telling me this in certain investigations I was making." Moore then explained that, when he wrote *The French Connection*, "it was obvious that [the NYPD] did not even come close to touching the top man." Moore explained that all the Frenchmen and their American associates prosecuted in the case were "fairly far down the ladder."

Moore then disclosed that he had been given tantalizing tidbits of information about the identities of the shadowy figures behind the arrested French operatives but that he was prevented from writing about them. Moore explained: "Just at the end of the case, Detective Eddie Eagan found a photograph strongly suggesting that there was a high-level French figure who had been given the orders that were carried out by the underlings who had been ensnared by the NYPD drug bust. Moore claimed, "when they took his picture down to police headquarters and started processing it, all of a sudden the word came through from some much higher headquarters to drop the whole investigation and forget it...."

Moore further disclosed to Barsha that, in the final draft of *The French Connection*, he included this information about the detectives on the case being told to go no further with it. However, as Moore explained, "at the last minute, they made me take it out; the cops begged me, they said we'll get in trouble. We weren't supposed to tell you about that anyway." He said that, among other details, he was asked not to disclose the fact there was a "continuing investigation" of the upper echelons of the French–Corsican drug cartel, who had been identified only as "John Doe" defendants in a sealed indictment.

Moore said he acceded to the detectives' pleas to "excise it from the book." However, Moore told Barsha on camera that he had "nevertheless worked with the police to try to find out where and at what point high up the man was." But he never was able to identify this person. Still, he believed this mystery man was "very closely associated with either the President of France" or "one of his Cabinet members."

Moore candidly admitted that, while the book and film were hugely successful, the prosecution of the participants involved was far less satisfactory. The case against one of the defendants, Joel Weinstock, was dismissed for "lack of proper evidence." Another defendant received a suspended sentence with no jail time after pleading to a misdemeanor charge. A third defendant also received a substantially reduced sentence. Only one of the defendants prosecuted paid any meaningful legal penalty–a four-year sentence in federal prison on a conspiracy charge. None of the French-based masterminds or kingpins were ever apprehended.

Over the years, Moore dropped tantalizing "clues" in testimony before Congressional committees regarding the identity of the "brains" of that organization. For example, Moore testified to a Congressional committee about the photo shown to him by Detective Egan of the two Frenchmen having dinner in a Manhattan restaurant. Only one of them could be identified: Jean Jehan. The other man in the photograph was identified to Moore only as "an official in Michelin Tire Co."–was never arrested or even identified.[2] Moore also testified about another photo shown to him by the NYPD detectives. This picture clearly depicted Weiller and a previously unidentified young woman, who Moore immediately recognized as Patricia Richardson.

The French Government "Stonewalls" the Investigation

French authorities remained equally tight-lipped about their open "investigation" of the "French Connection" kingpins. The photos and other evidence in the French government file were never publicly disclosed, and the various French investigations–like the American ones–died quiet deaths, leading nowhere.

When French government officials were finally asked whether Paul-Louis Weiller was one of those depicted in the matchbook photograph shown to Robin Moore or whether he was ever investigated for his complicity in the French Connection, the question was dismissed out of hand. Their only official public comment was: "Mr. Weiller's respectability is beyond question."

Jerry Barsha and The New York Times later reported one small crack that eventually appeared in the French Government's stone wall of silence regarding Weiller's involvement. An article published in the New York Times on July 30, 1975, revealed the French police issued a report in 1973, concluding that there was a distinct "possibility" of "the participation of Patricia Richardson in drug trafficking." The French police report recommended that "surveillance of the activities of Patricia Richardson in the United States would be desirable." The French police also found that "a network of drug traffickers is believed to exist in the Dutch zone of St.

Robin Moore in Vietnam with the Green Berets, c. 1965. Copyright unknown. Courtesy of Paul Davidson.

Martin, which is directed toward the United States from France via Philipsburg, St. Martin."

However, at the hearings held by the New York State Senate Subcommittee on Crime, state and federal drug agency officials admitted that their investigations had been cursory at best. No surveillance of Richardson had ever been conducted. Jacques Kiere, who helped lead the original BNDD investigation, would even go so far as to say that he had never seen the French police report before.

Barsha's Second T.V. Interview with Spector and Moore

On August 11, 1974–the day following Barsha's blockbuster premiere interview with Robin Moore and Spector–Barsha interviewed Moore again on air during his evening T.V. 3 news broadcast. The segment began with an introductory statement by Moore: "What you're about to see on T.V. 3 Total News with Jerry Barsha will undoubtedly shock you, but I believe it to be true. I've known Bill Spector for almost two years. We've worked very closely together, and I think he has uncovered and exposed the real French Connection at last."

Barsha then gave what he described as a "bombshell" breaking news story. "The Mob has put out a contract to kill Spector and Moore," adding: "steps have already been taken to have federal officials provide protection."

Barsha further reported on his August 11 T.V. news broadcast that, after the story aired the previous night, he was contacted by 30-year-old William Stratton of Sandy Pond, New York. Stratton told Barsha that he had information going back five years about illegal narcotics shipments through his area. Stratton said one method used involved dropping bags of drugs by private airplane.

Barsha also interviewed Moore again, and Moore expressed the opinion to Barsha that Spector's story had the ring of credibility, especially since Spector was a car dealer, which gave him the advantage "of having cars go back and forth into Canada and the United States. Nobody stopped his vehicles." Moore concluded that Spector's story was consistent with "the pattern, the continuing pattern, of narcotics smuggling."[3]

Barsha's Subsequent T.V. Broadcasts

On August 13, 1974, two days later, Barsha promised his viewers that "the story of the Real French Connection, which is enormous in its totality, will be told to the finish, in the days, weeks, and months to come."

Shortly after that, during his August 18, 1974, show, Barsha addressed a reoccurring question from his show's viewers, which was "why the story had not appeared anywhere else besides T.V. 3?" Barsha said that he could not answer for any other media outlets, but "rest assured we have not been bought off and the story will continue in the days to come."

Barsha's News Broadcasts Make Waves from Washington to the U.K.

As Barsha's continuing T.V. coverage gained momentum, it created considerable turmoil both in the U.S. and the U.K. According to Sybil Leek, an English journalist for the London Times, Spector had "stirred up a hornet's nest" in the U.K. by alleging that there was an "English Connection" to the international conspiracy he had uncovered. Spector was charging that a "wealthy Englishman with vast international holdings" had been one of the financial backers of the drug smuggling operation. Although Spector did not identify this person by name, Spector had long shared his suspicion with law enforcement that, besides Weiller, one of the wealthy financiers of the Unione Corsc's drug empire was Sir Charles Clore, a prominent British financier. Spector also alleged that he had information about his ex-wife's involvement with Clore and that he had turned this information over to the DEA and other government investigators, which later proved to be true.

Barsha's dogged reporting also led to a flurry of national and international attention. In its May 12, 1975, issue, Newsweek magazine ran a story with the questioning caption: "A Nixon Connection?", saying that Senator Buckley's probe had sparked investigations by the Syracuse Police, State Police, and others and that some believed that the investigation would reach as high as former President Nixon.

The national exposure generated by the Newsweek story triggered a story appearing in New York Newsday, reporting that there was an ongoing investigation of John Bartels, the DEA Administrator, and that there were "four separate investigations into the DEA–two by the Justice Department, one by Senator Henry Jackson's Congressional Committee, and one by Senator James Buckley." According to the Newsday article, Senator Buckley's materials had been shared with the New York State Select Committee on Crime. It was also reported that the Select Committee had served some subpoenas.

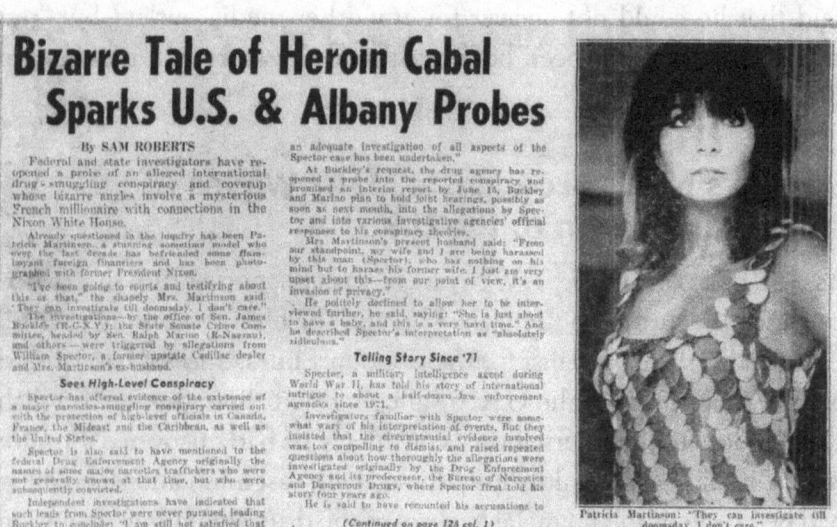

Sam Roberts, "Bizarre Tale of Heroin Cabal Sparks U.S. & Albany Probes," New York Daily News, June 8, 1975.

The Sunday edition of the New York Daily News contained a story entitled, "Bizarre Tale of Heroin Cabal Sparks U.S. and Albany Probes." A photo of Patricia Richardson (using her new married name of "Martinson") was included in the Daily News story, and she was quoted as saying: "They can investigate until doomsday. I don't care." Patricia's husband was reported as saying that Spector's allegations were "just harassment." According to the article, Senator Buckley's investigation had been prompted by the Senator's belief that "Spector's charges and evidence did not get a thorough investigation four years ago."

In response to the relentless reporting by NBC affiliate T.V. 3, as well as the articles and questions being raised by Newsweek, Newsday, and the New York Daily News, U.S. Attorney General Edward Levi ordered the formation of a "special investigative team" of federal agents to replace the federal agents who had been working on the case, who were under fire for allegedly failing to investigate Spector's allegations seriously. However, as with every other investigation, the Attorney General's investigation fizzled out within months of the press release announcing it.

Eventually, as the publicity and news coverage regarding Spector's allegations died down, even Jerry Barsha had to throw in the towel and move on to other stories. Weiller, Richardson, and their entire crime syndicate continued to operate unscathed.

Chapter 12:
The 1978 Coast Guard Hearings

On Wednesday, July 19, 1978, hearings chaired by Congressman Mario Biaggi of New York began in Washington, D.C., before the Coast Guard Subcommittee of the House of Representatives. The ostensible purpose of the subcommittee hearings was to consider legislation to expand the authority of the U.S. Coast Guard to interdict ships suspected of narcotics trafficking outside the 12- mile limit. However, a major sub-theme of the hearings was to determine why the investigations of Spector's allegations had gone nowhere since the 1975 hearings headed by Senator Buckley.

As Congressman Biaggi stated on the first day of the hearings, as of 1978, drug smuggling was big business, amounting to some $170 billion annually. That was larger than the operating budget of the U.S. Defense Department at the time. Congressman Biaggi described the U.S. borders as "an open sieve for smugglers to penetrate at will."[1]

Throughout the early 1970s, the Unione Corse expanded its operations in Central and South America, forging alliances with local drug syndicates in Paraguay, Brazil, and other countries. It also recruited a small air force of *contrabandista* pilots. They flew back and forth between Latin America and the U.S., carrying loads of narcotics to the U.S. and bags of cash back south. This multifaceted approach minimized the risk of overreliance on cars, boats, and commercial airlines, the main smuggling methods used by the Unione Corse throughout the 1960s.

The Unione Corse had suffered a temporary setback in 1970 when President Georges Pompidou of France ordered a major "housecleaning" of the SDECE, the French counterintelligence agency, and appointed a new chief, Alexander de Marenches.[2] In 1965, the SDECE, working with Mossad and The C.I.A., had relied on connections with the French-Corsican mob to kidnap and execute a Moroccan leftist politician named Ben Barka. Barka, an anti-colonial politician

Farabola. "Fotografia Press Photo Vintage 1969 Antoine Pinay con Georges Pompidou, Parigi. "Photograph courtesy of Farbola. (PDM).

friendly with Malcolm X and Che Guevarra, had presented a threat to continued French influence in Morocco through his critiques of the loyal royal family.

The Barka scandal, along with the SDECE's widespread use of underworld assassins and reliance on funding from the opium trade in Indochina, led to de Marenches decision to fire half of his agency in an attempt to clean house.[3]

Marenches' mass-firing was only partially successful. In 1971, over $12 million worth of high-grade heroin was found hidden in a Volkswagen camper shipped from France to Port Elizabeth, New Jersey. A massive firestorm of charges and recriminations erupted between the U.S. and French law enforcement officials following the arrest of Roger DeLouette. He claimed to be a former agent of the SDECE sent to pick up the heroin-laden car.

DeLouette soon began accusing other agents and officials associated with the French intelligence organization of being complicit in the drug smuggling conspiracy. Exposure of the corruption in the French intelligence services also had severe repercussions in the U.S. The U.S. Attorney Herbert J. Stern, whose offices were in Newark, New Jersey, stated in an interview that DeLouette had been ordered by Col. Paul Fournier of SDECE to pick up the drug-filled "Volkswagen camper." He claimed Fournier had been working for many years with French intelligence under an alias. Stern even went so far as to disclose that Fournier's real name was "Paul Ferrer," and that this senior French official had changed his name to hide his shady past.

Stern demanded that the French authorities extradite Fournier/Ferrer to the U.S. In a letter to Investigating Magistrate Gabriel Roussel in Paris, U.S. Attorney Stern said that he was forwarding the transcript of the arraignment proceedings in which a guilty plea was entered by DeLouette. At the two-hour arraignment proceedings, U.S. District Judge Frederick B. Lacey extensively questioned DeLouette until he established that DeLouette's charges against Fournier were valid. The proceeding transcript included details of a polygraph test the Justice Department gave DeLouette, as well as documentary evidence supplied by Stern's top aide, Jonathan L. Goldstein.

In November 1971, Colonel Roger Barberot of the Bureau of Agricultural Production Development, an SDECE front, said there was massive corruption in the agency and that he supported Stern's claims about Ferrer. Among other things, he confirmed that French agents within the intelligence agency had, for many years, coordinated their "investigations" with the Unione Corse. This allegation had the ring of truth about it, since virtually none of the French investigations of heroin smuggling ever went anywhere.

In November 1972, the "Volkswagen drug deal" was tied to another French citizen, Christian David. He operated throughout South America on behalf of the French-Corsican syndicate and reported directly to Richardson and Weiller. David was arrested in Brazil on heroin trafficking charges, and was then handed over to the U.S. to face trial for drug trafficking.[4] Christian David admitted to Brazilian police (after being tortured) that he was, in fact, a major drug smuggler, and that had been paid $150,000 to assassinate Ben Barka, the charismatic Moroccan opposition leader. According to Christian David, he doused Barka's corpse in lye and buried it in a Parisian suburb.[5] He was also wanted in France for murdering a police commissioner and faced the guillotine if extradited there.[6]

At this time, the FBI attempted to prosecute August Ricord, a top-level Unione Corse member who organized *contrabandista* operations in Paraguay and was extradited to the U.S. in 1972. While awaiting extradition, David was repeatedly grilled by DEA, FBI, and CIA agents. He gave them some tantalizing information on rivals in the drug smuggling trade. Still, he refused to provide the names of any of the upper echelon members of the Unione Corse. To do so would breach the "Code of Honor" he had sworn to keep. Any breach of that

Code would have meant an automatic death sentence at the hands of a fellow prisoner once he was turned over to the French law enforcement officers. Instead of cooperating with the police, David spent his time in prison threatening other witnesses in the Ricord trial to prevent them from testifying.[7]

However, David did tell an intriguing (but most likely apocryphal) tale to Stephen Rivele, an investigative journalist with a strong interest in the assassination of President John F. Kennedy. David told Rivele that he had information on the Kennedy assassination, in return for which he wanted a deal with the U.S. government to block his extradition to France. After that, through Rivele's efforts, a federal judge temporarily halted David's extradition, finding that David's information was sufficiently credible to warrant further investigation.

David told Rivele that President John F. Kennedy's assassination had been organized by Antoine Guerini, the Corsican crime boss in Marseille. And that after David had turned down the "hit" contract on President Kennedy, it was "accepted" by Lucien Sarti and two other members of the Marseille mob. According to David, Sarti and two accomplices were the ones who shot and killed Kennedy from behind the wooden fence on the grassy knoll in Dallas on November 22, 1963. David's story about the assassination and Rivele's subsequent investigation were the basis for the 1988 T.V. documentary, *The Men Who Killed Kennedy*. The Warren Commission had steered completely clear of this assassination theory, probably because there was no evidence or witnesses available at the time to pursue this line of inquiry.

After multiple suicide attempts while in custody, Christian David eventually pleaded guilty to the trafficking charges in the U.S. and successfully avoided extradition to France (and his likely execution there). He later offered to assist with investigations into heroin smuggling. He told his interrogators that the DEA had "screwed up the investigation" into Spector's allegations.[8]

Undercover Investigator Larry Spivey

One of the first witnesses to testify at the 1978 Coast Guard Hearings was Larry H. Spivey, a former undercover investigator with the Georgia Bureau of Investigation (GBI).[9] As a secret agent, Spivey had frequently traveled to Guatemala, Mexico, Jamaica, and other locations in Central and South America as part of the efforts by U.S. law enforcement agencies and the GBI to interdict the northward flow of narcotics. Spivey testified that, before meeting Spector, he worked on various state and federal cases, including those involving narcotics smuggling, counterfeiting, grand theft, prostitution, and gun running.

On April 27, 1977, Spivey first met with Spector after reviewing a book manuscript that Spector was trying to get published. Spivey introduced Spector to his publisher, who was about to publish a book on Spivey's exploits as an undercover narcotics agent. However, after reviewing Spector's manuscript, Spivey also felt that much of Spector's allegations and documentation warranted further investigation. Spivey decided to contact William Lynch, then head of the Organized Crime Division of the U.S. Department of Justice, to speak with him about Spector's claims.

During a telephone call, Spivey gave Lynch a thumbnail sketch of Spector's allegations. including his ex-wife's involvement in a major narcotics trafficking organization operating in the U.S. Spivey gave Lynch his opinion that there may be a great deal of truth to Spector's allegations. The basis for Spivey's endorsement of Spector's story was that he had recently received confirmation from low-level narcotics dealers about the existence and extensive operations of this French-Corsican syndicate.[10] Spivey had even received reliable information that the Unione Corse had its own fleet of aircraft to facilitate its narcotics trade.

Obviously intrigued, Lynch gave Spivey permission to contact Assistant U.S. Attorney James E. Baker, who was assigned to the U.S. Attorney's Office for the Northern District of Georgia. He urged Spivey to call him right away, which Spivey did. Baker and Spivey agreed to meet in a motel room that Spivey and his law enforcement colleagues used to make a series of arrests earlier in the day. After the other agents left, Baker told Spivey he had been briefed on Spivey's phone call with Lynch. He added that the "Mike Kalmbach" who Spivey had identified as approaching him about a drug deal was the son of Herbert W. Kalmbach, former President Nixon's attorney.[11] Baker said one of the highest priorities the U.S. Justice Department wanted to pursue in connection with the information provided by Spivey and Spector was whether Mike Kalmbach had any association with the shadowy French-Corsican drug syndicate.

In the intervening period, from 1972 to 1977, the White House changed hands twice, and the country was in considerable upheaval. In the wake of the Watergate scandal, Nixon resigned on August 8, 1974, and was replaced by his Vice-President, Gerald Ford. Democrat Jimmy Carter defeated Ford in the 1976 presidential election and was inaugurated on January 20, 1977, as the country's 39th President.

The Justice Department, working under the new Democratic administration, had a strong motivation to investigate Herbert Kalmbach's son. His father had been convicted in connection with several secret funds he controlled as finance chairman of the Committee to Re-elect the President (CREEP) during Nixon's 1972 re-election campaign. Herbert Kalmbach had served six months in jail and was fined $10,000 for operating an illegal campaign committee and illegally "selling" an ambassadorship in return for a $100,000 payment.[12] Kalmbach was later linked to a secret $500,000 fund used to finance sabotage and espionage operations under the direction of Donald H. Segretti, another Nixon lawyer.[13] He was also responsible for raising $220,000 in "hush money" to pay off the Watergate burglars.[14]

In addition to working with AUSA James Baker regarding Spector's allegations, on May 4, 1977, Spivey met with Steve McClintic, a DEA official who Spivey had been told had close ties to the White House. They met at the Army-Navy Club at 17 and "I" Streets in Washington, D.C. According to Spivey, McClintic "was agitated and extremely nervous."[15] Spivey asked McClintic if he would be willing "to cooperate with a highly enough placed task force in an investigation." McClintic agreed but startled Spivey by asking about "the possibility of immunity" for himself. Spivey could not even begin to imagine why McClintic—a past White House aide during the Nixon era—would feel that he needed a grant of immunity, unless, of course, McClintic had personal criminal involvement in the international drug conspiracy or "coverup" Spector talked about.

While in Washington, Spivey also met with Richard Ray, an aide to Senator Sam Nunn of Georgia. Ray suggested Spivey turn Spector's information over to Senator Jackson's Committee, which was investigating allegations of corruption and wrongdoing at the DEA. Spector and Spivey also went to see Owen Malone, chief counsel for the McClellan Committee, formally known as the U.S. Senate Select Committee on Improper Activities in the Labor or Management Field.

According to Spivey, the people he established contact with at these Congressional investigative committees agreed they had a serious "law enforcement problem on their hands," alluding to a possible coverup and corruption by the DEA. Richard Ray of Senator Nunn's office recommended that Spivey "turn the matter over to the Justice Department" and keep him and Senator Nunn "in the loop."[16] Mr. Ray then made an appointment for Spivey with Mike Egan, the Associate Attorney General.

That afternoon, Spivey met with Mike Egan and was introduced to the Deputy Attorney General, Peter F. Flaherty, and the Chief of the Criminal Division, Benjamin Civiletti. Flaherty introduced Spivey to William Tyson, an attorney with the Justice Department, with instructions that he should discuss the matter with Tyson. During the ensuing conversation, Spivey suggested that he could take Spector and some of his records to Atlanta to discuss the issue further with Jim Baker.

Assistant Attorney General Benjamin Civiletti in 1979. ("De Delegatie van de Verenigde Staten, in Het Midden Minister van Justitie Benjamin Civiletti | Nationaal Archief" n.d.)

Tyson agreed to this proposal and promised to get in touch with Jim Baker and authorize him to meet with Spivey and Spector.

The following Saturday morning, May 7, 1977, Spector and Spivey arrived in Atlanta, where they were met at Hartsfield Airport by Jim Baker and an FBI agent. At the U.S. Attorney's Office, they were also joined by an agent with the Bureau of Alcohol, Tobacco, and Firearms (ATF). They then began to debrief Spector and go through his material.

Their first marathon session lasted until 4 a.m. Sunday morning. Spector and Spivey then checked into the Intown Motor Inn nearby, and the two agents went home. Jim Baker joined them again the following day and continued the debriefing. Spector left Baker with copies of the material he had brought along and seven tape recordings. Spector and Spivey then took separate flights back to New York that evening. Before they left, Baker asked Spivey to get in touch with Owen Malone and ask him to send copies of the Jackson Committee hearing on Vesco and "anything else he thought would help."

Later, when Spector and Spivey testified at the Coast Guard hearings, Congressman Biaggi asked them whether he discussed his allegations with any "high government officials." In response, they confirmed that they had discussed the allegations with Mike Egan, the Deputy Attorney General, and with Ben Civiletti. Spivey specifically testified that Egan had directed Civiletti to "look into it."

Spivey also testified he had checked with Detective Sonny Grosso of the NYPD regarding Spector's allegations. According to Spivey, "Sonny was able to corroborate some of what Mr. Spector has alleged." Spivey also confirmed to the Coast Guard Subcommittee that he had been a contract employee of the CIA for many years. Unfortunately, he had no records to corroborate this, since he had been "paid in cash."

Since the U.S. Attorney's Office for the Southern District of New York had been involved in previous investigations of Spector's allegations in 1974 and 1975, Spivey took it upon himself to contact John "Rusty" Wing, one of the Assistant U.S. Attorneys in that office. A meeting was arranged between Spivey and Wing. According to Spivey's testimony, Wing's first question at the meeting was, "What do you know about Robert Vesco and the CIA?"[17] Spivey told him he knew very little, but that he and Spector strongly suspected efforts by the U.S. government to extradite Vesco had been intentially unsuccessful. Both Spivey and Spector strongly believed that there were powerful forces in the CIA, BNDD/DEA, and other U.S. agencies that did not want Vesco to be extradited for fear of what he would say. When Spivey asked if any further effort had been made to extradite Vesco, Wing vaguely assured him that another effort was "underway."

But when Spivey asked if Vesco's attorney had been in touch about a possible "deal," Wing smiled and said he couldn't say anything more.

Spivey then called Edward Bennett Williams, Vesco's attorney, and arranged a meeting at Williams' law office in Washington. At the meeting, Spivey – at Williams' suggestion - first "retained" Williams as his attorney for $1, so that the conversation would be subject to the attorney-client privilege. Spivey suggested to Williams that Jim Baker could be assigned "to look into" the issue of Vesco's extradition. Perhaps "some sorta deal" could be reached whereby Vesco could provide critical information in return for immunity or a favorable plea deal. Williams listened carefully, took some notes, but did not say much more than that he had been retained by Vesco for the sole purpose of "helping make his peace with the U.S. government." Spivey told Williams it was unlikely that the U.S. government would give Vesco "total immunity" in return for his testimony about corruption within the relevant U.S. agencies. Williams responded that Vesco wanted "the best deal he can get." Spivey then asked Williams if a meeting could be arranged between Baker and Vesco to determine the value of Vesco's knowledge and testimony (often referred to as a "proffer"). Williams assured him that such a meeting would be "extremely possible." Spivey concluded the meeting by promising to have Baker get in touch with Williams if the Justice Department decided to go ahead with such a meeting.

Baker then sent a memo up the chain of command in the Justice Department on June 1, 1977, asking for formal authorization to investigate the allegations raised by Spector and Spivey. Baker's memo recapped the findings made by Saffir and Buckley about a potential coverup at the DEA that had not been thoroughly investigated. He connected this to the DEA's mishandling of the Peroff-Vesco affair.

Baker also spoke to former lead Watergate Prosecutor Henry Ruth. Ruth indicated the DEA coverups may have had a CIA link, and that "cut-offs of DEA investigations" into Spector's claims occurred "because of national security and the possible exposure of CIA activities."[18] Baker concluded his memo by asking to be sent to Washington to investigate Spector's claims.

After waiting patiently for two weeks without an answer, Spivey decided to use his Georgia political connections with the Carter White

House to "get things moving." Carter had surrounded himself with a cadre of "good old boys" from Georgia who agreed to come to Washington to "shake things up" and maintain his aura of authenticity.

According to Spivey's testimony at the Coast Guard hearings, he made sure that President Carter, Hamilton Jordan (his chief advisor), and Frank Moore (Assistant to the President for Congressional Liaison) knew about Spector's allegations. In addition, the Justice Department was dragging its feet in investigating the matter.

Spivey also met with legendary Washington Post investigative reporter Jack Anderson and his chief assistant, Les Whitten. According to Spivey, they agreed to "raise hell if this thing got shoved under the carpet again."[19] He next contacted Everett Clark and Nick Harrock of Newsweek, Newsday bureau chief Marty Schramm, and Craig Hume of the Atlanta Constitution. Leaving no stone unturned, Spivey also briefed Senators Nunn and Talmadge and Senator Strom Thurmond, the ranking minority member of the Senate Judicial committee.

Attorney General Griffin Bell in 1977. Courtesy of the US Department of Justice.

Spivey and Spector then put together a list of 165 people, including addresses and phone numbers, who confirmed that they would be available to "testify concerning the various cases and the obstruction of justice." They sent the list to Attorney General Griffin Bell with an impassioned cover letter dated July 14, 1977, imploring him to reopen the investigation. In addition, they threatened if the Justice Department did not act expeditiously, they would make sure that it would be "tried by the House, the Senate or the press." In conclusion, Spivey signed off by writing: "I wish you the best of luck as Attorney General and God speed. Nothing would make me happier than to return my attention to my own business and let James Baker and the Justice Department continue working on this problem. I agree with your position on drugs and hope you agree with my opinion on the matter. William Spector's case is one of eight such cases, and I'm appalled that such a thing as has obviously happened can and did happen in our country."[20]

In response, the Narcotics and Dangerous Drugs section of the Justice Department requested that Jim Baker and Spivey come up to Washington and fill them in on Spector's allegations. The meeting, however, was destined to go poorly. On July 18, 1977, Baker and Spivey met with an attorney in the Office of Drug Abuse Law Enforcement named Tom O'Malley. O'Malley told them that the DEA had adequately investigated Spector's claim of a French-Corsican heroin smuggling ring in the past and that "there was really nothing to it."[21] As far as the DEA was concerned, the capture of August Ricord in 1972 had decapitated the Unione Corse.

Spivey, strongly sensing the Justice Department had no real interest in the investigation, pointedly asked O'Malley whether he would be personally involved in the investigation, and whether he was willing to "investigate his friends." In other words, Spivey accused O'Malley of being complicit in the coverup surrounding Spector's allegations. O'Malley told Spivey it was "none of his business" whether he would be investigating his colleagues or friends. So, Spivey refused to provide any of Spector's information to O'Malley or other D.O.J. officials whom he did not trust.

At this point, O'Malley brought Spivey to see William Lynch, the head of Narcotics and Dangerous Drugs at the D.O.J. Their conversation did not go any better. Spivey told Lynch that he expected an impartial investigation into Spector's claims and that this might require D.O.J. agents to disqualify themselves from investigating the case if it concerned their personal associates. Lynch, like O'Malley, refused to answer whether he would investigate his friends. He told Spivey to talk to his boss, Ben Civiletti, the Assistant Attorney General heading the Criminal Division at the D.O.J.

Civiletti told Spivey and Baker that he was too busy to meet with them and assigned them to meet with his Special Assistant, William

Brady. Brady, a veteran criminal investigator, was much less combative than his D.O.J. colleagues. He was sympathetic to Spector's claims because "John Bartels, former Director of the Drug Enforcement Administration, had barely missed being prosecuted when he was fired."[22] He assured Spivey he would attempt to get Baker assigned to investigate the Spector case. Further, Spivey should "not continue to press this thing and risk all that [he] stood to gain through the potential success" of his forthcoming book.[23] While Spivey took this as well-intentioned advice, in reality it was a veiled threat: if he continued to press for a full investigation of Spector's allegations, the U.S. government might figure out a way to "spike" his book deal, and it might never be published.

After meeting with Brady, Baker was called into a private meeting by Lynch and O'Malley. They accused Baker of being manipulated by Spector and Spivey, reiterating the line that the DEA had adequately investigated Spector's allegations and raked him over the coals for being so "gullible." O'Malley and Lynch pointed to Spivey's trip to Washington alongside Baker as "evidence" that Baker was sharing too much information with Spivey and Spector. This suspicion was groundless, however, since O'Malley himself had set up an appointment with Spivey, and Baker had not coordinated privately with Spivey in planning their trip. Nevertheless, in light of the increased hostility Baker was getting from his superiors at the D.O.J., Baker asked to withdraw from the case rather than risk ruining his promising career while chasing Spector's claims.

To mitigate any potential damage to his career, Baker wrote a voluminous letter to William Brady, Special Assistant to the Assistant Attorney General Ben Civiletti. In his letter, Baker stated that Lynch's conclusions about him being "captured" by Spector and Spivey were "without foundation."[24] He pointed out to Brady that the DEA's supposed 7000 hours investigating Spector's complaints was "impressive." But he raised the question of how the investigation was conducted, and the fact that many of the questions that were raised were left "unanswered."[25]

Baker concluded his letter by saying, "I cannot comprehend how any investigation [of Spector's claims] could proceed," but stopped short of recommending it be halted.[26]

> DEPARTMENT OF JUSTICE,
> Washington, August 18, 1977.
>
> Mr. LARRY H. SPIVEY,
> New York, N.Y.
>
> DEAR MR. SPIVEY: Your letter of July 14, 1977, to the Attorney General has been referred to this office for reply.
>
> Since this past spring, when you first brought to the attention of the Department of Justice your allegations of illegal acts and cover-ups in Federal narcotics enforcement, the Criminal Division has reviewed the investigation conducted some years ago when William Spector first made these small allegations. We have concluded that this earlier investigation was exceedingly vigorous and thorough. We concur in the conclusion reached at that time that the information in our possession is not a sufficient basis for any criminal prosecutions and does not warrant further investigation of this matter.
>
> You indicated in your recent interviews with Justice Department officials that you possess additional facts relevant to the Spector allegations. After more than two days of meetings, however, you have declined to provide any specific information to Criminal Division attorneys. In the absence of any new facts, the Criminal Division will abide by its earlier decision not to investigate the matter further. You may be interested to know that in a letter to me dated July 27, 1977, Assistant United States Attorney James E. Baker also recommended this result.
>
> Very truly yours,
>
> WILLIAM J. BRADY,
> Special Assistant to the Assistant
> Attorney General, Criminal Division.

Letter from William J. Brady to Larry H. Spivey, August 18, 1977. Quoted in Congress, House, Committee, Seaborne Drug Smuggling Problems, 62–63.

Spivey, who had not spoken with Baker since their trip, was greatly surprised when he received a response to his letter to the Attorney General from William J. Brady, Special Assistant, as follows:

One of several things unusual about Brady's letter was it ignored the fact that the Spector case was *just one of eight similar cases* pointing to DEA coverups that Spivey had brought to the attention of the Justice Department. Nevertheless, the letter only addressed what the Justice Department deemed to be the lack of merit of the Spector case. There was no mention of the other seven cases and whether or not they were properly investigated.

Secondly, the letter suggested that Jim Baker had made a negative recommendation regarding the Spector allegations. While Baker said he was "unaware of the existence of any evidence or witnesses" capable of proving Spector's claims, he never recommended that the investigation be terminated. As a highly skilled lawyer and careful writer, the purpose of Baker's letter to Brady was to artfully distance himself from Spivey's investigation. This made sense, given Spivey's bitter confrontation with D.O.J. officials. But he explicitly *did not* recommend the D.O.J. stop pursuing the Spector case.

When he testified before the Coast Guard Hearings, Jim Baker was asked by Congressman Biaggi whether he personally believed that Spector's allegations "merit further investigation."[27] Baker replied that, while he was "not trying to dodge the question," he did not know "whether I would investigate Spector's allegations. What I would first do would be to determine whether or not they had already been investigated." He reiterated that Spector had spent most of the decade requesting a proper investigation, and Baker expressed skepticism regarding the DEA's claim to have spent 7,000 hours investigating Spector's case. Baker also questioned the veracity of the DEA's claim that they had a large file on Spector. Despite repeated requests, the file had never been turned over to investigators outside the DEA.

Baker's healthy scepticism regarding the DEA's claim to have properly investigated Spector's allegations was strongly supported by the 1975 Buckley investigation, which established that the DEA's alleged "thorough investigation" into Spector's allegations was a figment of the agency's imagination. Buckley's 1975 investigation demonstrated that the DEA was suppressing evidence in the Spector case, such as the French police reports of 1971 and 1973. Baker also knew the DEA had done the same in the Vesco-Peroff affair. In that case, DEA agents refused to put Vesco's name down in writing after he was mentioned by an infamous heroin smuggler. The "bottom line" of Baker's preliminary investigation into Spector's claims showed the DEA sabotaged any

Democratic Congressman for the Bronx Mario Biaggi. Courtesy of U.S. Congress.

investigation that threatened Nixon, including his allies in the Unione Corse: Patricia Richardson and Paul-Louis Weiller.

In addition to his live testimony in response to questioning by Congressman Biaggi, Baker submitted a June 1 letter into the Committee's Congressional record, concluding that Senator Buckley's 1975 investigation into Spector and Senator Jackson's probe into the DEA's mishandling of the Vesco-Peroff affair supported his view that Spector's allegations had never been fully or properly investigated. In short, even though Baker knew that it would be personally perilous for him to continue pushing for a full investigation and feared reprisals from his superiors at the D.O.J., he still refused to publicly disavow Spector or say that the investigation should be closed.

Detective Stephen Balducci and the 1975 NYPD Investigation into Richardson

The Coast Guard hearings did not break much new ground concerning additional evidence against those at the top of the French-Corsican narcotics pyramid. The hearings did confirm, however, that no real effort had been made to gather evidence against the people and organizations providing the financing or running the supply chain of narcotics smuggled into the U.S.

Detective Stephen Balducci opened his statement at the Coast Guard hearings by asserting that Spector's case concerned people who were so powerful, insulated, and "untouchable" that they could never be properly investigated. He described them as "the people we never really arrest."[28] His testimony and that of Officer Gilbert "Sonny" Hight provided some insight into how their ability to fully investigate Spector's allegations had been restricted during the time that they had been assigned to work with the New York State Senate Select Committee on Crime. Balducci testified the NYPD officers working with the Committee coordinated almost exclusively with Leonard Saffir of Senator Buckley's office. The investigative materials they developed did not go into the NYPD's files or the databases of other law enforcement organizations, such as the DEA. This resulted in a complete lack of coordination with the ongoing DEA and other investigations regarding Spector's allegations. However, this had the beneficial effect of insulating the NYPD investigators from the pressure campaigns by the White House, CIA, and DEA that had halted previous investigations into Patricia Richardson and Paul-Louis Weiller.

At one point, the NYPD officers recounted how they "wired up" Spector to tape a conversation between himself and John Stevenhagen, who had lived with Patricia Richardson in St. Martin after she left Spector. During the undercover operation, the NYPD officers became aware that Spector was under surveillance by another law enforcement agency, which turned out to be the DEA. Spector was being followed by both DEA and NYPD officers. Oddly, neither force had prior knowledge of the other's active surveillance of Spector in New York City. This highlighted the lack of cooperation between federal and local law enforcement agencies regarding the investigation of Richardson, Weiller, and the drug smuggling operations of the Unione Corse in the U.S.

As Detective Balducci described it at the Coast Guard hearings:

> "This one particular day [Spector] walked up to Fifth Avenue and this fellow followed him, walked by him and another woman walked up and stood next to Spector. Across the street, another fellow appeared, took pictures, and then this woman crossed the street, walked away with the guy and jumped into a cab and took off. We followed the other fellow who originally followed him and this fellow went back to Mellon's. At that time we dropped that and picked up Spector."[29]

Detective Balducci and the NYPD squad assigned to the case found out later that while they were scouring New York for Patricia Richardson, the DEA had secreted her in a hotel room on the orders of DEA Group Supervisor John J. O'Neal. This caused quite a flurry. It was revealed that O'Neal and another DEA official, John Coleman, had picked up Patricia Richardson and kept her in hiding for an extended time. As a result, Richardson was unavailable for questioning by the NYPD officers assigned to line up the witnesses for the State Select Committee hearings.

Balducci further testified at the Coast Guard hearings that, despite making some arrests, "we never reached the top. We never really touched the people who supplied all the narcotics, who supplied all the financing for them." Balducci went on to say that, despite their hard work with the Buckley investigation, there was no follow-up. They never received instructions on how to follow up or whether there should be any follow-up investigation. This was despite a report dated August 1, 1975, concluding with the following recommendation to the NYPD

> 7. Due to the continuing investigation and the contradicting testimonies of the witnesses, which related generally to Patricia Martinson's movements in and out of the country, her possession of large amounts of U.S. Currency on several occasions, a conspiracy to have William Spector murdered and her acquaintance with various persons of questionable character, one of whom was Marcel Boucan who is currently serving a prison sentence in France for possession of over 900 pounds of pure heroin, and pending further developments, and direction from the Chief Counsel of the New York State Select Committee on Crime, and U.S. Senator Buckley, it is the opinion of the assigned investigators that the investigation remain active and I concur. All surveillance and investigative reports relative to this investigation are on file at the Intelligence Division.
> 8. For your information.
>
> JAMES B. MEEHAN,
> *Deputy Chief.*

James B. Meehan, "Update on Operation Sunshine," Quoted in Congress, House, Committee, Seaborne Drug Smuggling Problems, 87.

Deputy Commissioner to continue the investigation:

Ultimately, considering the lack of impetus from federal authorities, Officer Hight expressed pessimism about the likelihood of catching the kingpins of international drug smuggling:

> "We are very frustrated because organized crime is well organized. Your financier of narcotics is very well insulated. He never comes directly in contact with the drug himself. He deals through a right-hand man who deals through another one, and so on down the line. Money doesn't have a name on it …. So there is no way of really identifying these people."

Spector's Testimony

On July 27, 1978, Spector testified extensively at the Coast Guard hearing, detailing the information and assistance he had previously given to several Congressional committees.[30] He also testified about a request by Senator Robert Dole, asking whether he was the U.S. officer that had taken the surrender of the commanding general of the Hungarian 5th Army at the end of World War II. After confirming to

Senator Dole that he was, in fact, that U.S. officer, Spector explained to the Congressional panel at the Coast Guard hearings that he had been asked to testify at a federal court proceeding in Kansas City regarding the issue of whether the Crown of St. Stephan turned over to him and other U.S. officers should be returned to Hungary.

Spector explained to Congressman Biaggi and the other subcommittee members that the commanding general of the Hungarian forces fighting a rear-guard action at the time had custody of the Crown of St. Stephan, which to Hungary represented the equivalent of the U.S.'s Declaration of Independence. As Spector explained it, "Hungarian history and legend has it that whoever owns that crown or has possession of that crown is the legitimate king of Hungary. It is a symbolic symbol." When Russian forces tried to penetrate the area, Spector and the U.S. forces with him "turned them back." The crown was then transferred to the Isle of Capri, off Naples in Italy, and then brought to the United States where it was deposited in Fort Knox, Kentucky. In 1978, Jimmy Carter ordered that the U.S. return the Crown to the people of Hungary, despite protest from the Hungarian-American diaspora who feared it falling into Communist hands.

At the hearings, Spector also discussed assisting the Senate Government Operations Permanent Investigations Subcommittee regarding the "Peroff-Vesco affair." Spector stated that he provided the Committee with information showing who at the DEA had hired Frank Peroff. Spector claimed Steve McClintic and Kevin Gallagher of BNDD - the U.S. government principals who directed Peroff's activities - had "cut him loose" after he insisted that Vesco was involved in the major drug deal under investigation.

Spector also testified as to how he had worked closely with the Watergate Special Prosecutor's Office. He explained he provided the office with information surrounding the cash contributions from Paul-Louis Weiller and others to the Nixon campaign. Spector also recounted that after the "Saturday Night Massacre," Assistant Watergate Prosecutor Carl Feldbaum called him. Feldbaum informed Spector they were turning his "conspiracy case" over to the U.S. Attorney's Office for the Southern District of New York. Spector thought this meant a decision had been made to pursue the investigation into the illegal contributions made by Weiller and others to the Nixon campaign. He felt certain the New York federal prosecutors would be pursuing it as a conspiracy case.[31]

However, when Spector was asked by a member of the Committee about what happened to the federal prosecutor's investigation in New York, all Spector could say was, "To date–nothing, except certain material of mine, was subpoenaed by the grand jury. Other witnesses were subpoenaed by the grand jury. Certain of that material—as a matter of fact, the material which was submitted and taken from me by the grand jury–later was found reposing with the Drug Enforcement Administration in their offices in New York City with the group headed by a man by the name of John Coleman."[32]

In response to Congressman Biaggi's question about who he spoke to at the DEA, Spector identified John Coleman and a "Mr. Doonan," an investigator with the U.S. Attorney's Office. According to Spector, the response he got was as follows: "Sir, we have our own methods," suggesting that they did not want to make Spector privy to the specifics of the investigation they were conducting.

Spector also gave the Committee the details on how his ex-wife left him and what she had left behind. He said that after he had been gone from the house for only a few hours, he found the house had been cleaned out upon his return. However, he testified that he found "a certain series of what I call diaries" and that they contained a list of names, some of which Spector knew. But others were names of people he had no idea Patricia Richardson knew or had been involved with. According to Spector, the most notable of the unfamiliar names was that of Yusef Beidas, President of Intra Bank. Information regarding Paul-Louis Weiller was also written down, along with references to Marcel Boucan and others known to be drug smugglers. After Spector read his name, a check on Beidas showed he had run Intra Bank from Beirut, Lebanon. It disclosed that he had been indicted for "bank fraud, white slavery, and heroin smuggling."[33] In response to Congressman Biaggi's question about the outcome of the charges against Beidas, Spector replied: "He was murdered." According to Spector, Richardson's diary showed that she had been with Beidas when he was attacked. Like in a James Bond movie, they had "escaped by the laundry chute."

Spector further postulated that Beidas had been murdered by Eduardo Baroudi. Although the official report of Beidas' death described it as a "suicide or heart attack," the CIA apparently considered it a homicide.[34]

Spector also testified that his ex-wife's papers included the name of Robert Abramovici. The latter Spector claimed he had known of since his days working as an OSS agent. Spector said Abramovici (who also used the alias "Robert Adam") "was involved in gun running, money changing, and other matters touching on affairs which are still classified top secret today." Abramovici became a famous arms dealer after helping negotiate the Czech-Israeli arms shipments of 1947-1949.[35]

Spector also testified that the name of Marcel Boucan was mentioned in his ex-wife's papers. This was the same person whose shrimp boat, the *Caprice de Temps*, had been seized with a record-breaking cache of heroin off the coast of Marseille by French authorities. Also mentioned was the name of Henri Helle, the owner of the Pirate Hotel in the French West Indies, who was a known smuggler dating back to the 1950s.

Spector explained that the French police had issued a report regarding Boucan, Helle, and "a woman by the name of Patricia Richardson." This report was given to the BNDD in April 1971. However, multiple DEA agents who worked on Spector's case testified before State Senate Select Committee hearings in 1975 to have never seen it before. Spector also said that he had in his possession "a picture from 1964 tying a Paul-Louis Weiller to Marcel Boucan and to Patricia Richardson," which he gave to the Committee as evidence. However, it was not made publicly available in the hearing records.

When questioned about the financial kingpin of the Unione Corse, Spector's answer was unequivocal: "Paul-Louis Weiller—to the best of my knowledge—is the key financier of the international drug syndicate."

Spector further testified about his knowledge of the yacht *Samana*, owned by James Frankel, the C.E.O. of Resorts International, which had a resort in the Bahamas, also bearing the name "Samana." Spector informed the Committee that Frankel's wife, Nicole, "was given in marriage to James Frankel by Paul-Louis Weiller." According to Spector, the yacht *Samana* was seized off the coast of Puerto Rico in 1971 with a load of marijuana "emanating from the French West Indies." Soon thereafter, Nicole got into a fight with her friend Patricia Richardson at the St. Martin airport. After seeing that Richardson was wearing her stolen clothing, as detailed in chapter two of this book, Nicole Frankel told NYPD investigators in 1975 that Patricia Richardson and herself had both been "protégés" of Paul Louis Weiller. She also testified that Richardson was an international jewelry smuggler involved in a scheme to move gems into the U.S. from Mexico.[36]

Finally, Spector presented the Committee with a map pinpointing "proved and known narcotic and banking routes used by the Weiller group, ranging from Hong Kong to Paris, France." This map depicted "the narcotics and financial activities radiating from France into the French West Indies, pointing north to Canada and the United States, links extending from the Middle East and Hong Kong." According to Spector, "top leaders of international cartels have so injected themselves into international banking and business that no attempt has been made to expose them. One will find that there are no Mafia, as such, in the top echelon of organized crime. Instead, one must look to a man called Paul-Louis Weiller, associated with the Unione Corse of France."[37]

The testimony of another witness, John Coleman, who had previously testified at the State Senate Select Committee hearings in 1975, was introduced at the 1977 Coast Guard hearings.[38] Coleman testified about a search of the residence in Guadeloupe where drug trafficker Boucan frequently resided before the seizure of a large stash of heroin aboard his ship uncovered a piece of paper with the handwritten name "Richardson" on it. Coleman further testified that they found marine navigation charts aboard Boucan's boat, the *Caprice des Temps*. The majority covered the French West Indies and the area of the waters surrounding the Miami peninsula. They correctly assumed that the vessel was headed from Marseille in that direction with its secret cargo of heroin. The most likely route would have been through the Straits of Gibraltar, down through the Canary Islands, and then crossing from the Canaries to the West Indies. Coleman said that, at that time of the year, the waters were very calm and suitable for the vessel to cross.

Boucan admitted to making two previous trips across the Atlantic, each time carrying 100 kilograms of heroin from France to the United

States by way of the West Indies, and each time coming into Miami and up the Miami River and discharging at a commercial boatyard.

McClintic Testifies Against Spector

Stephen McClintic also testified at the Coast Guard hearings. It was a thinly veiled attempt by the federal agencies that had suppressed Spector's allegations to destroy Spector's reputation and to irreparably smear him.[39] McClintic was particularly critical of Spector's dealings with the Watergate Special Prosecutor's Office. He testified that "Spector, in his efforts to get attention at whatever level he could, would naturally reach as high as he could…. That is what led him to Archibald Cox's office and Mr. Jaworski's office, to get attention wherever he could."[40]

McClintic also expressed disbelief about Spector's testimony that Weiller and Nixon had a longstanding relationship and that they had at least several meetings together. However, an increasing amount of evidence was coming to the attention of the Congressional committee about this relationship between Weiller, Richardson and Nixon. For example, Patricia Richardson's landlady, Leta Meyers, swore in an affidavit that Richardson had boasted to her of being present at a meeting between Paul-Louis Weiller and Nixon. Richardson showed Meyer a photo of her with Weiller and Nixon and said, "she saw big money pass between these two men."[41] Meyers' testimony, which had been made without Spector's prompting, strongly reinforced his claim that Richardson had, in fact, witnessed the illegal cash transaction between Weiller and Nixon.

McClintic, despite being considered a key figure in the case by Spivey and Spector, was not thoroughly questioned by Representative Biaggi or the other House committee members. Although Spivey alleged McClintic had asked about the possibility of immunity for cooperating with an investigation, the Committee never asked McClintic about this. Nor was McClintic questioned about the DEA files he had produced to Senator Buckley's office in 1975, which were later suppressed by the DEA. Most notably, Leonard Saffir had testified in 1975 that McClintic himself proved that DEA Director John Bartels Jr. had lied to Buckley's office and the State Senate Committee on Crime concerning his contacts with the Watergate Special Prosecutor's office. Nevertheless, McClintic was not asked at the Coast Guard hearings about what really happened to those "missing" DEA records and whether he knew of their whereabouts.

After his brief testimony condemning Spector, McClintic retired from the stand and disappeared from public life. He died in 1991 and is buried at Arlington National Cemetery.

***

Although the 1978 Coast Guard hearings shed some additional light on Spector's allegations, they ended inconclusively. No clear record could serve as a basis for a criminal indictment of Patricia Richardson, like all the other investigations of Weiller, Nixon, or anyone else. While the members of Congress conducting the hearings expressed interest in Spector's claims, they failed to meaningfully question McClintic, despite the numerous inconsistencies between his hearing testimony and prior statements on the subject. With the conclusion of these hearings, Spector's case was never again investigated by any relevant authorities.

Conclusion

William H. Spector died a frustrated and bitter man on September 21, 1995, at St. Joseph's Hospital in Syracuse, New York. He remained alienated from his children with Patricia Richardson, who was not even mentioned in his obituary. He had spent the last 23 years of his life seeking some degree of justice and retribution against an ex-wife. She had turned his life upside down and used his Cadillac-Oldsmobile dealership to transport narcotics undetected across the U.S.-Canadian border. She had utterly destroyed his flourishing car dealership by manipulating the business's financial records to carry out a massive bank fraud. Spector suffered the ignominy and humiliation of being charged and convicted of the scam. No one believed that Patricia Richardson could carry out such a sophisticated fraud scheme without his knowledge.

Spector's longstanding campaign to expose the ties Weiller and Richardson had with the French-Corsican mob and heroin trafficking was never able to get off the ground, despite attention from several Congressional investigations, a significant commitment of resources and political capital by Senator Buckley's office, and at least one New York State Senate investigation. After all this, Spector's reputation was left in tatters. The FBI, DEA, and other federal and state agencies closed ranks, labeling him a deranged "psycho" who should not be taken seriously.

Jerry Barsha, Spector's friend, and longtime Syracuse radio and TV journalist, died at the Cleveland Clinic on September 10, 2009. In the end, Barsha firmly believed that Spector's story was true. The fact his hard-hitting and intrepid coverage of the story was not followed up by other media outlets didn't shake his confidence in the quality of his reporting. Barsha was a maverick for most of his career and disdained "herd" journalism. This kind of coverage led many reporters to only cover stories that everyone else was reporting on. Without question, herd journalism was certainly a factor in the decisions by most media outlets to ignore Spector's allegations and the substantial evidence supporting it. Robin Moore, an acknowledged expert on French organized crime and its multi-faceted approach to the trafficking of narcotics into the U.S., voiced his unequivocal endorsement of Spector's story. But even this high profile endorsement was not enough to break the "code of silence" that every federal investigation agency was enforcing.

Meanwhile, Patricia Richardson, Paul-Louis Weiller, and the Unione Corse flourished under the protection of the CIA and its French government equivalent. In contrast, the DEA continued its focus on Mexican, Colombian, and other drug cartels that were the major competitors of the Marseille-based French-Corsican syndicate.

Weiller died in Geneva, Switzerland, on December 6, 1993, at the ripe old age of 100. He was mourned throughout Europe as a French national hero and one of the great industrialists, philanthropists, and arts patrons in the post-World War II era. No mention was made, of course, in any of the many obituaries and biographies written about him regarding his leadership position in the Unione Corse and the fact that he was an international drug kingpin.

Although she has been out of sight for many years, it is said that Patricia Richardson Martinson lives a quiet life of elegance in her villa in St. Martin. Now in her 70's, she apparently still makes occasional trips to Paris and New York to do some shopping and to visit her wide circle of wealthy and distinguished friends. It is doubtful she thinks too often of Spector and his crusade to expose her and her organization. I suppose when she does give it a fleeting thought, a smile must come to her lips. She had been forced to face so many Congressional committees, investigators, and reporters. Yet, no one seemed to be able to lay a glove on her. She had outwitted them all.

Who says that crime doesn't pay?

Chronology

1914–1918 (World War I)

- Paul–Louis Weiller becomes one of France's top aviators and heavily decorated war hero.

1922

- Paul–Louis Weiller and his partner, designer Marcel Bloch, take over and reinvigorate the famous Societe Gnome et Rhône motor works.
- Weiller marries Princess Alexandra Ghika, a member of the Romanian nobility.

1925

- Weiller acquires Companie Internationale de Navigation Aerienne (CIDNA) and establishes the first regular European commercial flights.

1930

- U.S. Federal Bureau of Narcotics established within US Treasury Department.

1932

- Weiller and Princess Ghika are divorced. Weiller marries the world-famous Greek model and Miss Europa 1931, Alika Deplarakou.

- Weiller is briefly jailed after being accused of conspiring to transfer stock in the French Aeropostale company to Deutsche Lufthansa, Germany's flag carrier.

1933

- Weiller joins the Board of Directors of Air France.

1940

- After Nazi Germany overruns France, Weiller is arrested by the French Vichy government and stripped of his French citizenship.

1942

- Weiller escapes from prison, fleeing first to Morocco, then to Cuba, Mexico, and Canada. He eventually joins the Free French forces under General Charles de Gaulle in London and soon becomes de Gaulle's financier.

- INTERPOL headquarters is moved to Berlin. The agency comes under control of two Nazi Gestapo officers, Ernst Kaltenbrunner and Reinhard Heydrich.

- French Resistance fighters machine gun the HQ of pro–German PPF in downtown Marseille.

1943

- Corsican resistance cells begin an uprising against the Nazi occupation of the island.

1944

- Weiller gains entry to the US at the request of the Soviet Union.

- Weiller returns to Cuba, where he establishes a working relationship with mob leaders Meyer Lansky, Santos Trafficante, and Carlos Gambino.

- Lt. William H. Spector is assigned to a secret intelligence unit of the OSS in Bucharest, Romania.

- The Battle to liberate Marseille starts in August 1944. Barthélemy Guérini of the Unione Corse supplies intelligence, arms, and men to Gaston Defferre's Socialist militia.

- CRS (Compagnies Republicaines de Securite) is formed, primarily by communist resistance fighters, to restore public order and round up Nazi collaborators.

1945

- In April, a left-wing coalition wins the mayoral race in Marseille, electing Gaston Defferre as mayor of Marseille.

- In June, Navy legal officer Lt. Richard Nixon reviews the wartime record of Karl Blessing.

- The French–Corsican syndicate (Unione Corse) and members of the Roman Catholic clergy (led by Croatian Franciscan priest Father Krunoslav Draganović) establish the "Ratline" to smuggle high level ex–Nazis to South America

- In August, U.S. Intelligence officers arrange for Nazi Lt. General Reinhard Gehlen to be transported to the US.

- In September, following V–Day and the end of World War II in Europe, Lt. William Spector and other U.S. wartime intelligence operatives are asked to stay on in Europe to help with the process of denazification and to secure control of as many Nazi scientists and secrets as possible before the Soviets can get them.

1946

- In January, President Truman establishes the National Intelligence Authority, the successor to the OSS and direct precursor to the CIA.

- In June, France volunteers to host a revived INTERPOL. Many ex–Nazis and Vichy French Nazi collaborators continue working with the organization.

- In November, the Communist candidate for mayor of Marseille is elected.

- Richard Nixon is elected as a Republican candidate for the U.S. Congress from his home district in California.

1947

- Paul–Louis Weiller returns to his villa in Provence, France. He re-organizes Air France and is appointed as a director of several major French companies, including Renault, Michelin, and Peugeot.

- French–Corsican operatives of the Unione Corse travel to the U.S. to establish a Marseille–New York heroin trafficking network.

- Congressman Richard Nixon joins the House Un–American Activities Committee (HUAC).

- In October, municipal elections in Marseille lead to the election of conservative candidate Michel Carlini as mayor.

- On November 12, protestors in Marseille gather to demand the release of sheet metal workers arrested for attacking a tram. Two workers escape police custody. A large crowd of demonstrators gathers outside Marseille city hall and storm the waterfront areas controlled by the Guerini mob, who are viewed as anti–union. Multiple demonstrators are wounded, and one is killed.

- On November 13, the Communist newspaper *La Marseillaise*'s posts a headline denouncing the conservative mayor Carlini of Marseille, and alleging that Guerini's men had attacked municipal councilors and protestors.

- The local labor confederation calls a general strike, bringing Marseille to a standstill.

- On November 14, the Leftist labor confederation CGT calls for a national general strike, and by the end of the month, 3 million French workers are on strike.

- On November 16, two police officers testify to seeing the Guerini brothers shooting into the crowd of protesters, but then retract their testimony after receiving death threats.

- U.S. Intelligence Agents William Spector, E. Howard Hunt and James Angleton are ordered to go to Marseille to do whatever was necessary to open the port up to shipping.

- In late November, the Marseille Accord is struck between Gaullist French conservatives represented by Paul-Louis Weiller, the CIA represented by James Angleton and William Spector, and the Unione Corse syndicate controlled by the Guerini clan. Force Ouvriere, an anti-communist labor union, is formed with CIA funding.

- On December 9, the Marseille general strike is abandoned.

- On December 10, charges are dropped against the Guerini brothers for allegedly shooting into the crowd.

1948

- In May, Congressman Nixon co-sponsors the "Mundt-Nixon Bill" to combat "internal communist subversion."

- In August, Nixon gains national prominence as a HUAC member breaking the Alger Hiss spy case, where former State Department official Whittaker Chambers alleged that Hiss, a former US official, was a Soviet spy and had received secret documents and microfilm hidden in a pumpkin patch.

- In November, the presidential election defeat of New York Governor Thomas Dewey, the Republican candidate, to President Truman is blamed on the Democrat-leaning "Jewish vote." Republicans formulate a plan to counter with the "Ethnic vote" of Eastern European immigrants to the U.S., including ex-Nazis, Fascists, and anti-Soviets.

Ex–Waffen SS, fascists, Croatian ex–Nazis, and pro–fascists are courted by the Republicans, especially by Richard Nixon.

1950

- Senator Joseph McCarthy of Wisconsin takes up the anti–Communist cause. He starts a "Red Scare" by alleging that there were thousands of closet Communists and Communist sympathizers in the military and the US government.

1952

- In preparation for the 1952 Eisenhower–Nixon campaign, Nixon and the Republicans form an "Ethnic Division" in the Party. They recruit displaced Fascists, anti–Communists, and ex–Nazis who are in the U.S. Nixon wins the support of ex–Romanian industrialist Nicolae Malaxa, who has a close relationship with Romania's Nazi regime and who escaped to the U.S. with over $200 million in U.S. dollars. To get the money "unfrozen," Malaxa receives legal support from Sullivan & Cromwell, which has close ties to the Dulles brothers. Nixon helps Malaxa form a corporate "front," Western Tube Corp., based in California. Western Tube and its officers become some of Nixon's major financial donors.

1953

- U.S. Col. Edward G. Lansdale makes a six–week tour of Indochina for the CIA. He reports that French officers bought the entire annual opium harvest for sale and export from Saigon. Dubbed "Operation X," this opium trafficking operation involves the Unione Corse and French intelligence officers. The opium is transported by ship to Marseille. It is then converted to heroin in labs throughout the city and its suburbs and shipped to the U.S. and other North and South American markets.

1957

- In January, Howard Hughes loans $205,000 to bail Donald A. Nixon–Richard Nixon's brother–out of a failed "Nixon's drive-in restaurant" venture in Whittier, California. It is suspected that Hughes made the loan to get closer to then Vice President Richard Nixon.

1960

- The Ogdensburg Bridge is built over the St. Lawrence Seaway, separating the U.S. and Canada. It quickly becomes the chief conduit used by Patricia Richardson and her cohorts in the Unione Corse for the flow of narcotics stashed in automobiles coming across the Canadian–U.S. border.
- In November, Nixon loses a close presidential race to Democrat John F. Kennedy.

The early 1960s

- Patricia Richardson arrives in Paris from St. Martin to pursue a modeling career and rise up the Unione Corse's international drug operations ladder. She soon becomes the "protégé" of Paul–Louis Weiller, using his connections with Air France to establish heroin trafficking routes from Paris to Montreal and other major cities.
- Weiller creates the Stewart Modeling Agency in Paris, partly to provide Richardson a platform for her modeling career. It also is used by the Unione Corse to expand their heroin trafficking network.

1962

- In November, Nixon loses a close campaign for Governor of California to Democrat Pat Brown.

1965

- On March 14, Nixon meets with Weiller at a dinner party hosted by John Shaheen, an oil executive and major Republican donor. Nixon sends Weiller a letter the following day to arrange for another meeting in Paris.

- In June, Nixon joins Weiller in Rome for the wedding of his son, Paul–Annik Weiller, to Olimpia Torliona, the granddaughter of the Spanish Queen Victoria Eugenia.

1968

- On July 13, Patricia Richardson, Paul–Louis Weller, Bebe Rebozo, and Richard Nixon dine at La Côte Basque restaurant in Manhattan and seal a $2 million cash donation for Nixon's presidential campaign.

- On November 5, Richard Nixon is elected President, defeating Vice President Hubert Humphry. Nixon relies heavily on recruited ex-Nazis and fascists for his 1968 campaign, including war criminal Ivan Docheff, the head of the "American Friends of the Anti–Bolshevik Block of Nations" (ABN). Docheff is invited with other ex-Nazis and fugitive fascists to a "prayer meeting" at the White House to celebrate "Captive Nations Week."

1969

- The book, *The French Connection*, written by Robin Moore, is published. It recounts the notorious "French Connection" case in 1963, where two NYPD Detectives investigated a drug trafficking scheme involving hidden bags of heroin in an automobile imported from France. The book was later used as the basis of the famous movie of the same name, released in 1971, starring Gene Hackman.

- On January 20, Richard Nixon is sworn in as the 37th President of the United States. His best friend and bagman, Bebe Rebozo, moves into the White House shortly thereafter to act as unofficial liaison with Cuban and Italian mob bosses and the Unione Corse.

Nixon soon announces his "War on Drugs," aimed at suppressing the black community, anti-war activists, and the Mexican and South American cartels threatening the Unione Corse's grip on the international heroin trade.

- On September 21, Nixon's White House tries to prove it is "tough on crime" by launching "Operation Intercept" along the Mexican border. It is a massive "stop and search" operation designed to crush or impede drug flow from Mexico, which was interfering with the more established Unione Corse narcotics operations.

- In November, Spector and Patricia Richardson are married, moving to Ogdensburg, New York.

- The Unione Corse successfully expands its heroin smuggling operations on the U.S.–Canadian border by using Spector's Cadillacs and other vehicles to move heroin from Montreal over the Canadian border to New York and other points on the East Coast of the U.S.

1970

- In October, Congress passes the Comprehensive Drug Abuse Prevention and Control Act.

1972

- After Patricia Richardson leaves him, Spector complains about his ex-wife and her narcotics trafficking to local police, Syracuse police, New York State Bureau of Criminal Investigation, U.S. Customs and Immigration and Naturalization Service (INS), and the Bureau of Narcotics and Dangerous Drugs.

- In March, Marcel Boucan is arrested in Marseille with the largest heroin haul to date: over 450kg of pure heroin worth billions. The arrest is "authorized" by the Unione Corse because Boucan's "freelance" operation did not have their approval.

- During the summer, the Bureau of Narcotics and Dangerous Drugs (BNDD) inspection unit uncovers BNDD's involvement with CIA-sponsored drug operations in Latin America. BNDD Director Ingersoll and CIA Director Helms concoct a scheme to disband the BNDD inspection unit and replace it with a new "counter–intelligence" unit within BNDD staffed primarily by CIA officers who continue to report to the CIA.

- On June 17, the White House "Plumbers" break-in at the Democratic Party headquarters in the Watergate complex. A few days later, The Washington Post reports the connection between the Watergate burglars to former CIA Agent E. Howard Hunt and Nixon's Special Counsel Charles Colson.

- In November an investigation of French–Corsicans in South America reveals information about a vehicle with drugs being shipped to New York. The Unione Corse organization running the smuggling operation is headed up by Christian David, a French–Corsican with close ties to Richardson and Weiller. However, David refuses to "rat" on the organization's higher–ups, although he claims the JFK assassination was carried out by the French–Corsican mob. This story became the basis for the 1988 TV documentary, *The Men Who Killed Kennedy*. David also confirms to U.S. investigators that the DEA "screwed up" the investigation of Spector's allegations.

- Mary Jo Ottman travels with Patricia Richardson to St. Martin. When she returns to the U.S., her bags are packed by Richardson, and when she lands at JFK Airport in New York, her bags are unpacked by Richardson's associate, Louis Marcel, a Pan Am agent. He takes a valuable necklace from Ottman's bag after assaulting her.

- On November 22, *La Samana*, a boat owned by James L. Frankel (husband of Patricia's friend), is seized off Puerto Rico with a large stash of marijuana, but Mr. Frankel is never charged.

1973

- Spector complains to the Watergate Special Prosecutor's staff about Patricia Richardson and the absence of any real federal investigation of her organized crime and narcotics trafficking connections.

- In February, U.S. financier Robert Vesco flees the country to avoid arrest on security fraud charges. Vesco spends the next 15 years on the run, moving from one Central American country to the next. He makes arrangements for significant cash contributions to President Nixon through Nixon's nephew, Donald A. Nixon. While in Central America, Vesco establishes close ties with Richardson, Weiller, and other Unione Corse top leadership members.

- Vesco, Richardson, and Weiller meet at Norman's Cay in the Bahamas, the private island of Carlos Lehder Rivas, a German–Colombian drug lord, neo–Nazi, and co–founder of the Medellin Cartel. They establish a working relationship between their two organizations, and both agree to use Norman's Cay as a transit point for narcotics trafficking. Weiller and Richardson authorize their Montreal organization to work with Vesco on financing various heroin deals.

- In July, smuggler–turned–informant Frank Peroff records a phone call with Montreal mobster Bouchard. He tells Peroff that Vesco is providing the financial backing for a major heroin deal that Peroff was supposedly working on. Peroff turns the tape recording over to U.S. narcotics agents. This information, however, is never included in official reports since no one in the Nixon White House, Justice Dept., or any other federal agency want Vesco to be apprehended and placed in U.S. custody, for of fear what he might disclose about the CIA and White House's association with the Unione Corse and other organized crime groups.

- On July 1, the same day that Nixon is forced to endure the humiliation of ending the U.S. involvement in Vietnam, he issues an Executive Order creating the DEA without Congressional authorization. By signing "Reorganization Plan No. 2", Nixon–with the stroke of a pen—begins a brand—new law enforcement apparatus empowering the executive branch to operate domestically and overseas.

- On July 18, Peroff—now worried he was being sabotaged by the CIA—attempts to contact the Watergate Special Prosecutor Archibald Cox. Hearing nothing back, he follows DEA instructions to fly to Costa Rica to meet with LeBlanc and Vesco. He was directed to pick up the money for the heroin deal, fly to Europe to meet Bouchard and exchange the money for heroin, then fly back to North America.

- On July 22, Peroff's travel plans are interrupted when he is arrested in New York on some old warrants pending with Orange County Sheriff's office in Orlando, Florida. He is transported to the Queens County House of Detention, and is only later released to DEA custody after promising to "cooperate" with the DEA and "do what he was told." The DEA stops providing protection to Peroff and his family, even though his cover as an undercover informant has been blown.

- On October 20, the "Saturday Night Massacre" occurs when President Nixon orders U.S. Attorney General Elliot Richardson to fire Special Prosecutor Archibald Cox, who was investigating the Watergate break–in and its connections to the Nixon White House. Richardson refuses to fire Cox and resigns instead. Nixon then orders Deputy Attorney General William Ruckelshaus to fire Cox, but Ruckelshaus refuses and resigns. Solicitor General Robert Bork then carries out the order to fire Cox. A firestorm of protest erupts in Congress and across the country.

- On October 21, the morning after the "Saturday Night Massacre," William Spector speaks by phone with Henry Ruth, Archibald Cox's chief assistant. Ruth tells Spector that they are locked out of their offices and that he should call Carl Feldbaum, another lawyer working with the Special Prosecutor's office. When Spector calls Feldbaum, he is informed that the Nixon White House is trying to cover up or destroy any documents incriminating President Nixon. These documents include Spector's information on the cash payoffs made to the Nixon presidential campaigns in 1968 and 1972, as well as the connections that Nixon and Rebozo had with organized crime and ex–Nazis. Feldman suggests that Spector leave the country and "lie low" for a while.

- In late October, Spector flies to Caracas, Venezuela, paying cash for his ticket in the hope of avoiding detection. However, his reservation is tracked by the NCIS computer interlocks with the airline reservation systems. His departure from the U.S. and destination is reported to the FBI, the Washington DC police, and other law enforcement agencies. Arriving in Caracas, Spector receives an "urgent" message from the U.S. Embassy, telling him to return to the U.S. to meet with Senator Henry Jackson, Chairman of the Senate Governmental Committee

- On October 30, the Nixon impeachment process gets started in Congress.

- On November 1, Leon Jaworski is appointed as the new special prosecutor.

- In late November, Spector joins forces with Newsweek reporter Everett Clark, who has reported on Nixon's ties to organized crime.

- On December 26, Spector meets in Washington, D.C. with investigators from Senator Jackson's Committee, who tell him that the White House denied any knowledge of "Steve McClintic" ever being on the White House staff or liaising with the DEA.

1974

- Spector provides information to the U.S. Attorney's Office, Southern District of New York about Patricia Richardson and the cover–up by federal investigators of the connections that organized crime has with the CIA and federal narcotics law enforcement organizations.

- The DEA wiretaps Spector's phone, despite publicly denying that they were conducting any investigation of him and his claims of corruption and cover–ups by the DEA and other federal agencies.

- On March 23, Carl Feldbaum of the Special Prosecutor's office tells Spector that his office is "bogged down" in the legal battle over the disclosure of the Watergate tapes the Nixon White House was refusing to turn over. Spector is told that the U.S. Attorney's Office for the Southern District of New York is taking over the investigation of his allegations.

- On late March, Spector meets in Manhattan with Asst. U.S. Attorney John "Rusty" Wing, lead attorney in the Mitchell, Stans, and Vesco case. Spector gives him critical documents, tape recordings, and a world map pinpointing every bank and flight route used by the Unione Corse.

- Spector meets with Senator James Buckley's chief assistant, Leonard Saffir, who takes Spector's allegations seriously regarding Spector's ex-wife's involvement with heroin trafficking and the BNDD/DEA's mishandling of the case.

- On May 27–Memorial Day weekend 1974–Spector meets with Steve McClintic on Nantucket Island, off the coast of Massachusetts. McClintic tells Spector that he had prepared a letter in response to Archibald Cox requesting Spector's DEA files. However, the letter was never sent to the Special Prosecutor's office, and the DEA never sent Spector's files to them. McClintic further confirms that the Unione Corse's drug operations were "off limits for national security reasons." McClintic finally admits to Spector that his actual employer was the CIA.

- On August 9, Richard Nixon resigns as President of the US and is replaced by his Vice President, Gerald Ford.

- On August 10, Jerry Barsha of Syracuse TV 3 news breaks the story that Spector's Cadillac dealership in Ogdensburg, NY, was used by Richardson to smuggle vast quantities of drugs. Barsha also interviews Robin Moore, who gives Spector his wholehearted endorsement.

- On August 11, Moore says during a TV interview with Barsha, "it is my opinion that [Spector] has uncovered and exposed the real French Connection at last."

- On August 24, Barsha reports during his TV 3 news broadcast that federal authorities had seized a third airplane belonging to fugitive financier Vesco and that some of the material taken from Vesco's plane connected to Vesco's financing of a drug smuggling conspiracy across the Canadian border into New York.

- On September 1, Barsha's news broadcast raises a connection between the Watergate burglary and Spector's allegations of an international narcotics conspiracy with links reaching the Nixon White House and a $2 million cash "contribution" to Nixon's 1968 presidential campaign.

1975

- On February 9, Barsha reports in his TV 3 broadcast that the indictment of Yusef Beidas of Intra Bank on charges of heroin smuggling, gun running, and human trafficking.

- On February 23, Spector appears before a St. Lawrence County judge for sentencing after a jury found him guilty on fraud charges relating to a bank loan to his car dealership. Spector blames the financial fraud on his ex-wife Richardson, but the jury does not believe him.

- In March, the Jackson Committee report criticizes the DEA response to Peroff's information about Vesco's possible involvement in financing heroin trafficking transactions.

- During April, the Watergate Special Prosecutor's office confirms they had difficulty getting the DEA to give them a report on Spector, implying that there was a cover-up by the agency.

- Senator James Buckley and Ralph J. Marino, Chairman of the New York State Senate Select Committee on Crime, join forces. They share resources to investigate and hold hearings on Spector's allegations.

- On May 12, Newsweek magazine runs a story with the caption: "A Nixon Connection?" The article says the Buckley probe sparked investigations by the Syracuse Police, State police, and others and some believed the investigation could reach as high as former President Nixon.

- On May 31, New York Newsday publishes an article, "Drug Chief's Ouster Stems from Scandal," reporting that the firing of DEA Director John R. Bartels, Jr., triggered by reports of corruption in the agency.

- On June 8, the New York Daily News publishes an article, entitled "Bizarre Tale of Heroin Cabal Sparks US & Albany Probes." The report, with a photo of Patricia Richardson, quotes her as saying, "They can investigate till doomsday. I don't care."

- During July, U.S. Attorney General Edward Levi orders the formation of a new "special investigative team" of federal agents to work on the case regarding Spector's allegations.

- At Senator Buckley's direction, Leonard Saffir travels to France to investigate Spector's allegations, including the review of French police reports showing details of the French police investigation of Richardson and her associates Henri Helle and Marcel Boucan. The DEA denies receiving these reports, which are inexplicably missing from the DEA files.

- On July 28, the New York State Select Committee on Crime starts three days of hearings on Spector's allegations, with substantial press coverage. John Maynard Langford testifies that Richardson approached him about hiring someone to murder Spector.

- John Stevenhagen submits a sworn declaration implicating Richardson in narcotics trafficking but later recants his testimony, saying he only signed the statement to stop Spector from "badgering" him. Potential star witness Mary Jo Ottman fails to appear at hearings, reportedly having suffered a "nervous breakdown." Richardson denies all allegations under oath of any involvement in drug trafficking, alleging that Spector had tried to kill her by attempting to throw her in the St. Lawrence River and trying to run her over with his car. Richardson does, however, confirm that she met with Richard Nixon and others before the 1968 presidential election. She concludes her testimony by saying that she and her current husband plan to retire to a "modest" home on St. Martin, which is later reported to be worth $10.7 million.

- On July 30, The New York Times publishes an article reporting that a 1973 report prepared by the French police for U.S. drug enforcement officials–presented at the State Select Committee hearings–concluded that the participation by Richardson in drug trafficking seemed "possible" and recommended surveillance of her. However, no such surveillance was conducted.

- On July 31, at the conclusion of State Select Committee hearings, Senator Buckley and others promise that the investigation will continue, but there are no additional hearings and there is no record of a final report. Indeed, copies of the hearing transcripts and of the investigation appear to have been removed from the New York State Senate files and remain "unavailable."

1977

- During July, Spector contacts Larry H. Spivey, a former undercover agent for the Georgia Bureau of Investigation (GBI).

- On April 27, Spivey meets with Spector, and then contacts William Lynch, the head of the Organized Crime Division of the U.S. Justice Dept. about Spector's claims.

- On May 4, Spivey meets in Washington, D.C. with Steve McClintic, a State Department officer (and CIA agent) assigned to the BNDD as State Dept. liaison. Spivey also has several other meetings with government officials, including Mike Egan, Associate Attorney General, and Assistant Attorney General Benjamin Civiletti. Spivey later testifies at the 1978 Coast Guard Hearings that there was general agreement that there was "a serious law enforcement problem" and a possible cover–up and corruption within the DEA regarding its handling of the investigation of Spector's allegations.

- On May 5, Spector meets with Richard Rey in Senator Nunn's office and asks whether he thinks Spector's information should be turned over to the Jackson Committee or the Dept. of Justice. Spector also meets with Owen Malone, Chief Counsel for the McClellan Committee, and Mike Egan, Associate Attorney General, Deputy Attorney General Flaherty, and Ben Civiletti, Chief of the Criminal Division.

- On May 7, Spector and Spivey meet in Atlanta with James E. Baker, Assistant U.S. Attorney for the Northern District of Georgia. Spector leaves three briefcases of information regarding his allegations against Richardson, Weiller, and the Unione Corse.

- On May 28, Assistant U.S. Attorney Baker meets with Henry Ruth of the Watergate Special Prosecutor's Office, who mentions that the DEA's mishandling of the investigation into Spector's allegations may be due to "national security and possible exposure of CIA activities."

- On June 1, AUSA Baker sends a memo up the chain of command in the Justice Dept. asking for formal authorization to investigate the allegations raised by Spector and Spivey, including the alleged cover up and corruption by the DEA, and links between the CIA and drug trafficking.

- On July 14, Spivey and Spector send a letter to Attorney General Griffin Bell imploring him to reopen the investigation and threatening that if the Justice Dept. does not act expeditiously, the matter would be "tried by the House, the Senate or the press."

- On July 18, AUSA Baker and Spivey meet in Washington, DC with Tom O'Malley and William Lynch of the Narcotics and Dangerous Drugs section of the Justice Dept., and William Brady, a prosecutor with the Criminal Division. Spivey is warned "not to continue to press this thing and risk all that he stood to gain through the potential success" of his forthcoming book.

- On August 18, Spivey receives a letter from William J. Brady of the Justice Dept., stating that the "earlier investigation" of Spector's allegations "was exceedingly vigorous and thorough" and that it "does not warrant further investigation…."

1978

- On July 19, Congressional Hearings are held in Washington, D.C. before the Coast Guard Subcommittee of the House of Representatives, regarding proposed legislation and the possible mishandling federal investigations of Spector's allegations.

- NYPD Detective Stephen Balducci testifies regarding Spector's allegations: "Our conclusion was that there was a possibility that there was an international conspiracy" and that the follow-up to the French Connection case had "never really touched the top. We never really touched the people who supplied all the narcotics, who supplied all the financing for them." Detective Balducci also testifies that there was no coordination between the NYPD, which was working with Leonard Saffir of Senator Buckley's office, and the DEA. He recounted how, for example, they "wired up" Spector to speak with John Stevenhagen at J.G. Mellon's Restaurant in New York City, but then realized that Spector was being followed by agents later disclosed to be from the DEA. Also, he testified that, while they were looking for Richardson to interview her, the DEA had hidden her in an undisclosed location for an extended period of time.

1982

- Vesco moves to Cuba to obtain medical treatment, where he is visited by the President's nephew, Donald "Don-Don" Nixon. The two of them cook up an "immunotherapy cancer cure" scheme designed to defraud investors. Vesco introduces Donald Nixon to Fidel and Raul Castro, but when the Cuban government finds out the clinical trials on the therapy cure are being manipulated, they arrest Vesco, his wife, and their associate, rogue CIA agent Frank Terpil. Donald Nixon flees Cuba.

1985

- On December 20, an Associated Press article reveals the dirty little secret of drug smuggling by the CIA and its assistance of the Contra rebels in Nicaragua with their cocaine smuggling operation into the West Coast of the U.S.

1989

- Richardson and Weiller use their influence with the Cuban government to have Vesco's "freelance" narcotics operation in Cuba shut down and Vesco arrested. Vesco then enters into a 50–50 financial arrangement with Richardson and Weiller whereby the Unione Corse will get 50% of the profits from Vesco's narcotics operation in Cuba and Central America.

1993

- On December 6, Paul–Louis Weiller dies and is honored as a national hero.

1995

- On September 21, William Spector dies, a lonely and bitter man.

2008

- On May 9, The New York Times erroneously reports Vesco's death in a Cuban hospital five months earlier, but there is no death certificate or other documentation establishing his demise. According to Vesco associate Frank Terpil, Vesco fled to Sierra Leone. What is not reported is that Richardson and Weiller helped arrange for his transit out of Cuba.

Appendix

Articles used for reference in chapter 11.

Newsweek, May 12, 1975

Frank Zarb

Donald Rumsfeld

RUMSFELD'S DREAM

With Treasury Secretary William Simon already acting like a political entry in his native New Jersey, the man most likely—and eager—to succeed him is Presidential chief of staff Donald Rumsfeld. "Rummy wants it bad," says a friend of the onetime Illinois congressman, adding that he thinks the Treasury post would give him the exposure to Wall Street and Big Business that he wants and would be a long stride toward his next goal, the governorship of Illinois. The betting is that Rumsfeld's successor would be energy chief Frank Zarb, who has impressed President Ford with both his loyalty and his skill in maneuvering on Capitol Hill.

A WATERGATE DIVIDEND

Missouri's Democratic Rep. William Hungate may be the first to win tangible political rewards from his role in last year's impeachment hearings. His work—and TV exposure—as a member of the House Judiciary Committee during the 1974 impeachment proceedings against Richard Nixon have prompted Missouri party chieftains to urge the folksy Hungate, now 52 and in his seventh term, to run for governor next year. Should he run, his likely opponent will be incumbent GOP Gov. Christopher (Kit) Bond.

MY MAN, MY MONEY, MY MOVIE

Superstar Barbra Streisand has found a way to quiet Hollywood's misgivings about having boyfriend Jon Peters produce and direct her next movie—a multimillion-dollar remake of "A Star Is Born." Despite their eagerness for the Streisand box-office magic, movie moguls have been loath to entrust the venture to Peters, a former hairdresser. The singer plans to overcome objections by investing her own money in the film.

A NIXON 'CONNECTION'?

Efforts by New York Sen. James Buckley to learn whether Richard Nixon's campaign managers knowingly accepted money from international drug operators have sparked five additional inquiries. Buckley and his staff have spent weeks trying to verify such allegations, which grew out of a three-year investigation by a former military-intelligence officer. The senator's work has prompted parallel probes by the Syracuse, N.Y., police, the New York State police, the New York State Commission of Investigation, a New York State Senate crime committee and the Federal Drug Enforcement Administration.

Connors and Borg

CONNORS'S NEXT CHALLENGER

Sweden's Björn Borg, currently ranked fourth in world tennis, may be Jimmy Connors's next challenger. Promoters in Sweden want to stage a $400,000, winner-take-all match there later this year. The Swedish Lawn Tennis Association, however, threatens to block the event, partly because such matches are not sanctioned internationally but also because the association was kept out of the arrangements. If the LTA succeeds, the promoters plan to switch the match to Monaco, where Borg has now settled for tax reasons.

CHEMICAL-WAR GAMES

While the U.S. has officially renounced first-strike use of chemical weapons, the Soviet Union thinks differently, according to top NATO officials. During a recent Russian war game, NATO intelligence has learned, Soviet forces opened their simulated attack on Western Europe by blanketing Denmark with a gas that renders its victims unconscious for 48 hours.

—JOHN A. CONWAY with bureau reports

"A Nixon 'Connection'?" *Newsweek*, May 12, 1975.

Clues Point To Drug Plot, Prober Says

By SAM ROBERTS

A Senate investigator concluded yesterday that "there was an international narcotics conspiracy of major proportions in existence in 1971 and 1972" that federal and state probers ignored or covered up.

Leonard Saffir, top aide to Sen. James Buckley (R-C-N.Y.), said that he and other investigators had reached that conclusion after following leads supplied by William Spector, a former upstate auto dealer. Spector has told of a drug-smuggling conspiracy whose trial extended to St. Martin in the Caribbean, France, the Middle East, Montreal and New York State.

Patricia Martinson, Spector's stunning ex-wife, has been questioned in the inquiry. Her flings with flamboyant foreign financiers aroused hs suspicion. Mrs. Martinson, who has lunched at Cote Basque with former President Nixon and others, was friendly with such fat cats as the late Lebanese banker Yusif Bedas and French multimillionaire Paul Louis Weiller.

The allegations of a major worldwide drug ring

1 of 3 Sam Roberts, "Clues Point to Drug Plot, Prober Says" New York Daily News, June 9, 1975.

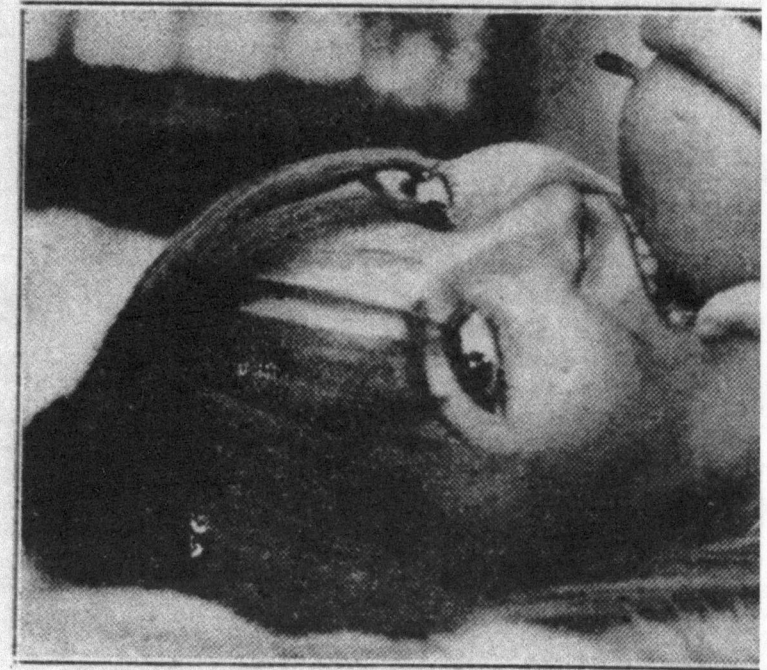

Patricia Martinson—denies an

and the accusations of coverup were disclosed yesterday by The News.

Mrs. Martinson has denied any sinister connections, and her present husband says Spector "has nothing on his mind but to harass his former wife." He described Spector's conspiracy theories as "absolutely ridiculous."

Hearings into Spector's allegations and the response to them by official agencies are expected to be held as early as next month by Buckley and the State Senate Crime Committee, headed by Sen. Ralph Marino (R-Nassau).

Among those whose names have been dropped in the alleged conspiracy have been Marcel Boucan, whose shrimp boat was seized in Marseilles with a

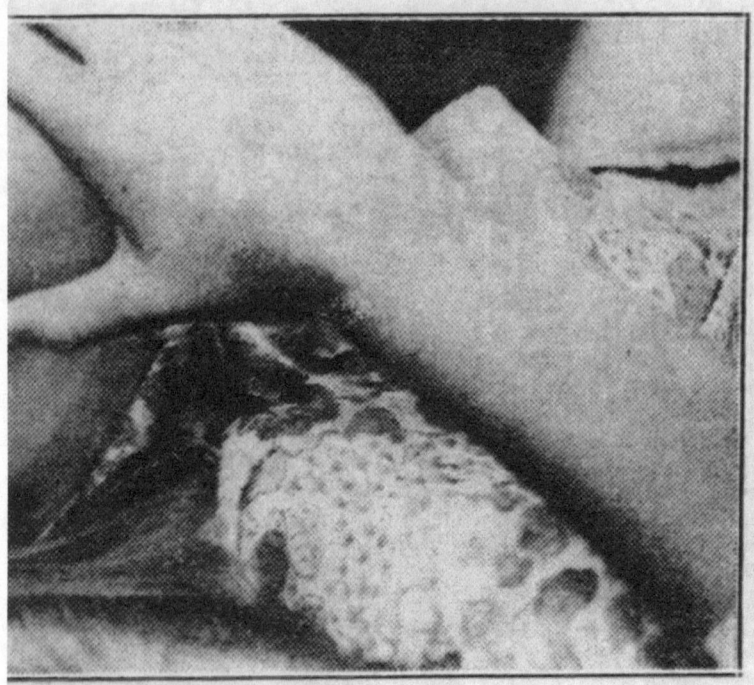

any sinister connections.

record cargo of 937 pounds of heroin in 1972 and who admitted that he had delivered 220 pounds worth more than $25 million to Miami a year earlier.

Another who is said to have figured in the alleged drug smuggling cabal was Conrad Bouchard, a reputed Canadian underworld figure. An undercover agent has said that Bouchard told him an associate of fugitive financier Robert Vesco was also involved in heroin smuggling.

Mrs. Martinson lived with Spector at Ogdensburg near the Canadian border until their separation. After she left him, investigators said, she lived in a $100-a-month apartment in Syracuse without a telephone until her divorce was made final.

Drug Chief's Ouster Stems From Scandal

The Los Angeles Times

Washington—Behind the ouster Thursday of federal drug enforcement chief John R. Bartels Jr. is a Justice Department effort to take decisive action before Senate investigators air further allegations of misconduct and mismanagement in Bartels' 4,000-member agency.

A secret Justice Department report—called "explosive" by one source—is said to back up claims that Bartels was not moving aggressively to clean up the Drug Enforcement Administration, a two-year-old division of the department. Those claims had been made by two veteran law enforcement officials whom Bartels moved out of the agency last December.

Congressional sources said yesterday that the Senate permanent investigations subcommittee also has obtained evidence that some top officials of the agency have consorted with convicted gamblers and persons allegedly linked to criminal activities, and that the agency formed questionable alliances with gambling casinos in an effort to penetrate alleged narcotics rings. The Senate committee will resume its' hearings June 9.

The DEA turmoil comes as the drug enforcement picture is particularly bleak. Turkey, which had stopped growing opium poppies, has resumed production of this major heroin source and use of the narcotic is increasing in the United States.

Bartels, 41, was replaced by Henry S. Dogin, 40, a deputy assistant attorney general in the Justice Department's criminal division who has been supervising narcotics and dangerous drug prosecutions. Dogin will serve as acting administrator until President Ford nominates a successor for Bartels.

It was learned that Attorney General Edward H. Levi actually had asked White House Chief of Staff Donald H. Rumsfeld to request Bartels' resignation during a telephone conversation last week. A source familiar with the Levi-Rumsfeld discussion said Levi framed the issue in terms of morale. Levi allegedly said that dissension within the agency was so high that Bartels' energies were dissipated. The Justice Department spokesman said, "there was no allegation of misdeeds or corruption on the part of Bartels." A Senate source also indicated that no evidence of corruption has been found involving Bartels, but that the subcommittee was probing charges from inside the agency that Bartels failed to act on reports of misconduct by subordinates.

One of these charges centered around the alleged conduct of Vince Promuto, a former football player with the Washington Redskins who was Bartels' director of public affairs. Promuto, who has since moved to the agency's New York office, was said by District of Columbia police to have associated, while at the agency's headquarters, with convicted gamblers and other disreputable persons. Promuto has acknowledged he knew three Washington gamblers but said he had no financial dealings with them. Promuto is expected to be a key witness at the upcoming Senate hearings.

Earlier probes by the Senate committee have revealed that fugitive financier Robert L. Vesco paid $3,000 in 1972 to have federal drug agents search his New Jersey home and office for hidden electronic bugging devices. Vesco at that time was a major contributor to the reelection campaign of then-President Richard M. Nixon. A year later, according to the Senate panel, agency officials ignored charges by a government informant that Vesco was involved in a heroin-smuggling scheme. Bartels had been director of the federal organized crime strike force in New Jersey.

"Drug Chief's Ouster Stems from Scandal," *New York Newsday*, May 31, 1975.

Endnotes

Chapter 1

1. U.S. Central Intelligence Agency, Review of the World Situation as it Relates to the Security of the United States, CIA 3, 17 December, 1947.
2. ibid.
3. Wisner's career in intelligence lasted into the 1950s. He reportedly took part in multiple CIA-led coup d'etats including overthrowing Prime Minister Mossadegh of Iran and President Arbenz of Guatamela. Following a mental-breakdown induced by the failed Hungarian Revolution in 1956, Wisner retired and eventually took his own life in 1965. See Dill, Josh "Parties, Politics, and Press on P Street," Volume XLIIII, Issue 4 (September 2019), https://cagtown.org/wp-content/uploads/2020/07/cag092019.pdf, Retrieved September 27, 2021.
4. U.S. Congress, House, Committee on Merchant Marine and Fisheries, Subcommittee on Coast Guard and Navigation *Oversight of Seaborne Drug Smuggling Problems in the United States and Consideration of Legislation Proposed to Facilitate Coast Guard Drug Law Enforcement on the High Seas*, 95th Cong., 2nd sess., 1978, 124-125
5. CIA Memorandum to the Forty Committee (National Security Council), presented to the Select Committee on Intelligence, United States House of Representatives (the Pike Committee) during closed hearings held in 1975. The bulk of the committee's report that contained the memorandum was leaked to the press in February 1976 and first appeared in book form as *CIA – The Pike Report* (Nottingham, England, 1977). The memorandum appears on pp. 204-5 of that book.
6. Luciano maintained that he was American and, after his death in Italy in 1962, his family buried him in Middle Village, Queens.
7. Charles Tilly and Edward Shorter, *Strikes in France, 1830-1968* (Cambridge: Cambridge University Press, 1984), 137.
8. Alfred McCoy, *Politics of Heroin in Southeast Asia* (New York: Harper & Row, 1972), 33.
9. *Milieu* is the French term for "underworld" or "organized crime."
10. McCoy, *Politics of Heroin in Southeast Asia*, 31.
11. Rural Corsicans actually managed to launch a successful resistance to the Italian invasion in 1942, even taking parts of the island back from Italian forces by the summer of 1943.
12. *See* Maurice Agulhon and Fernand Barrat, *CRS à Marseille: "le police aux service du peuple," 1944-1947* (Paris: Presses de SciencesPo, 1971).
13. U.S. Office of the Chairman of the Joint Chiefs of Staff, *The Joint Chiefs of Staff and the First Indochina War, 1947-1954*, (Washington D.C.: Office of Joint History, 2004), 21. https://www.jcs.mil/Portals/36/Documents/History/Vietnam/Vietnam_1947-1954.pdf
14. "VIETNAM-DRUGS: Colonial Era Opium Trade Still Haunts Hanoi Today" *Inter Press Service*, July 16, 1996. http://www.ipsnews.net/1996/07/vietnam-drugs-colonial-era-opium-trade-still-haunts-hanoi-today/
15. Greg Lockheart. Review: *Quand L'Opium Finançaçit La Colonisation en Indochine: L'élaboration de la régie générale de l'opium (1860 à 1914)* by Chantal Descours-Gatin, *Journal of*

Southeast Asian Studies Vol. 25, No. 2 (September 1994), 463-465. https://www.jstor.org/stable/20071688

16 French police in Corsica still largely leave local organized crime alone, rarely arresting anyone over murders on the island. *See* Martin Buckley "Are Corsica's Militants and Mafia a Thing of the Past?" *BBC News*, November 1, 2014. https://www.bbc.com/news/magazine-29662561

17 For example, in 1934 Sabiani publicly defended Carbone and Spirito after their financial advisor was found mutilated and displayed on a railroad track. "On the morning of 3 April 1934 the walls of Marseille were plastered with massive posters claiming that 'Carbone and Spirito are my friends' and threatening that the wrath of Sabiani would fall on any who touched a hair on their heads." *See* Simon Kitson, *Police and Politics in Marseille, 1936-1945*, (Leiden: Brill Publishers, 2014).

18 C. L. Sulzberger, "Tempest in an Opium Pot," *The New York Times*, November 26, 1971. https://nyti.ms/3uDfazj; "The World: The Milieu of the Corsican Godfathers," *Time Magazine*, September 4, 1972. http://content.time.com/time/subscriber/article/0,33009,910391-2,00.html

19 Tolson and Hoover ate together twice a day, vacationed together, and are now buried only a few yards apart. Anthony Summers, "The Secret Life of J Edgar Hoover," *The Guardian*, December 11, 2011.

20 The United Press, "2 U.S. Crews Back French Strike, Bar Troops From Unloading Ships," *The New York Times*, November 19, 1947.

Chapter 2

1 U.S. Congress, House, Committee on Merchant Marine and Fisheries, Subcommittee on Coast Guard and Navigation *Oversight of Seaborne Drug Smuggling Problems in the United States and Consideration of Legislation Proposed to Facilitate Coast Guard Drug Law Enforcement on the High Seas*, 95 Cong., 2 sess., 1978, 83.

2 Another model, "Tish Martinson, who came to Paris to model at age 15, tells how, when she was a teen-ager, Weiller gave dinner parties for her." *See* "A Man Of Many Houses Collector Of Homes Shares Them With Famous Friends" *Town and Country*. Published in *The Orlando Sentinel*, February 18, 1986. https://www.orlandosentinel.com/news/os-xpm-1986-02-15-0200120061-story.html

3 ibid.

4 "The automobile is one of the greatest means of smuggling large quanitities... [it's] a very difficult thing to try and discover that type of concealment." – Albert Seeley, Special Agent in Charge of the Office of Investigation at JFK Airport *quoted in* U.S. Congress, House, Committee, *Seaborne Drug Smuggling Problems*, 16.

5 Edward Kirkman and Henry Lee, "Agents Seize Heroin Worth Record 22M". *New York Daily News*, 27 June, 1968. This same method of transport was used in another infamous seizure of heroin. Later, in April 1971, a Volkswagen Camper van carrying 96 pounds of heroin was shipped from France to New Jersey. *See* John L Hess, "French Official Supports U. S. Charges in Narcotics Case Here," *The New York Times*, November 20, 1971. *And* U.S. Congress, House, Committee, *Seaborne Drug Smuggling Problems*, 15.

6 U.S. Congress, House, Committee, *Seaborne Drug Smuggling Problems*, 83.

7 ibid. 149.

8 Approximately $13,000 now, adjusted for inflation

9 U.S. Congress, House, Committee, *Seaborne Drug Smuggling Problems*, 84.

10 ibid. 83.

11 Marcel, born Louis Moscovch, was an Argentinan immigrant operating in the U.S. under a false name after racking up large debts. It is believed that he was paid by Richardson to retrieve the necklace she used Ottman to bring back to the U.S.

12 U.S. Congress, House, Committee, *Seaborne Drug Smuggling Problems*, 83.

13   Just a week prior, Frankel's boat Samana was caught off the coast of Puerto Rico stuffed to the brim with marijuana. Frankel, of course, was not on the boat and therefore avoided arrest.
14   U.S. Congress, House, Committee, *Seaborne Drug Smuggling Problems*, 142.

Chapter 3

1   U.S. Congress, House, Committee on Merchant Marine and Fisheries, Subcommittee on Coast Guard and Navigation *Oversight of Seaborne Drug Smuggling Problems in the United States and Consideration of Legislation Proposed to Facilitate Coast Guard Drug Law Enforcement on the High Seas*, 95th Cong., 2nd sess., 239-240.
2   "Lazare Weiller," Assemblée National (website), accessed December 9, 2021, https://www2.assemblee-nationale.fr/sycomore/fiche/%28num_dept%29/7385
3   "Stock Certificate for Société des Moteurs Gnome et Rhone," Smithsonian Online Virtual Archives (website), accessed October 12, 2021, https://sova.si.edu/record/NASM.XXXX.0892
4   Germany's industrial heartland, the Ruhr valley, was home of multiple uprisings by Spartacists and Red Guard militias following the First World War. France also invaded and occupied the Ruhr between 1923-1925 after Germany defaulted on their reparation payments owed as part of the Versailles treaty.
5   William Neubauer, "Activities of I.G. Farbenindustrie in the United States, 1929 until March 11, 1942" (University of Richmond, Honors Thesis, 1969), 20.
6   "Evidence Forged in French Air Case," *The New York Times*, October 6, 1932. https://timesmachine.nytimes.com/timesmachine/1932/10/07/105874099.html?pageNumber=2
7   "50,000 French Jews Hit By New Decree" *The New York Times*, October 8, 1940
8   "Marcel Dassault," Dassault Aviation (website), accessed October 12, 2021, https://www.dassault-aviation.com/en/passion/history/men/marcel-dassault/
9   Weiller's mother was not so lucky, and, after being interned by the Vichy Regime, was deported to Auschwitz where she died in 1944. Little is known of what happened to his wife Aliki, or his children in this time, although she was reportedly attending high society banquets in New York City by October 1941. *See* "Dinners are Held Before Premiere," *The New York Times*, October 29, 1941.
10   Chapman, *State Capitalism and Working-Class Radicalism in the French Aircraft Industry*, (Berkeley: University of California Press, 1990).
11   "Paul Louis Weiller, French businessman of questionable loyalty, departed for Havana and reportedly arrived in Mexico City on October 5, 1942. He is stopping at the Maria Cristina Hotel, a favorite Nazi stopping place, supposedly to await his wife, … who is planning a trip to Mexico because of Weiller's inability to get a Visa to enter the United States." *From* Tenth Naval District Counter Intelligence Section, *Monthly Summary*, Office of Naval Intelligence, November 1942.
12   Was Weiller, in fact, the "unidentified" Michelin officer in the photo with John Jehan, which Detective Egan showed to Robin Moore? U.S. Congress, House, Committee, Seaborne Drug Smuggling Problems, 85.
13   "Air France Employee Accused in Smuggling Attempt — Seized at Airport," *The New York Times*, March 23, 1961. https://timesmachine.nytimes.com/timesmachine/1961/03/23/118029308.html?pageNumber=23
14   U.S. Congress, House, Committee, Seaborne Drug Smuggling Problems, 85, 240.
15   U.S. Congress, House, Committee, Seaborne Drug Smuggling Problems, 75.

Chapter 4

1   Thomas O'Toole, "Operation Ratline Was Barbie's Ticket Out," *The Washington Post*, August 21, 1983.

2 Paul E. Lyon, "History of the Italian Rat Line," Austria: 430th Counter Intelligence Corps, April 1950. https://web.archive.org/web/20071008205604/http://www.jasenovac-info.com/cd/biblioteka/pavelicpapers/army/ar0002.html
3 Mark Aarons and John Loftus, *Unholy Trinity: The Vatican, The Nazis, and the Swiss Bankers* (revised ed.), (New York: St. Martin's Press, 1998).
4 ibid. supra, footnote 1
5 ibid.
6 Kevin Ruffner, *Foraging an Intelligence Partnership: CIA and the Origins of the BND, 1945-49*, CIA History Staff, 1999, xvi.
7 Quoted in Scott Anderson, *The Quiet Americans: Four CIA Spies at the Dawn of the Cold War – A Tragedy in Three Acts*. (New York: Knopf Doubleday, 2020)
8 Scott, Peter Dale. Scott, "Why No One Could Find Mengele: Allen Dulles and the German SS.", " *The Threepenny Review*, no. 23 (1985): 16–18. http://www.jstor.org/stable/4383422.
9 Shraga Elam and Dennis Whitehead, "In the Service of the Jewish State" *Haaretz*, March 29, 2007. https://www.haaretz.com/1.4813593 (retrieved October 18, 2021)
10 For instance, French authorities requested as early as 1947 that the U.S. extradite Barbie to face justice for the crimes he committed in France. The French Embassy in Washington D.C. noted in 1949 that "despite repeated requests, American occupation authorities in Germany have not to date arrested and surrendered this war criminal...." U.S. Department of Justice, Criminal Division, *Klaus Barbie and the United States Government A Report to the Attorney General of the United States* (Washington D.C.: DOJ, 1983), 87. https://www.justice.gov/sites/default/files/criminal-hrsp/legacy/2011/02/04/08-02-83barbie-rpt.pdf
11 After the initial success of Germany's invasion of Russia, dubbed "Operation Barbarossa," Gehlen attempted to form a Slavic Army of Liberation composed of anti-communist Eastern Europeans to aid the Wehrmacht as auxiliaries. Hitler's view of Slavic people as subhuman and only controllable through violence and terror led him to scrap Gehlen's plan, despite Gehlen already having over 100,000 Russians willing to sign up. Arthur Cox, "Super Spy, Strange Ally" *The Washington Post*, April 8, 1972.
12 Matthew Aid, *It Did Not Begin With Snowden: The Declassified History of American Intelligence Operations in Europe: 1945-2001*, (Leiden: Brill, 2014), 22-23.
13 "Silicon Valley Felt Touch of ex-Nazi Masquerader," *San Jose Mercury*, November 20, 1981. http://www.lamoth.info/?p=digitallibrary/getfile&ibid.=6499. Courtesy of the LA Museum of the Holocaust.
14 This villa hosted the infamous 1942 Wannsee Conference, where Nazi leadership outlined their Final Solution to the Jewish Question, putting into motion the climax of Nazi industrialized genocide.
15 Simon Wiesenthal, *Recht, nicht Rache: Erinnerungen*. (Frankfurt am Main/Berlin: Ullstein, 1992), 315.
16 National Commission on Law Enforcement and Social Justice, *The Ajax File: An Analysis of Interpol's Failure to Combat International Drug Trafficking.*" Courtesy of The Weisberg Collection. Hood College, Frederick, MD, USA. http://jfk.hood.edu/
17 M, Barnett and L. Coleman, "Designing Police: INTERPOL and the Study of Change in International Organizations," International Studies Quarterly, No. 49 (2005), 593.
18 Elmer B. Staats, *United States Participation in INTERPOL, the International Criminal Police Organization*, (Washington, D.C.: GAO, 1976), 13, 76-77. Accessed October 19, 2021, https://www.gao.gov/assets/ibid.76-77.pdf

Chapter 5

1 Mark Aarons and John Loftus, *The Secret War Against The Jews: How Western Espionage Betrayed The Jewish People*. (New York: St. Martin's Press, 1994), 221.
2 Adam LeBor, "Overt and Covert", *The New York Times*, November 8, 2013. https://www.nytimes.com/2013/11/10/books/review/the-brothers-by-stephen-kinzer.html

3   Mark Stout, "The Pond: Running Agents for State, War, and the CIA. The Hazards of Private Spy Operations," *Studies in Intelligence* 48, no. 3 (2004), https://www.cia.gov/static/d08a4f7735c47a7c025d22ca60a2e3c7/the-pond.pdf (accessed October 20, 2021).
4   Aarons and Loftus, *The Secret War Against The Jews*, 222.
5   "Malaxa Wins Permanent Home in U.S.", *The Washington Post*, September 9, 1958.
6   Howard Blum, *Wanted! The Search for Nazis in America* (New York: Quadrangle/The New York Times Book Company, 1977), 119.
7   ibid. p. 120
8   Vladimirov, Katya, "General Nicolae Rădescu: New Sources, New Perspectives, 1940s–1950s" *Faculty Publications* 103, (2018), 610-627.
9   "Romania's 'Ford' Wins Conditional Reentry to U.S.," *The Washington Post*, December 17, 1955.
10 "Nixon-Malaxa Link Denied by Attorney", *The New York Times*, October 10, 1962.
11 Jack Anderson, "Nixon Helped Rich Nazi Stay in U.S.," *The Washington Post*, November 16, 1979. Anderson also wrote a November 1971 expose of Nixon's Nazi connections that appeared in the Washington Post at the same time as the November 1971 Republican convention. The article mentioned Pasztor by name, including a detailed description of his wartime activities in Hungary.
12 Adam Nagourney, "In Tapes, Nixon Rails about Jews and Blacks," *The New York Times*, December 10, 2010.
13 Ken Ringle, "Shaken Foundation," *The Washington Post*, April 9, 1997. https://www.washingtonpost.com/archive/lifestyle/1997/04/09/shaken-foundation/1eaca3e1-77a9-4700-8c6a-ac658e5d9e9c/
14 Aarons and Loftus, *The Secret War Against the Jews*, 297.
15 Liddy confirmed this himself in his autobiography (the name of which was inspired by a Nazi propaganda film): "I had taken my children to see Leni Riefenstahl's cinematic masterpiece Triumph of the Will. I called the National Archives and set up a special showing for the White House staff. About fifteen people attended" and, at the end of the film "from the rear of the audience came an awed "Jesus! What an advance job!" G. Gordon Liddy, *Will: The Autobiography of G. Gordon Liddy*, (New York: St. Martin's Press, 1996), 156.

Chapter 6

1   "Oilman Betting New Paper Will Succeed in New York City," *Tuscaloosa News*, Tuesday, October 16, 1973
2   Correspondence; Richard Nixon to Paul-Louis Weiller, 15 March 1965, Wilderness Years: Series I: Sub-Series A: 1963-1965, Box 36, Weiller, Commandant Paul-Louis, Richard Nixon Presidential Library and Museum, Yorba Linda, CA, Presidential Materials
3   U.S. Congress, House, Committee on Merchant Marine and Fisheries, Subcommittee on Coast Guard and Navigation *Oversight of Seaborne Drug Smuggling Problems in the United States and Consideration of Legislation Proposed to Facilitate Coast Guard Drug Law Enforcement on the High Seas*, 95th Cong., 2nd sess., 1978, 240.
4   Daily Diary; President Richard Nixon's Daily Diary April 1, 1970 – April 15, 1970, Box RC5, White House Central Files, Nixon Presidential Library. *See also* Correspondence; "Invites to Tricia's Wedding," from unknown to Pat, April 12, 1971, Box 41, Folder 17, Contested Materials Collection, Nixon Presidential Library.
5   Dan Fulsom, "Gangster in the White House," *Crime Magazine*, September 11, 2009.
6   "I am also aware of the fact that after an article was published on Mr. Rebozo I got instructions that one of the authors of that article should have some problems. I did not know how to deal directly with the situation. I discussed it with Mr. Caulfield. I was reluctant to call Mr. Walters, who was the head of the Internal Revenue Service and suggest that he do anything about this." U.S. Congress, House, Committee on the Judiciary (1973). *A Resolution Authorizing And Directing The Committee On The Judiciary To Investigate Whether Sufficient Grounds Exist For The House Of Representatives To Exercise Its Constitutional Power*

To Impeach Richard M. Nixon President Of The United States Of America, 93rd Cong., 2nd sess., 1974, 166.

7 Quoted in Fulsom, "Gangster in the White House."
8 David Binder, "Bebe Rebozo, Loyal Friend in Nixon's Darkest Days, Dies at 85," *The New York Times*, May 10, 1998. https://www.nytimes.com/1998/05/10/us/bebe-rebozo-loyal-friend-in-nixon-s-darkest-days-dies-at-85.html
9 "At Key Biscayne, according to a Secret Service source, Nixon once lost his temper during a conversation about Cambodia. "He just got pissed," the agent quoted eyewitnesses as saying. 'They were half in the tank, sitting around the pool drinking. And Nixon got on the phone and said: 'Bomb the shit out of them!'" "If the president had his way,' Kissinger growled to aides more than once, 'there would be a nuclear war each week!'" *quoted in* Anthony Summers and Robbyn Swan, "Drunk In Charge (Part Two)," *The Guardian*, September 2, 2000. https://www.theguardian.com/weekend/story/0,3605,362958,00.html

Chapter 7

1 "Opinion - An Opioid Crisis Foretold" *The New York Times*, April 21, 2018; George Fisher, "The Drug War at 100", *Stanford Law School Legal Aggregate Blog*, December 19, 2014. Accessed December 10, 2021. https://law.stanford.edu/2014/12/19/the-drug-war-at-100/
2 "I have been obliged to have recourse to opium .... It has taken away my appetite and so impeded my digestion that I am become totally emaciated, so that little remains of me but a skeleton covered with a skin." Benjamin Franklin, *The Life of Benjamin Franklin, Written by Himself, Volume 3, 4th edition, revised and corrected*, (Philadelphia: J.B. Lippincott Company, 1902).
3 *Opium Throughout History* (website), PBS Frontline, 1998. Accessed October 8, 2010. https://www.pbs.org/wgbh/pages/frontline/shows/heroin/etc/history.html
4 In 1971 it was estimated that between 10-25% of enlisted soldiers in Vietnam were using heroin, with some units reporting up to 50% of their men on Heroin. Alvin Shuster, "G.I. Heroin Epidemic in Vietnam," *The New York Times*, May 16, 1971.
5 *Thirty Years of America's Drug War, a Chronology* (website), PBS Frontline, 1995. Accessed December 10, 2021. https://www.pbs.org/wgbh/pages/frontline/shows/drugs/cron/
6 *Timeline: America's War on Drugs* (website), NPR, April 2, 2007. Accessed December 10, 2021 https://www.npr.org/templates/story/story.php?storyId=9252490
7 German Lopez, "Was Nixon's war on drugs a racially motivated crusade? It's a bit more complicated," *Vox*, March 29, 2016.
8 "Nixon Adviser Admits War on Drugs was Designed to Criminalize Black People," *Equal Justice Initiative*, March 25, 2016.
9 *See, for example* "Nixon Tapes Reveal Anti-Semitic, Racist Comments," *The Daily Beast*, August 21, 2013. Accessed November 11, 2021, https://www.thedailybeast.com/cheats/2013/08/21/nixon-tapes-reveal-anti-semitic-racist-comments.
10 "The Impact of the War on Drugs on U.S. Incarceration," *Human Rights Watch*, May, 2000. Archived from the original on November 28, 2008. Accessed October 20, 2021.
11 N.B. This speech was prepared by Stephen McClintic. "The President's Remarks to Senior United States Narcotics Control Officials Attending the Conference at the Department of State. September 18, 1972" *quoted in* U.S. Congress, House, Committee on Merchant Marine and Fisheries, Subcommittee on Coast Guard and Navigation *Oversight of Seaborne Drug Smuggling Problems in the United States and Consideration of Legislation Proposed to Facilitate Coast Guard Drug Law Enforcement on the High Seas*, 95th Cong., 2nd sess., 1978, 161-163.
12 "The Milieu of the Corsican Godfathers," *Time Magazine*, September 4, 1972.
13 ibid.
14 *United States of America, Appellee, v. Antoine B. Rinieri*, Defendant-Appellant., 308 F.2d 24 (2nd Cir. 1962).

15 Richard Nixon, *Special Message to the Congress on Drug Abuse Prevention and Control*, June 17, 1971 The American Presidency Project (web) https://www.presidency.ucsb.edu/node/240245; "Nixon Calls War on Drugs," *The Palm Beach Post*, June 18, 1971; Emily Dufton "The War on Drugs: How President Nixon Tied Addiction to Crime," *The Atlantic*, March 26, 2012.
16 According to G. Gordon Liddy, a senior Nixon advisor and Watergate accomplice, this was exactly the point: "as Liddy pointed out in his autobiography, the goal of Operation Intercept was not, in fact, to freeze the flow of drugs. "For diplomatic reasons the true purpose of the exercise was never revealed. Operation Intercept, with its massive economic and social disruption, could be sustained far longer by the United States than by Mexico. It was an exercise in international extortion, pure, simple, and effective, designed to bend Mexico to our will." *Quoted in* Doyle, "Operation Intercept."
17 ibid.
18 Douglas Valentine, "Creating a Crime: How the CIA Commandeered the DEA," *Dissident Voice*, September 19th, 2015; *see also*, Douglas Valentine, *The Strength of the Wolf: The Secret History of America's War on Drugs* (Brooklyn: Verso, 2004); Douglas Valentine, *The Strength of the Pack: The Personalities, Politics, and Espionage Intrigues that Shaped the DEA* (Walterville: TrineDay, 2009); and https://www.douglasvalentine.com
19 Alain Labrousse, "Uncle Sam's Junk," *Index on Censorship* 28, Issue 5 (1999), 100–105. https://journals.sagepub.com/toc/ioca/28/5
20 The National Security Archive, "Fighting The War In Southeast Asia, 1961-1973," *National Security Archive Electronic Briefing Book* 248, April 9, 2008. https://nsarchive2.gwu.edu/NSAEBB/NSAEBB248/.
21 Valentine, *The CIA as Organized Crime*, Chapter 12.
22 Douglas Valentine, "Creating a Crime," *Counter Punch*, September 11, 2015.
23 ibid.
24 The National Security Archive, "JFK and the Diệm Coup," *National Security Archive Electronic Briefing Book* 101, November 5, 2003. https://nsarchive2.gwu.edu/NSAEBB/NSAEBB101/index.htm.
25 Tim Weiner, "Lucien Conein, 79, Legendary Cold War Spy," *The New York Times*, June 7, 1998.
26 Bart Barnes, "Lucien E. Conein Dies at 79: Fabled Agent for OSS and CIA," *The Washington Post*, June 6, 1998.
27 Alfred W. McCoy, *The Politics of Heroin in Southeast Asia*, (New York: Harper & Row, 1972), 210-213.
28 "Creation of the DEA" (website), DEA. Accessed October 24, 2021, https://www.dea.gov/highlight-topics/dea-anniversary.
29 United States. Congress. House. Permanent Select Committee on Intelligence *Report on the Central Intelligence Agency's Alleged Involvement In Crack Cocaine Trafficking in the Los Angeles Area*, 106 Cong. 2 sess., 2000, 281, 296.
30 Valentine, *The CIA as Organized Crime*, chapter 12.
31 United States, Congress, Senate, Committee on Government Operations, Permanent Subcommittee on Investigations, *The Robert Vesco Investigation*, 93 Congr. 2 sess., 1974, 111.
32 ibid.
33 Brian Barger and Robert Parry, "Reports Link Nicaraguan Rebels to Cocaine Trafficking," *Associated Press*, December 20, 1985.
34 John Lichfield and Tim Cornwell, "America has fought the wrong war. Did US policy in central America in the 1980s assist the growth of the Colombian cocaine cartels?" *The Independent*, 26 August, 1989.
35 ibid.
36 ibid.
37 Barger and Parry, "Reports Link Nicaraguan Rebels to Cocaine Trafficking."
38 ibid.

Chapter 8

1. Marc Lacey and Jonathan Kandell, "A Last Vanishing Act for Robert Vesco, Fugitive," New York Times, May 3, 2008.
2. "Vesco Hired Nixon Nephew After U.S. Inquiry Began," The New York Times, May 4, 1973.
3. United States. Congress. Senate. Committee on Government Operations, Permanent Subcommittee on Investigations, The Robert Vesco Investigation, 93rd Congr. 2nd sess., 1974, 8, 46.
4. Joseph Sullivan, "Sears Is Suspended as a Lawyer For Transmitting '72 Vesco Gift," The New York Times, October 1, 1976.
5. "Learning to love exile," Time Magazine, February 9, 1976.
6. T. Noah, "Know Your Fugitive Financiers!" Slate, February 20, 2001. Accessed December 10, 2021, https://slate.com/news-and-politics/2001/02/know-your-fugitive-financiers.html.
7. Christopher Woody, "Meet The Cocaine-Addled, Hitler-Obsessed Drug Smuggler Who Tried To Take Down Pablo Escobar," The Independent, March 22, 2017.
8. Ron Word, "Prosecutor Identifies Vesco as Co-Conspirator for First Time," Associated Press, December 10, 1987.
9. U.S. Congress, House, Committee on Merchant Marine and Fisheries, Subcommittee on Coast Guard and Navigation Oversight of Seaborne Drug Smuggling Problems in the United States and Consideration of Legislation Proposed to Facilitate Coast Guard Drug Law Enforcement on the High Seas, 95th Cong., 2nd sess., 1978, 150.
10. U.S. Congress, House, Committee, Seaborne Drug Smuggling Problems, 244.
11. Wallace Turner, "2 Agencies Explain End of Drug Inquiry With Link to Vesco," The New York Times, November 27, 1973.
12. ibid.
13. Morton Mintz, "Drug Scheme Link to Vesco Undoes An Undercover Man," Washington Post, November 26, 1973.
14. John Crewdson, "Senate Study Calls U.S. Drug Agents Lax in Checking Alleged Link of Vesco to Heroin," The New York Times, March 9, 1975.
15. DEA Official George Brosnan, quoted in Wallace, "Two agencies Explain."
16. The rumors and allegations against Director Bartels were investigated by Andrew C. Tartaglino, the D.E.A.'s inspector general, who testified before the Jackson Committee that Bartels had tried "to frustrate, impede and obstruct" an investigation of Mr. Promuto's alleged links to crime. Senator Jackson commented that, if true, Bartels' actions constituted an obstruction of justice. "The evidence that has been brought out … would indicate that there was a conscious, premeditated plan involving misconduct at the highest levels of the D.E.A.," Jackson said. Under pressure, Bartels resigned as D.E.A. Director, although he escaped prosecution.
17. Larry Rohter, "Robert Vesco, the Fugitive Financier, Goes on Trial in Cuba on Fraud Charges," The New York Times, August 2, 1996.
18. Terpil joined the CIA in 1965, but in 1980, he fled the country after being indicted for illegal arms dealing. He was sentenced to 53 years in prison in absentia, with the federal judge commenting that Terpil's profession was "trading in death and destruction." E.R. Shipp, "2 Fugitive Gun Agents Denounced By Judge; Terms Set At 53 Years," The New York Times, June 9, 1981.
19. Rohter, "Robert Vesco, the Fugitive Financier."
20. ibid.
21. Larry DuBois and Laurence Gonzales, "The Puppet and the Puppetmasters," Playboy, September 1976.
22. Carl Stern, "Howard Hughes Contribution / Kalmbach Version," NBC Evening News, April 10, 1974. Courtesy of the Vanderbilt Television News Archive.
23. Rohter "Robert Vesco, the Fugitive Financier."

24 Arthur Herzog, Vesco, His Rise, Fall and Flight (New York: Doubleday, 1987).
25 S.S. Anreder, "Vesco's legacy: International Controls Corp. hopes to live it down," Barron's, April 17, 1978.
26 Michael Carlson, "Obituary: Robert Maheu," The Guardian, August 20, 2008.
27 Marc Lacey and Jonathan Kandell, "A Last Vanishing Act for Robert Vesco, Fugitive," New York Times, May 3, 2008.
28 "Frank Terpil: How a CIA spy went rogue to court the world's worst dictators," The Guardian, March 6, 2016.

Chapter 9

1 U.S. Congress, House, Committee on Merchant Marine and Fisheries, Subcommittee on Coast Guard and Navigation *Oversight of Seaborne Drug Smuggling Problems in the United States and Consideration of Legislation Proposed to Facilitate Coast Guard Drug Law Enforcement on the High Seas*, 95th Cong., 2nd sess., 1978, 241-253.
2 U.S. Congress, House, Committee, *Seaborne Drug Smuggling Problems*, 247.
3 John Crewdson, "Senate Study Calls U.S. Drug Agents Lax in Checking Alleged Link of Vesco to Heroin," *The New York Times*, March 10, 1975.
4 United States, Congress, Senate, Committee on Government Operations, Permanent Subcommittee on Investigations, *The Robert Vesco Investigation*, 93 Congr. 2 sess., 1974, 82.
5 Crewdson, "Senate Study."
6 United States. Congress. Senate. Government Operations, *The Robert Vesco Investigation*, III.
7 It was widely known in U.S. intelligence circles that, when Carlucci was working at the U.S. Embassy in the Congo, Patrice Lumumba, the first prime minister of that country, was executed in January 1961 based on a CIA directive approved by the White House authorizing Lumumba's "termination with extreme prejudice." David Akerman, "Who Killed Lumumba?" *BBC*, October 21, 2000.

Chapter 10

1 Lee Dembart, "The Model, the Drug Ring And the Big Evidence Hunt," *The New York Times*, June 12, 1975.
2 James L. Buckley, "Why Richard Nixon Should Resign the Presidency," *The National Review*, April 12 1974.
3 ibid.
4 "August 9th in History: The Resignation of Richard Nixon," *Huff Post*, August 9, 2016.
5 U.S. Congress, House, Committee on Merchant Marine and Fisheries, Subcommittee on Coast Guard and Navigation *Oversight of Seaborne Drug Smuggling Problems in the United States and Consideration of Legislation Proposed to Facilitate Coast Guard Drug Law Enforcement on the High Seas*, 95th Cong., 2nd sess., 1978, 136.
6 ibid. 136
7 ibid. 137
8 ibid. 138
9 ibid.139
10 ibid.
11 ibid.
12 ibid.
13 ibid. 140
14 ibid.
15 ibid.
16 Larry Collins and Dominique Lapierre, "The French Connection—In Real Life," *The New York Times*, February 6, 1972.
17 "The DEA Years," DEA, N.D., 33. https://www.dea.gov/sites/default/files/2021-04/1970-1975_p_30-39_0.pdf.

18. Fred Guilledoux, "L'Alliance Mortelle De Robert Blémant Et Des Frères Guérini," *La Provence*, August 24, 2010.
19. F. C., "M. Marcel Francisci Poursuit «Politique-Hebdo» En Diffamation," *Le Monde*, February 20, 1974.
20. "Marcel Francisci Shot Dead; Tied to 'French Connection'," *The New York Times*, January 16, 1982.
21. U.S. Congress, House, Committee, *Seaborne Drug Smuggling Problems*, 142.
22. Dembart, "The Model, the Drug Ring."
23. ibid.
24. Martin Tolchin, "Drug Trafficking Charges Denied by Model at Inquiry," *The New York Times*, July 31, 1975.
25. ibid.
26. U.S. Congress, House, Committee, *Seaborne Drug Smuggling Problems*, 244.
27. Tolchin, "Drug Trafficking Charges Denied."
28. Martin Tolchin, "Syracuse Man Says Ex-Wife Is Worldwide Drug Trafficker," *The New York Times*, July 29, 1975.
29. ibid.
30. U.S. Congress, House, Committee, *Seaborne Drug Smuggling Problems*, 188.

Chapter 11

1. Much of this chapter is based on notes and transcripts of on-air TV interviews during 1974 and 1975 by Jerry Barsha of William Spector and Robin Moore, as well as transcripts of tape recordings made by Spector.
2. It is worth noting here that Paul Louis Weiller held a directorship in the Michelin Tire and Rubber Company. *See* U.S. Congress, House, Committee on Merchant Marine and Fisheries, Subcommittee on Coast Guard and Navigation *Oversight of Seaborne Drug Smuggling Problems in the United States and Consideration of Legislation Proposed to Facilitate Coast Guard Drug Law Enforcement on the High Seas*, 95th Cong., 2nd sess., 239.
3. Robin Moore spent several frustrating decades after the publication of *The French Connection* trying to find the evidence that would conclusively identify Weiller as the mastermind of the Unione Corse, and Richardson as a member of its inner circle. However, he was never able to do so. That portion of the French Connection case remained unsolved as of Moore's death on February 21, 2008.

Chapter 12

1. U.S. Congress, House, Committee on Merchant Marine and Fisheries, Subcommittee on Coast Guard and Navigation *Oversight of Seaborne Drug Smuggling Problems in the United States and Consideration of Legislation Proposed to Facilitate Coast Guard Drug Law Enforcement on the High Seas*, 95th Cong., 2nd sess., 1978, 7-8.
2. Norman Pomar and Thomas Allen, *The Spy Book*, (New York: Random House, 1997), 498.
3. John Hess, "French Aid Backs U.S. in Drug Case," *The New York Times*, November 19, 1971.
4. "F.B.I. Asked for 3," *The New York Times*, November 18, 1972.
5. U.S. Congress, House, Committee, *Seaborne Drug Smuggling Problems*, 136.
6. Robert McFadden, "Heroin Smuggler Chooses U. S. Prison Over Guillotine," *The New York Times*, December 2, 1972.
7. Paul Montgomery, "Narcotics Smuggler Accused Of Threatening Witness in Jail" *The New York Times*, December 5, 1972.
8. U.S. Congress, House, Committee, *Seaborne Drug Smuggling Problems*, 136.
9. U.S. Congress, House, Committee, *Seaborne Drug Smuggling Problems*, 18-41.
10. ibid. 22.

11 This allegation appears to have been a fabrication by Spivey, since Kalmbach did not have a son named Mike, at least according to his obituary. Baker later testified that he never thought this was the same Kalmbach family and that Spivey had fabricated it.
12 Karen de Witt, "Watergate, Then and Now. Who Was Who in the Cover-Up and Uncovering of Watergate," *The New York Times*, June 15, 1992.
13 "Payment reported," *The Dallas Morning News*, March 8, 1973.
14 Larry Eichel, "The 'duality' that made the man: Richard Milhous Nixon, 1913-1994," *Philadelphia Inquirer*, April 24, 1994; "Watergate figures! Where are they? What do they say?" *Associated Press*, June 14, 1982.
15 Congress, House, Committee, *Seaborne Drug Smuggling Problems*, 30.
16 ibid.
17 ibid. 38
18 ibid. 60-62
19 ibid. 38
20 ibid. 36-39
21 ibid.
22 ibid. 40
23 ibid.
24 ibid. 62-65
25 ibid. 64
26 ibid. 65
27 ibid. 59-70
28 ibid. 70-87.
29 ibid. 79.
30 ibid. 120-151.
31 ibid. 125-126.
32 ibid.
33 "White slavery" was a term used to describe human trafficking. ibid., 127.
34 ibid. 140.
35 Amos Ettinger, *Blind Jump: The Story of Shaike Dan*, (Cornwall Books, 1992), 265-270.
36 Congress, House, Committee, *Seaborne Drug Smuggling Problems*, 85.
37 ibid. 123-124.
38 ibid. 172-198.
39 ibid. 157-163.
40 ibid. 160.
41 ibid. 149.

Kenneth overlooking the city of Marseille.
Photo courtesy of Susan McCallion

Kenneth Foard McCallion is a highly respected civil litigator who has worked on some of the most notable cases in U.S. legal history over the past 50 years. A graduate of Yale University and Fordham Law School, McCallion began his career as a prosecutor for the U.S. Department of Justice and the New York State Attorney General's Office, specializing in high-profile organized crime, racketeering, and counter-intelligence cases. Since entering private practice, McCallion has specialized in international human rights, environmental law, and complex litigation. He is an Adjunct Professor at Cardozo Law School in New York City and has lectured at Fairfield University. A prolific author, this book represents McCallion's 8th publication. When he is not writing or practicing law, Ken can be found sailing, biking, playing tennis, or walking the family dogs, Skipper and Tango, along with tending to Spot, the cat. He also enjoys traveling with his family throughout Europe, including Marseille.

www.KennethMcCallionAuthor.com

Kenneth overlooking the city of Marseille.
Photo courtesy of Dean McCallon

Kenneth Read McCallion is a widely recognized trial litigator who has tried some of the most complex cases in U.S. legal history over the past 30 years. A graduate of Fordham University and Fordham Law School, McCallion began his career as a prosecutor for the U.S. Department of Justice and the New York State Attorney General's Office, specializing in high-profile organized crime, racketeering, and corruption investigations. Since entering private practice, McCallion has modeled an intersection of human rights and international law, and complex litigation. He is a Ad Junct Professor at Cardozo Law School in New York City, and was engaged in Fall of Crotch? A prolific author, this book represents McCallion's 8th publication. When he is not writing or practicing law, Ken can be found sailing, biking, or jogging or walking the family dogs, Skipper and Tango, along with tending to Spot, the cat. He also enjoys traveling with his family throughout Europe, including Marseille.

www.KennethMcCallionAmbass.com

www.ingramcontent.com/pod-product-compliance
Lightning Source LLC
Chambersburg PA
CBHW010003110526
44587CB00023BA/3995